PROTECTING RIGHTS AND FREEDOMS
Essays on the Charter's Place in Canada's Political, Legal, and Intellectual Life

In his introduction to this collection of essays by constitutional experts, Philip Bryden says that Canadians can be proud of their commitment to the protection of rights and liberties in the Charter. Canada, he believes, is a better place to live than it would be otherwise. Nevertheless, as the essays in this book reveal, the case in favour of the Charter is not simple or one-sided. For instance, Kim Campbell, minister of justice at the time of writing, and Jeffrey Simpson of the *Globe and Mail* express concern that the Charter promotes a rights discourse that threatens to overwhelm the ordinary politics of recognizing and accommodating different interests. Dean Lynn Smith of the University of British Columbia law faculty observes that Charter rights are better understood as complementing than as supplanting traditional mechanisms.

The authors, diverse in background and outlook, reflect varying points of view but share a significant degree of consensus on issues that need to be addressed.

PHILIP BRYDEN is Professor, Faculty of Law, University of British Columbia, and Past President, British Columbia Civil Liberties Association.

STEVEN DAVIS is Professor of Philosophy, Simon Fraser University.

JOHN RUSSELL is Research Associate, Mansfield College, Oxford University, and Vice-President, British Columbia Civil Liberties Association.

PHILIP BRYDEN
STEVEN DAVIS
JOHN RUSSELL
EDITORS

PROTECTING RIGHTS AND FREEDOMS

Essays on the Charter's Place
in Canada's Political, Legal, and
Intellectual Life

UNIVERSITY OF TORONTO PRESS
Toronto Buffalo London

© University of Toronto Press Incorporated 1994
Toronto Buffalo London
Printed in Canada

ISBN 0–8020–2902–7 (cloth)
ISBN 0–8020–7410–3 (paper)

∞

Printed on acid-free paper

Canadian Cataloguing in Publication Data

Main entry under title:

Protecting Rights and Freedoms

Includes bibliographical references and index.
ISBN 0–8020–2902–7 (bound) ISBN 0–8020–7410–3 (pbk.)

1. Canada.   Canadian Charter of Rights and Freedoms.   2. Civil rights –
Canada.   3. Canada – Politics and government – 1984   .*   4. Canada –
Politics and government – 1980–1984.*   I. Bryden, Philip, 1953–   .
II. Davis, Steven, 1937–   .   III. Russell, John, 1956–   .

KE4381.5 1994   323'.0971'09048   C93–094984–6
KF4483.C519P7 1994

This book has been published with assistance from the Canada Council and
the Ontario Arts Council under their block grant programs.

CONTENTS

ACKNOWLEDGMENTS

The papers in this volume originated in a conference which was held in Vancouver in May 1992. The conference was sponsored by the British Columbia Civil Liberties Association and the Philosophy Department of Simon Fraser University. The editors would like to thank the federal Department of Multiculturalism and Citizenship, the Social Sciences and Humanities Council, and the Dean of Arts at Simon Fraser University for their financial support for the conference and the volume that resulted from it.

The editors also would like to thank Linda Hurd, Margaret Johnston, Mary Wang Ward, John Westwood, and Russell Woddell for their help with the conference, and Lindsey Thomas Martin and Eleanor O'Donnell for their help with producing the volume.

CONTRIBUTORS

PHILIP BRYDEN
Professor, Faculty of Law, University of British Columbia;
Past President, British Columbia Civil Liberties Association

RT. HON. KIM CAMPBELL
Former Prime Minister of Canada

PETER H. RUSSELL
Professor, Department of Political Science, University of Toronto

LYSIANE GAGNON
Political columnist, *La Presse* and *The Globe and Mail*

JEFFREY SIMPSON
Political columnist, *The Globe and Mail*

LYNN SMITH
Dean, Faculty of Law, University of British Columbia

ANDRÉE LAJOIE
Professor, Faculty of Law, Université de Montréal

HENRY QUILLINAN
Doctoral student, Faculty of Law, Université de Montréal

PATRICK J. MONAHAN
Professor, Osgoode Hall Law School, York University

ROBIN ELLIOT
Professor, Faculty of Law, University of British Columbia

FRANK I. MICHELMAN
Professor, Harvard Law School, Harvard University

EDGAR Z. FRIEDENBERG
Emeritus Professor, School of Education, Dalhousie University

JAMES TULLY
Professor, Philosophy Department, McGill University
JOHN RUSSELL
Research Associate, Mansfield College, Oxford University;
Vice-President, British Columbia Civil Liberties Association

PROTECTING RIGHTS AND FREEDOMS

1   PHILIP BRYDEN

Protecting Rights and Freedoms: An Overview

> *"Protecting rights and freedoms" is a deceptively simple idea ... As Yvon Pinard, the government's House Leader, echoing so many of his colleagues, put it, "what is wrong with the fundamental freedoms of Canadian citizens being protected forever by the Canadian constitution?" What indeed could possibly be wrong with such a project if that was basically all there was to it?*
>
> Peter Russell, "The Political Purposes of the Canadian Charter of Rights and Freedoms" (1983) 61 *Canadian Bar Review 30*, at 43.

This book is a collection of essays that were originally presented at a conference organized by the British Columbia Civil Liberties Association (BCCLA) and the Simon Fraser University Philosophy Department in the spring of 1992 to celebrate the tenth anniversary of the proclamation of the Canadian Charter of Rights and Freedoms as part of the Canadian Constitution."[1] At least, when I and the other members of the BCCLA's board of directors who were involved in the organization of the conference began our planning, we thought of the Charter's tenth anniversary as an occasion for celebration. At the end of the day I remain of the view, both as a legal academic and as former president of the BCCLA, that we ought to take pride in the commitment Canadians have made to the protection of rights and freedoms in the Charter, and that the Charter has helped to make Canada a better place to live than it would be otherwise. Nevertheless, as the essays in this book reveal, the case in favour of the Charter is not as simple or as one-sided as those of us who support it sometimes like to believe.

Since its foundation in 1962, the BCCLA has been a proponent of the constitutional protection of civil liberties and human rights. When it became apparent in 1980 that the Trudeau government was committed to implementing a package of constitutional reforms that included an entrenched Charter of Rights and Freedoms, the BCCLA was one of many organizations across the country that were active in giving support to this initiative and in making suggestions concerning the content of the proposed Charter. Indeed, the BCCLA was one of a more select group of organizations that not only presented a brief to the Special Joint Committee of the Senate and the House of Commons on the Constitution, but was invited to appear before the committee as well.[2]

Not only has the Association promoted the creation of the Charter, it has been a reasonably successful Charter litigant, both as a plaintiff[3] and as a supporter of litigation brought by others.[4] In addition to being important in its own right, this litigation has helped to fundamentally alter the relationship between the Association and both the public and the government. As a successful litigant the BCCLA was newsworthy, and this has increased media interest in our views even when we are not going to court. Moreover, the enhanced public profile of the Association (along with the prospect of litigation if we detected a governmental infringement of rights protected by the Charter) has encouraged governments at all levels and of all political stripes to be prepared to consult with us when their actions or policies give rise to civil liberties or human rights concerns. Our membership has increased, our financial position has become more secure, we have been able to add more staff to handle increased demand for our services – all in all, the ten years between 1982 and 1992 were banner years for the BCCLA. A good deal of that success could be attributed, directly or indirectly, to the existence of the Charter.

However useful the Charter was in enhancing the BCCLA's abilities to accomplish its goals as an organization, we soon came to realize that these benefits did not come without cost. In particular, we became aware of the capacity of complex Charter litigation to consume the time, energy, and money of what remained a fairly small voluntary organization. In addition, experience quickly taught us that the types of questions that would have to be addressed using the Charter were more likely to involve the resolution of conflicting rights claims rather than the vindication of the rights of one individual or group. And most fundamentally, we were sufficiently humble to recognize that even if we were confident that the Charter was a good thing for the BCCLA and for our conception of a good society, that did not *necessarily* make it a good thing for Canadians as a whole.

Thus, as we moved further along in our preparation of the conference program, we came to see both the Charter's tenth anniversary and the conference itself as opportunities for a deepening of our understanding of the significance of the Charter rather than merely as occasions for breaking out the champagne. With this in mind, we decided to try to bring together a set of speakers who could offer a range of reflections on the Charter rather than a group who would simply praise it. Our view at the time was that a critical appreciation of both the strengths and limitations of the Charter would, in the long run, enhance rather than detract from the esteem in which the Charter was held in the minds of members of the Canadian public. My review of the essays we have been able to assemble has reinforced my own belief in the soundness of that judgment.

We realized that an abundance of material had been generated by and for members of the legal profession describing and subjecting to critical analysis the many decisions of Canadian courts interpreting the Charter. Likewise, we suspected that many individuals and organizations would be eager to provide us with an account of their own experiences, both positive and negative, with the Charter as a means of promoting (or subverting) their efforts to achieve their goals. Despite the significance of both types of account of the impact of the Charter on Canadian society, we decided to put together a program that attempted to put the Charter in a larger perspective. Of course, ten years is not a long time in the life of a nation or a constitution, and we understood that in asking our speakers to give us their sense of the "big picture" we were also asking them to walk a tightrope between banality and observations that would not stand the test of time. Nevertheless, it seemed to be a challenge that was worth putting forward, and I have been pleased by the willingness of our authors to avoid the tendency to err on the side of safe but uninteresting generalizations.

We organized the conference around three themes, and we have followed that organization in this book. The first theme was the impact of the Charter on Canadian political life; the second was the way the Charter had been interpreted judicially and how this had affected our sense of the significance of law within our system of government; and the third was the place of the Charter within a more general framework of ideas and intellectual traditions. I do not propose to use this introductory essay to provide a detailed analysis of each of the papers, but I do wish to make a few general observations about the relationships of the papers to each other within and across these three themes

The first part of the book, which contains five essays, deals with the impact of the Charter on Canadian political life. What especially distinguishes this group of essays is the diversity of the backgrounds of the authors, which influences both the content and the style of their remarks. Kim Campbell's observations are those of an elected politician who, as former minister of justice, had much direct experience of the constraints the Charter places on the federal government's ability to implement policy through law. Professor Peter Russell of the University of Toronto writes as a political scientist whose insightful analysis of the Trudeau government's political purposes in making the Charter the centrepiece of its program of constitutional reform[5] has itself become the starting-point for debate on the success or failure of the Charter as part of the Canadian political landscape. Lysiane Gagnon and Jeffrey Simpson bring the insights of political journalists who have gained national recognition and respect. And Dean Lynn Smith of the University of British Columbia Law Faculty is both an accomplished legal academic and (as a former president of the Women's Legal Education and Action Fund) a successful advocate of the use of the Charter to promote women's equality.

The choice of authors with different backgrounds and outlooks was, of course, deliberate, and it was made notwithstanding our recognition that it was likely to produce a certain discordance in the first section of the book between essays that were written in a journalistic style and those written by academics. What impresses me about the essays is that, despite these differences, the authors tend to reflect a significant degree of consensus on the issues that need to be addressed if we are to provide an adequate evaluation of the Charter's impact on Canadian politics.

The first of these issues is the concern, expressed most clearly by Kim Campbell and Jeffrey Simpson, that the Charter promotes a kind of rights discourse that threatens to overwhelm the ordinary politics of recognizing and accommodating the different interests that are bound to exist in a country as large and diverse as Canada. Given my earlier observations about the Charter and my position as past president of the BCCLA, I suppose it will come as no surprise when I say that I tend to agree with Lynn Smith's observations that the existence of Charter rights is better understood as complementing rather than supplanting more traditional political mechanisms for advancing the ideals that the Charter endorses, and that there is a useful place in our political system for both the discourse of rights and the discourse of interests. Where I think Charter sceptics may be on firmer ground is in suggesting that the popularity of the Charter is based precisely on its tendency to produce unrealistic expectations about what the rights guarantees of the Charter mean in practical terms. Thus, one might argue, it is the unrealistic expectations that the Charter induces that undermine the legitimate function of political debate and compromise. This is a significant though not, I believe, an insuperable argument, but I want to defer consideration of it until the conclusion of my remarks.

The second issue that the authors raise is the political significance of differences between the type of support the Charter enjoys in Quebec as opposed to the rest of Canada. Both Lysiane Gagnon and Peter Russell comment on Prime Minister Trudeau's use of the Charter as a means of convincing the people of Quebec to embrace his project of constitutional renewal, and they effectively expose the fallacy of the argument that people in Quebec are somehow less committed to the protection of our fundamental freedoms than other Canadians, an idea that had gained currency outside Quebec in the wake of the Bourassa government's response to the Supreme Court of Canada's striking down of Quebec's French-only sign laws.[6] What is equally apparent from their observations, however, is that acceptance of the notion of constitutionally protected rights and liberties has not translated, in Quebec at least, into an enhanced sense of identification with the Canadian nation-state whose constitution formally guarantees those rights. Thus it would seem that the question of whether the Charter will inevitably be a divisive rather than a unifying force in Canadian politics is likely to turn on whether the Charter is inextricably linked with a concept of the relationship between the citizen and the state that cannot be reconciled with a vision of Quebec as a distinctive community within Canada.

The third point that influences each author's assessment of the Charter's impact on Canadian politics is, naturally enough, his or her views of the practical significance of key judicial decisions applying the Charter. There are, of course, many types of yardstick against which the performance of our judiciary in interpreting the Charter can be measured. One can, as Lysiane Gagnon does in her criticism of the Supreme Court's refusal to accept the argument that Quebec's sign laws were an acceptable form of regulation of commerce rather than an infringement of free speech, abstract judicial decisions from their political consequences and assess them in purely jurisprudential terms. One can also focus on the immediate social impact of judicial decisions, as I think Peter Russell tends to do, or one can look more at the implications of judicial decisions for broader governmental management of social issues, which tends to be the approach taken by Kim Campbell and Jeffrey Simpson. Given the significance of this issue and the different impressions that the judicial record has made on our authors, I trust that the reader will indulge me if I take this opportunity to briefly put forward my own views on the subject.

I believe that over the first decade of the Charter's existence, the most important thing our courts have done using the Charter is to break up what I would describe as political logjams on a series of important social issues. Having overcome the forces of political inertia, however, the courts by and large have left governments with a significant amount of room to manoeuvre in moving the issue forward to a politically acceptable resolution of the problem.[7] The success of governments in creating satisfactory political solutions to these problems has been uneven, but my sense is that this has been attributable more to the strengths and weaknesses of the relevant political and bureaucratic actors than to the tightness of the constraints placed on these actors by the courts.

Let me give three illustrations of this process in action. The first, and most significant, concerns the Supreme Court of Canada's decisions in the area of abortion – *R. v. Morgentaler*[8] and *Tremblay v. Daigle*.[9] By the mid-1980s two things seemed painfully obvious about the restrictions on abortion that had been introduced in section 251 of the Criminal Code in 1969. The first was that the law was increasingly regarded as unsatisfactory by both supporters of women's reproductive choice and those who were committed to the protection of foetuses. The second was that no government seemed capable of mustering the political will to change the legislation. Whether or not this situation was politically intolerable can be debated endlessly, but a reasonable case can be made out that it was. By offering three different rationales for striking down section 251 of the Criminal Code, the Supreme Court majority in *Morgentaler* managed to destroy the political stalemate while at the same time leaving Parliament with a significant amount of leeway, should it choose to use it, for reasserting criminal law controls on abortion that could plausibly be supported as satisfying the requirements of the Charter. The Mulroney government seized this opportunity, albeit rather gingerly, and a lengthy and elaborate political debate ensued that ultimately led to the introduction, passage in the House of Commons, and defeat in the Senate of Bill C-43. While this debate was going on, the Court in *Daigle*, at least in practical terms, made sure that the courts would not undermine Parliament's effort to set standards for the availability of abortions by granting civil injunctions at the request of the fathers of foetuses that were about to be aborted.

Certainly, the overall effect of the *Morgentaler* and *Daigle* decisions was to create a new status quo that was favoured by pro-choice forces, and in and of itself this had considerable political significance. Nevertheless, this did not prove to be a position that was politically unassailable, as the narrow margin by which Bill C-43 was defeated demonstrates. Thus, I would argue, the political effect of the Supreme Court's abortion decisions was to create a climate in which a political solution in this controversial area could re-emerge. It is not obvious to me that this was a deliberate stratagem pursued by the court, and I am not going to argue that it is an entirely appropriate way for the court to see its role in Charter adjudication,[10] but it does seem to me that the most politically significant work that the courts have done in their first decade of interpreting the Charter follows this pattern.

The second example I would offer of judicial use of the Charter to break a political logjam is the BCCLA's successful challenge to British Columbia's electoral boundaries in *Dixon v. Attorney General of British Columbia*.[11] In the mid-1980s British Columbia's electoral system was widely understood to grossly overrepresent residents of rural British Columbia and underrepresent residents of rapidly growing suburban areas.[12] In addition, the province had developed a patchwork system of dual member ridings and there were suspicions that in at least some of these ridings the boundaries had been chosen to favour Social Credit candidates. Premier Vander Zalm, who was himself elected in 1986 in a dual member riding in the Vancouver suburb of Richmond, had promised to eliminate dual member ridings. In 1987 he appointed the Fisher Commission to make recommendations on how this should be done. Prior to the 1986 provincial election, the BCCLA had begun a lawsuit challenging the constitutional validity of the province's system of electoral boundaries on the basis that the guarantee of the right to vote found in section 3 of the Charter by implication required the electoral system to give equal weight to each citizen's vote. Given the pendency of this lawsuit, the Fisher Commission was also given the broader mandate of looking at the principles by which seats should be distributed across the province.

The Fisher Commission's report recommended a significant reduction in the disparity of the population base between ridings as well as the elimination of the dual member ridings. By the time the report was released in the spring of 1989, however, the government's ardour for electoral reform seemed to have cooled considerably, and it was far from clear that the political will to implement these recommendations would be forthcoming. It was in this state of political uncertainty that Chief Justice McLachlin of the British Columbia Supreme Court (now a member of the Supreme Court of Canada) released her judgment in *Dixon* finding that the existing system of electoral boundaries violated the Charter. Interestingly enough, Chief Justice McLachlin was not prepared to decide how this state of affairs should be remedied, though she did give a broad hint that the implementation of the Fisher Commission's recommendations would solve the problem, and in addition offered the BCCLA the opportunity to take further proceedings if the situation was not resolved within a reasonable period of time. Even at this point the government took its time in introducing legislation to alter the electoral boundary system, and the courts showed no great enthusiasm for moving the process along.[13] Eventually, however, the Fisher Commission's recommendations were implemented and the current system was in place in time for the 1991 provincial election.

The B.C. electoral boundaries dispute is an interesting illustration of the use of the Charter to break up a political logjam precisely because a political solution to the problem emerged relatively easily once the courts had intervened. My third example is chosen to show that the interaction between judicial and legislative solutions is not always so smooth. It concerns the Supreme Court of Canada's decision in *Singh v. Minister of Employment and Immigration*[14] striking down the refugee determination system that existed at the time on the basis that its failure to guarantee an adequate hearing to each refugee claimant violated section 7 of the Charter.

During the early 1980s there had been expressions of dissatisfaction with Canada's refugee determination process from inside as well as outside government, and it had been the subject of a series of reports that, for one reason or another, had not resulted in legislative action.[15] In handing down its decision in *Singh* in 1985, the court gave the government some general guidance on the elements a refugee determination system would require in order to pass muster under the Charter. But Parliament was still provided substantial room (in my view, at least) to replace the existing legislation with a scheme that satisfied the court's requirements and made sense from the point of view of sound public administration. Whether for reasons of political and bureaucratic ineptitude or because of a more deep-seated conceptual difficulty in marrying judicialized concepts of procedural fairness and mass-justice systems of adjudication, Parliament took three years to find a suitable replacement for the refugee determination system struck down in *Singh*, and that system has itself proved sufficiently unattractive that a further set of major revisions had to be undertaken.[16]

As is demonstrated by Kim Campbell's skilful handling, as minister of justice, of Bill C-49, the Mulroney government's legislative response to the Supreme Court of Canada's decision in *R. v. Seaboyer*[17] striking down the previous "rape shield" provisions of the Criminal Code, it is by no means impossible for a government to pursue its own law reform agenda in an area in which the courts have laid out some constitutional ground rules using the Charter. In fairness to the politicians and bureaucrats who were trying to develop a response to *Singh*, this way of thinking about the Charter was relatively unfamiliar in 1985. Moreover, one of the problems with trying to fix a system of mass adjudication on the run is that the claims keep piling up, which in the case of the Canadian refugee determination process resulted in the development of a parallel system of adjudication to deal with people whose claims were made prior to the coming into effect of the new system.[18] However one chooses to parcel out the responsibility for the difficulties the federal government experienced in coming to grips with the consequences of the *Singh* decision for the way Canada deals with refugee claimants, it was inevitable that some of the blame would be laid at the feet of the Supreme Court, and over time this may have helped to usher in a new and more conservative approach to the Charter described by the authors of the essays that make up the second part of the book. My point is simply that, for the first ten years at least, the Canadian judiciary has managed to breathe enough life into the Charter to make it politically meaningful while giving little evidence of a desire to usurp the role of elected officials in our democratic system of government.

This leads me to a discussion of the second part of the book, which is composed of three essays that deal more directly with the Charter as it has been interpreted by the courts. The authors, Professor Andrée Lajoie and doctoral student Henry Quillinan of the University of Montreal, Professor Patrick Monahan of Osgoode Hall Law School, and Professor Robin Elliot of the University of British Columbia, are accomplished constitutional law scholars and, as one might expect, they are reasonably consistent in their identification of the key Supreme Court of Canada decisions that need to be addressed in a discussion of the first decade of Charter interpretation by our courts. Likewise, they share a general view of how the court's approach to the Charter has evolved, one that is characterized by the supplanting of an early interventionist phase by a much more cautious use of the Charter outside the realm of criminal law and one or two other areas, with the watershed being marked by the 1986 decision in *Edwards Books*[19] upholding Ontario's Sunday closing laws from a challenge that they violated the Charter's guarantee of freedom of religion. Despite these similarities, each author manages to make a distinctive contribution to our understanding of the significance of this path of legal development.

The focus of the essay by Andrée Lajoie and Henry Quillinan is the way in which the wisdom and character of the individual Supreme Court justices, and the place each of them occupies within the decision-making structure of the court, has played a significant role in the development of Charter jurisprudence. Patrick Monahan, by contrast, concentrates on the expectations held by the politicians and others who were involved in

the creation of the Charter concerning the likely direction Charter jurisprudence would take, and explores the ways in which events have or have
not supported those expectations. Robin Elliot picks up the theme of the
expectations people had of the Charter, but the expectations he concentrates on are those of the legal professionals and academic commentators
on the Charter, and the ways in which the kinds of debates we have had
about the Charter differ from those he and others had anticipated in
1982.

The most important thing these essays help us to understand is that
the ideas that lie underneath the Charter are much more subtle, and in
the long run much more significant, than what sits on the surface. In particular, Robin Elliot's argument that the functions the courts perform in
interpreting the Charter include a good deal more than simply preventing governmental interference with legally recognized rights gives us a
whole new perspective on the expectations we ought to have of our
judges as they write Charter decisions. And if we begin to suspect that
these ideas were not in the forefront of the politicians' thinking when
they created the Charter, or even in the minds of the country's leading
academics as they originally contemplated the Charter, we are led naturally enough to ask ourselves, Where *do* these ideas come from?

This is, indirectly, the theme of the third part of the book, which
contains four essays that locate the constitutional protection of rights and
liberties within a broader set of intellectual traditions. In some respects it
is more appropriate to think of this section as containing two pairs of essays, though the first two relate to each other in quite different ways from
the second two. What the essays have in common is that they are not de-
scriptions of the way broader intellectual currents shape our thinking
about the Charter, but manifestations of those currents from which we
can derive approaches to the issues that are discussed more directly in the
first two parts of the book.

For example, neither Harvard Law School Professor Frank Michelman nor Dalhousie Emeritus Professor Edgar Friedenberg (himself an
American expatriate) purports to explain the relationship between Canadian and American thinking about the constitutional protection of freedom. Nevertheless, what they do discuss and how they discuss it
probably tells us more about the intellectual shadow that the American
Bill of Rights casts over the Charter than any direct account of the deri-

vation of the ideas that the Charter embodies. Frank Michelman's essay explores whether democracy should be considered as a right or merely as a background condition within which the rights set out in the American Bill of Rights or the Charter manifest themselves. The significance of this choice is then played out in the debate over the suppression of hate speech with the goal of enhancing the ability of the targets of hate speech to participate meaningfully in the discussions that are part of a democratic society. It is, in other words, an essay about how the retracing of our intellectual assumptions can lead us to new conclusions on issues that arise for judicial resolution, and as such has considerable resonance for a Canadian audience in the light of the Supreme Court of Canada's decision in *R. v. Keegstra*[20] upholding the Criminal Code's prohibition on hate speech. Edgar Friedenberg writes about the way in which the bedrock assumptions of our constitutional thinking – for example, the idea that freedom of expression is about preventing the suppression of information by government – can get in the way of the possibility of our using the Charter to address the practical problems facing contemporary Canadian society – for instance, the constraints on free expression that flow from mass media control of the dissemination of most of the information that is of political significance.

I see these essays as helping us to understand the influence of American ideas on the Charter because the defining assumptions about freedom of expression to which both authors react are quintessentially those of American constitutional jurisprudence. We may, as Frank Michelman suggests, be able to reconceptualize those ideas, but they remain the starting-point of our discussions, and this is a starting-point that is not in any obvious way geared to addressing the problems confronting Canadians in the 1990s as opposed to the problems facing Americans in the late eighteenth century. This is not to say that the Charter is not very useful as far as it goes, as Professor Friedenberg himself admits, but only to suggest that we might want to be a bit cautious about the types of expectations we have of the Charter.

The second pair of essays in this part, by Professor James Tully of the McGill University Department of Philosophy and by John Russell, Visiting Fellow at Mansfield College, Oxford and the BCCLA's vice-president, address at the level of ideas the question that Lysiane Gagnon and Peter Russell posed at the political level in relation to Quebec, namely, whether the Charter is compatible with the intellectual traditions and cultural aspirations of the French-speaking people of Quebec and the people of Canada's First Nations. James Tully approaches this question on the assumption that, if the Charter is understood as a manifestation of traditional liberal ideals that rest on a notion of Canada as a uniform society, these traditions cannot coexist. It is his thesis, however, that neither Canadian history nor our intellectual traditions compel such a view, and that we would be better served by embracing a concept of Canada as a pluralistic federation that recognizes the coherence of differential applications of the Charter within the different constitutive elements of the federation. John Russell seeks to avoid the conflict between liberal tradition and the aspirations of nationalistic minorities by arguing that at least some strands of liberalism are less antagonistic to such aspirations than is often supposed. Thus, Russell argues, the concepts of freedom, justice, and equality that the Charter endorses can be understood in a way that accommodates, at least to some extent, the notion of distinctive status for certain minority communities within Canadian society without abandoning the fundamental precepts of the liberal philosophic tradition.

I do not intend to attempt here to evaluate the arguments presented in these two papers – the merits of views set forth by the authors are more evident from a study of their own words than from mine. Nevertheless, I think it is instructive to relate their observations to the public debate that surrounded the unsuccessful attempts of the Mulroney government to amend the Canadian constitution pursuant first to the Meech Lake Accord and then to the Charlottetown Accord. For whatever reason, those of us who would like to find a way of reconciling the values expressed in the Charter with a sense that Canadians need to recognize the legitimacy of nationalistic aspirations among the people of Quebec and the First Nations have not been able to carry popular opinion. I am not suggesting that there were not plenty of other reasons for rejecting the constitutional proposals that were put forward in either round. Nevertheless, I do believe that a sense of the overriding significance of the Charter and a belief that the values the Charter expresses cannot be reconciled with "special status" for Quebec, First Nations people, or anybody else was a major factor in the defeat of those proposals, at least in the minds of many average Canadians. It is difficult, and perhaps impossible, to appreciate at this point what the defeat of the Charlottetown Accord in the referendum of 26 October 1992 means for our attempts to come to grips with the ambitions of nationalistic minorities, and it may be that the place of the Charter in these struggles will turn out to be insignificant. I suspect, however, that this will not be the case and that the position that these visions of Canada can be reconciled needs to be advanced more effectively than it has been in the past.

This brings me to my final observation, which touches on the purpose and overall thematic unity of this book. I believe strongly that the level of satisfaction that Canadians experience with the Charter inevitably will be shaped by the expectations they have for it. At the same time, the open-ended nature of what one scholar has called the "vague but meaningful"[21] guarantees that the Charter holds out makes the Charter a vessel into which Canadians can pour a vast range of hopes and fears. Our experience with the first ten years of the Charter has been that it is neither a guarantee that all Canadians enjoy the level of freedom, justice, and equality to which we may in our better moments aspire, nor a recipe for governance by the judiciary. Nevertheless, it is possible that the Charter's capacity to stir our imaginations, for good or ill, is precisely what gives it power as a symbol for Canadians, and that without a background of unrealistic expectation the Charter would not be a meaningful vehicle for such progress as it has made possible for people who could not make the wheels of our political system turn in any other way.

It seems to me that our authors are right to be troubled by this possibility. The problem with expectations that are not rooted in an understanding of the Charter's virtues and limitations as an instrument for promoting a good society is that these expectations can be destructive of our sense of commitment to the very institutions on which our ability to make such progress depends. The Charter can distract people from the pursuit of more productive channels for achieving their goals, and this disdain for traditional politics can help to sow the seeds of the kind of cynicism and contempt for politics that degenerates into a self-fufilling prophecy of a national political life that is indeed contemptible. Moreover, when the Charter and the courts fail (as they inevitably must) to live up to unrealistic expectations, the task of rebuilding the confidence of those who have been so disappointed in at least the possibility of a system of governance that meets their most urgent needs and aspirations is made that much more difficult.

I am not suggesting that we need to interpret the Charter in a narrow and technical way in order to stifle the capacity of the Charter to inspire our sense of commitment to the ideals it enshrines – quite the contrary. I do think we need to take a realistic look at the things that have been accomplished using the Charter and recognize that they are good and useful things, but that they do not exhaust our conception of what a good society is all about.

It is my sense that the only way this is going to happen is if those of us who support the Charter as a vehicle for social progress dedicate ourselves to the tasks of developing an understanding of what can and cannot be achieved using the Charter and of conveying that message to the Canadian public. This is not an easy or even a particularly enjoyable job for those of us who have occupied ourselves with the promotion and enhancement of the civil liberties and human rights of Canadians. An expression of outrage at the latest violation of an individual's rights makes better news copy than the patient plodding that is so often needed to understand a problem and to achieve results, and it is an all too common failing that we crave attention more than we desire success. Be that as it may, I believe that the development of a practical vision of the place of civil liberties and human rights in our democratic society is work that urgently needs to be done, and that it is the type of work that the BCCLA has been doing throughout its history. It is my hope that this collection of essays represents a step, even if only a small one, towards the achievement of that climate of understanding.

NOTES

1 Her Majesty Queen Elizabeth II signed a royal proclamation in Ottawa on 17 April 1982 bringing the Charter into force as part of the Constitution Act 1982. As Lynn Smith notes in her essay, even the observation of 17 April 1992 as the tenth anniversary of the Charter is slightly misleading, since the implementation of the equality rights found in section 15 of the Charter was delayed for three years, ostensibly in order to allow governments to review their legislation and repeal or replace any laws that offended the Charter's equality guarantees.

2 In December 1980, Professors David Copp and William Black appeared

before the committee on behalf of the BCCLA to present a paper entitled
"Comments and Recommendations on the Proposed Canadian Charter of
Rights and Freedoms: A Submission to the Parliamentary Committee
Studying the 1980 Constitutional Resolution."

3 The most prominent of these cases is the BCCLA's successful challenge of
British Columbia's electoral boundaries in *Dixon v. A.G.B.C.* (1989), 35
BCLR (2d) 273 (BCSC). The association also convinced the courts to in-
validate the provincial government's attempt to use regulations made under
the Medical Service Act to place strict limits on the availability of medicare
payments for abortions, but this case was argued on more traditional administrative law grounds rather than on the basis of the Charter. *British Columbia Civil Liberties Association v. A.G.B.C.* (1988), 24 BCLR (2d) 189
(BCSC). In the light of what follows, it is worth noting that the BCCLA deliberately adopted the strategy of refusing to invoke the Charter in the abortion funding case, in part at least because we did not want to force either
the courts or the government to approach the issue as one that was going
to be fixed in stone by a constitutional ruling. We believed, correctly as it
turned out, that if we were able to secure a quick and relatively narrow ruling invalidating the regulations, the political environment in the province
would force the government to reconsider its policy of restricting access to
abortion even though, from a strictly legal standpoint, it would have been
open to the government to reassert such controls in a slightly different fashion.

4 To give just two examples, the BCCLA provided legal assistance to the plain-
tiffs in *Re Hoogbruin and A.G.B.C.* (1985), 24 DLR (4th) 718 (BCCA), a
successful challenge to the absence of provision for absentee voting in B.C.
elections, and in *Austin v. Minister of Municipal Affairs* (1990), 42 BCLR
(2d) 358 (BCSC), in which the court ruled that a requirement that the cu-
rator of the provincial museum be a Canadian citizen violated the Charter's
equality guarantees. In addition, the BCCLA has twice appeared as an intervenor in Charter litigation before the Supreme Court of Canada: in *Reference re Provincial Electoral Boundaries (Saskatchewan)*, [1991] 2 SCR 158,
a case involving the one-person, one-vote principle explored in *Dixon*, and
in *R. v. Butler*, [1992] 1 SCR 452, in which the BCCLA attempted, unsuc-
cessfully, to persuade the Court that the obscenity provisions of the Criminal Code violated the Charter's guarantee of freedom of expression.

5 See P. Russell, "The Political Purposes of the Canadian Charter of Rights
and Freedoms," (1983) 61 *Canadian Bar Review* 30.

6 *Ford v. A.G. Quebec,* [1988] 2 SCR 712.

7 To employ Robin Elliot's very useful analysis of the functions the courts perform in Charter adjudication, these are instances where the judges have a prompting function. See Elliot's essay in this volume and, for a more extended treatment of this idea, R. Elliot, "Developments in Constitutional Law: The 1989–90 Term," (1991) 2 *Supreme Court Law Review* (2d) 83, at 154–71.

8 [1988] 1 SCR 30.

9 [1989] 2 SCR 530.

10 See P. Monahan, *The Charter, Federalism and the Supreme Court of Canada* (Toronto: Carswell 1987); J.H. Ely, *Democracy and Distrust: A Theory of Judicial Review* (Cambridge: Harvard University Press 1980).

11 Supra note 3.

12 In her judgment in *Dixon,* Chief Justice McLachlin notes by way of example that the riding with the lowest population had a population that was 86.8 percent below the average and the one with the highest population was 63.2 percent above the average. As she put it, in terms of voting parity, a vote in the least populous riding, Atlin, was worth 12.4 times as much as a vote in Surrey-Newton, the riding with the greatest population. 35 BCLR (2d) at 280.

13 Chief Justice McLachlin's decision was handed down on 18 April 1989. When the government gave no indication by May 1989 of its plans to comply with the decision, the BCCLA sought the assistance of the courts in enforcing the decision. In a ruling dated 1 June 1989, Mr. Justice Meredith of the British Columbia Supreme Court denied this application. *Dixon v. A.G.B.C.* (1989), 37 BCLR (2d) 231. The BCCLA filed an appeal of this judgment but the appeal was abandoned in the light of the subsequent passage of legislative amendments to the electoral boundary system that rendered the matter academic.

14 [1985} 1 SCR 177.

15 At page 219 of her judgment in *Singh,* Madame Justice Wilson refers to the comments on the refugee determination system made in 1980 by the chairman of the Immigration Appeal Board, Janet Scott, QC, who described the system as "highly unsatisfactory." In Chairman Scott's words: "Leaving aside any consideration of natural justice, the system is extremely cumbersome, and when we enter into the sphere of natural justice, open to criticism as unjust." Similar concerns were expressed in a number of other reports commissioned by the government, including the 1981 Employ-

ment and Immigration Task Force Report entitled "The Refugee Determination Process," W.G. Robinson's 1983 report on *Illegal Immigrants in Canada* (Ottawa: Enquiries and Distribution, Public Affairs Division, Employment and Immigration Canada 1983), and Ed Ratushny's study in 1984 entitled "A New Refugee Determination Process for Canada." Very shortly after the *Singh* decision was announced in April 1985, the government released Rabbi Gunther Plaut's report, *Refugee Determination in Canada: Proposals for a New System* (Ottawa: Supply and Services Canada 1985), which was destined to gather dust along with the others.

16 The most significant amendments to the refugee determination process were introduced in Bill C-55, which was given royal assent on 21 July 1988. SC 1988, c. 35. For an interesting description of at least some of the political manoeuvring associated with the amendment of the refugee determination process, see V. Malarek, *Haven's Gate: Canada's Immigration Fiasco* (Toronto: Macmillan of Canada 1987), especially pages 100–69. More recently, the Mulroney government introduced changes in the refugee determination process in Bill C-86, which was passed by Parliament after considerable public opposition and brought into effect on 1 February 1993.

17 [1991] 2 SCR 577.

18 See Refugee Claims Backlog Regulations, SOR / 86–701, which were later supplanted by the Refugee Claims Designated Class Regulations, SOR 90–40.

19 *Edwards Books and Arts Limited v. The Queen,* [1986] 2 SCR 713.

20 [1990] 3 SCR 697.

21 See N. Lyon, "The Teleological Mandate of the Fundamental Freedoms: What to Do with Vague but Meaningful Generalities," (1982) 4 *Supreme Court Law Review* 57.

I

The Charter
and Canadian
Political Life

Parliament's Role in Protecting the Rights and Freedoms of Canadians

I am delighted that the B.C. Civil Liberties Association has created this special forum for the thoughtful consideration of our first decade of experience with the Canadian Charter of Rights and Freedoms. People in central Canada are, of course, capable of forgetting that your organization was formed before the Canadian Civil Liberties Association. And I understand that it is one of your standing jokes that almost any club that springs up on Yonge Street is inclined to immediately dub itself the "Royal Canadian Something or Other." In any case, Canadians have now noticed your existence and special character – a process that has depended, at least to some extent, upon your own rather successful resort to the Charter as litigants. So I know that you, as civil libertarians, share the keen interest of government in the development of what might be called a "new Charter legal culture." And I am also sure – indeed, I am certain that it is part of the purpose of your arranging this conference – that you won't mind my being frank about some concerns I have about that culture and its direction.

As you might expect, this is an issue that confronts me daily as minister of justice and attorney general of Canada – the impact of the Charter on our system of government. The Charter is a very important part of the Canadian legal system and of our system of government generally. In the Charter's early years, the biggest challenge was to ensure that it was given real force, unlike the Canadian Bill of Rights, and that it was interpreted generously and purposively. The courts have met that challenge and met it well by giving the Charter a large and liberal interpretation. I hope that they will continue to do so.

In the second decade of the Charter, however, there is a second challenge – to ensure that the Charter advances the cause of good government in Canada, and helps to make our uniquely Canadian system of government function well. I would like to address three themes: first, that the Charter has given the courts new and expanded responsibilities; second, that unless we are careful, Canadians will increasingly look to the courts rather than Parliament to achieve social and political reform and to promote their rights; third, that we must articulate and respect an allocation of responsibility among the courts, Parliament, and the executive that reflects our Canadian traditions and circumstances and that assigns to each its proper role in this post-Charter era.

By giving Canadians constitutionally entrenched rights and freedoms, and by making these enforceable by the courts, the Charter has given the courts a much more powerful and visible role in our governmental system. It has also given the courts – which on the constitutional front were previously limited mainly to decisions about the division of powers – a substantive policy role, one that was previously reserved to Parliament. This has led to some tensions and to questions about the proper scope of judicial review in a parliamentary system. I think we must address these tensions. My concern is that unless Parliament and the courts understand and respect each other's role, we will evolve towards a system in which courts rather than democratically elected legislatures are seen as the primary protectors and promoters of our rights and freedoms.

In my view, this may be what is happening in the United States. Increasingly, Americans seem to be seeking social and political change through the courts. They may be doing so because they have lost faith in the capacity of the other two branches to achieve the results they desire. Consider, for example, the recent mass demonstrations in front of the United States Supreme Court on the abortion issue. I am concerned that similar developments are taking root here. We appear to have become increasingly rights-oriented, increasingly confrontational, and increasingly quick to look to the courts rather than to our elected representatives for social and political reform.

In my view, however, these trends are neither inevitable nor irreversible in Canada. Our adoption of an entrenched Charter of Rights does not mean that Canadians will *necessarily* become more litigious or that courts will *inevitably* replace legislatures as the agents of change: the decision is ours to make. While some hail these developments as proof of an increased sense of "ownership" in the constitution, I think we must be extremely careful not to disregard our constitutional history and attempt to understand our complex political and constitutional framework solely from a post-1982 perspective. In this regard, we must be mindful of one of the most distinctive aspects of Canadian political culture, namely, the relationship Canadians have with their government. Unlike their American counterparts, Canadian citizens have not perceived government as being antagonistic to their interests; on the contrary, there is a rich and deeply imbedded tradition of looking to government to protect a larger societal interest – of relying on government to advance and protect certain basic values. Social and income support programs, equalization payments, and regional diversification initiatives are but three of the many examples that could be cited. I do not think the Charter either represents or requires any radical break from this tradition. Indeed, I think it must be interpreted in the light of and consistently with this important element of the Canadian experience. The Charter is much more than a bulwark against the state; it is a statement of the positive relationship between citizens and state. We must remember that in Canada citizens have invoked state power as much as they have sought to limit it.

Against this background, then, what sort of institutional relationships are appropriate under the Charter? First, I think we must now accept that the Charter has given the courts a policy role, one that goes well beyond the mere adjudication of competing fact situations. Courts are now required to choose from among competing approaches and values. The real question, therefore, is not whether the courts are "making policy," but rather the appropriate limits of the courts' policy-making role. In considering the proper limits of the judicial policy function, courts must take into account three main factors. The first is *the nature of the issues.* Court cases are about the interpretation and the application of the law, usually to specific fact situations. They are, in my view, often inappropriate for deciding broad policy issues affecting a large number of people. The second is *the nature of the adversarial process itself.* The adversarial process has evolved over the centuries as a formalized process for re-solving disputes among parties by ensuring that the facts and the law relevant to the matter at hand are advanced and tested before an impartial arbiter. While this approach has proved its value in resolving differences of fact and in applying the law to those facts, it is not designed to ensure that all considerations relevant to value-laden policy decisions are identi-fied. Further, even if all those considerations are brought out, the adver-sarial process, with its win/loss result, is not then designed to lead to the finely crafted compromises that are required in our society, and that the parliamentary system is uniquely able to shape. Third, *the background of judges* is important. Judges are invariably eminent members of the bar, highly trained to deal with matters of law. They are, however, usually without training or experience in the broader exercise of policy formula-tion and may not be in the best position to benefit from those who are.

These considerations should, I think, constrain the policy involve-ment of courts. This is not to suggest that the courts should refrain from taking policy decisions where they have to, but rather that they should be very conscious of their role and of the limitations of the legal adjudicative framework within which they work.

If I appear to be placing considerable emphasis on the need for judi-cial restraint, I am. Bearing in mind the wide-ranging implications of ju-dicial decisions and the fact that those decisions are, to all intents and purposes, the final word as to the meaning of our constitution and the validity of governmental action pursuant to it, I think it important that courts approach their policy role with some degree of circumspection. It is natural for interest groups to demand more, but they are interested in specific results, not in the long-term health of the overall system. At the same time, we must acknowledge that the democratic process is imper-fect and at times fails to live up to its responsibilities to the individuals and groups it serves. To my mind, this is the reason why some form of judicial review is necessary. And if this is the raison d'être of judicial re-view, it equally provides guidance as to the proper limits of the judicial role.

As a general rule, I think judicial intervention will be most appropri-ate where it serves to strengthen the workings of the democratic process in order to correct failures within that process. On the one hand, courts can properly intervene where Parliament loses its way, either in disregarding fundamental values enshrined in the Charter or in failing to give sufficient regard to minority interests. Further, where a Charter defect is found, courts can provide guidance to Parliament by setting out the precise nature of the problem, thereby enabling Parliament to reformulate the legislation in a manner consistent with the Charter. In this way, courts can ensure that Parliament carries out its obligations under the Charter without intruding on Parliament's function.

On the other hand, it is particularly important that courts show restraint where their decisions will have fiscal implications. It must be open to Parliament to reassess fiscal priorities where Charter rulings affect the scope of government programs. The more that the courts become involved in the balancing of competing demands or political interests, the more they risk trenching upon the legislative domain. In this regard, I think there are real dangers to importing into Canada the so-called doctrine of extension, wherein courts become involved in the implementation of their own decisions. This doctrine is rooted in the American political and judicial context, with its elaborate system of checks and balances. It is based on concerns that are not part of Canadian reality or experience. We have a uniquely Canadian Charter, and Canadians are entitled to a uniquely Canadian rights jurisprudence. In this context, decisions as to the design of laws, policies, and of programs should, as a general rule, be left to Parliament within the constitutional framework as interpreted by the courts.

Let me give you a few examples of what I have been trying to say. First, let me refer to some instances in which courts may have been somewhat overzealous and risked encroaching upon Parliament's domain.

Section 7 guarantees the rights to life, liberty, and security of the person, and the right not to be deprived of those except in accordance with principles of fundamental justice. It is clear that the drafters of the Charter intended this section as a guarantee of a minimum level of procedural fairness. While the drafters' intent is not determinative, courts have in fact given it little weight. In the *B.C. Motor Vehicle Reference*, the Supreme Court rejected the argument of the attorney general of Canada and others that section 7 should be restricted to the examination of the procedural aspects of government action. Instead, the Court held that section 7 could also be used to review the substance of legislation. In so doing, the Court imported into Canada an American constitutional doctrine known as substantive due process. Not only is this contrary to what Parliament appears to have intended; the substantive use of section 7 is one of the chief bases of policy involvement by the courts and therefore one of the areas in which concern about the legitimacy of judicial review is most prevalent.

Another example is the series of cases in which the Court struck down the constructive murder provisions of the Criminal Code. In these decisions, rather than simply identifying the Charter defects and striking down the provisions, the Court effectively held that murder *had* to be defined in a certain way. In my view, the Court in so doing over-stepped the proper boundaries of the judicial function. It is for Parliament and Parliament alone to define what murder is. Having found Parliament's definition deficient, the Court should simply have struck down the provision and left it to Parliament to try again. The Court should set the basic limits, not define the optimum policy result.

Let me now give you an example of what I consider to be a more appropriate model for institutional relationships under the Charter. As most of you will know, the Supreme Court of Canada recently struck down what was commonly referred to as the "rape shield provision," which protected sexual assault complainants from being questioned about their sexual history. You will recall that the Court found that Parliament had gone too far in its attempt to protect victims of sexual assault, and had in fact violated the rights of accused persons to make full answer and defence. Significantly, while the Court provided some useful guidance as to what might be an appropriate way of balancing the competing interests, it did *not* attempt to strike this balance itself. It offered a fairly rich set of suggestions, but still left the final determination for Parliament to make, in accordance with its representative function.

In this instance, I believe the various branches of government worked cooperatively, as they were meant to do: the Supreme Court decision affirmed the principles on which Parliament had based its original provisions, but indicated how and why the actual balance struck was deficient. In so doing, it recognized the right and the responsibility of Parliament to go back and examine how best to achieve its objectives in a manner consistent with the Charter. This allowed us to go to the people who were most affected by the legislation and ask them for their opinions. It allowed us to engage in a truly democratic, consultative process whereby the views of many were considered and reflected in a legislative initiative that is consistent with the fundamental principles of the Charter. We have achieved protection for complainants and victims while at the same time respecting the right of the accused to a fair trial.

Besides illustrating an appropriate role for courts under the Charter, this example highlights the responsibilities of Parliament and the executive under the Charter, and the fundamental role of Parliament in fashioning social compromise and demonstrating leadership. Parliament has the vital and pre-eminent role in our constitutional system as an arbiter among competing interests in society. Our system of constitutional adjudication must recognize that the difficult political choices and decisions as to how to respond to social needs must remain in the hands of a government responsible through the House of Commons to the people of Canada. We must never lose sight of the central importance of the political process. Nor must we forget that it is legislatures – not courts – that are in the best position to assess competing demands and to conduct the necessary balancing of interests. In this regard, I think we often fail to give sufficient credit to our parliamentary process. It is this process alone that permits consensus decision-making, problem-solving, and public involvement – reflecting the spirit of practical compromise that is so fundamental to the Canadian way of doing things.

Parliament is, however, more than simply a broker among competing interests. It has a positive role to play as the guardian of the principal commitments of the Canadian community. It also has an enormously important creative role to play in giving material life to the aspirations of the Charter, a role that cannot be fulfilled by the courts. In a very real sense, Parliament and the executive side of government are on the front lines of rights protection in Canada. At the same time, democratic institutions must demonstrate that they deserve the trust, faith, and respect of Canadians. Parliament must *act* to promote the larger values and objects of the Charter. Parliamentarians have a vital responsibility to ensure that the laws they pass and other actions they take respect and advance Charter rights and freedoms.

I have begun to note a very disquieting trend among legislators to leave difficult decisions to the courts. There is a great temptation to avoid dealing with contentious issues by saying "Let's wait until the courts force us to act." This is a defeatist attitude and nothing less than an abdication of Parliament's role as the primary agent of social change in Canada. It ignores the responsibility of legislatures to craft the law – to determine both *what* should be done and *how* it is to be accomplished. We must never forget the profound responsibility of legislators to demonstrate leadership and to make the difficult choices required to govern a nation.

It will be obvious by now that I am trying to make a case for a coherent functional specialization among our governmental institutions in the application of the Charter. But there is one additional element that must not be forgotten, and that is the people whose welfare the Charter was designed to foster and protect. The people of Canada are the real beneficiaries of the Charter, and Canadians are, for good reason, justly proud of it. But the Charter's beneficiaries also have a responsibility. Just as courts must be responsible in their disposition of the Charter issues coming before them, so must Canadians be responsible in deciding which issues to put before the courts for judicial rather than political resolution. I would hope that Canadians will take their decisions carefully, having given due consideration to the effect of a particular course of actions on the welfare of our community and institutions. The question should never be: "Can we mount a winning Charter case?" but rather: "If we won this case with these particular pleadings, would we advance a vision of the Charter that is consistent with the set of principles and aspirations that our constitution was framed to conserve?" I know that this is asking a lot, but I strongly believe that those who go to law with a constitutional question must bear responsibility for the impact of their possible success on the vitality and health of the interrelated system of commitments and institutions that sustain our community. Power to win a Charter case makes you a player, and all the players in the constitutional game should bring a sense of citizenly proprietorship to the enterprise. If Canadians become too impatient with the workings of our democratic institutions, they will, as I implied earlier, lose their effectiveness.

What conclusions can we draw from what I have been saying? First, I think we must remain vigilant in ensuring that we do not become overly reliant on the courts to satisfy individual rights. We must not lose our ability to search for consensus and compromise. We must ensure that Canadians do not come to believe that public policy issues can be resolved only by a court decision. In particular, it is our duty to ensure that our political processes remain effective agents of social change, and that Canadians have confidence in the ability of those processes to advance the largest vision of public interest.

Second, we require an appropriate framework of institutional relationships between Parliament, the executive, and the courts. It is a framework based on a functional allocation of responsibilities. Each organ of government should encourage and assist the others to fulfil their roles while at the same time respecting the proper limits of its own function.

Third, there is a danger to democratic institutions of over-reliance on courts to effect social change. The long-term effect could be to debilitate the process of problem-solving and policy-making that lies at the heart of democratic governance and upon which its survival depends.

Fourth, we do our courts no favour in asking them to resolve what are essentially political questions. Besides demonstrating a lack of faith in political institutions, judicial involvement in political issues threatens the judiciary's legitimacy. There is a danger that courts will no longer be seen as impartial or neutral arbiters above the fray of political debate; instead, they may come to be perceived as active players in the political arena.

Fifth, the approach I am suggesting imposes a heavy responsibility on Parliament, parliamentarians, and the executive to ensure that democratic institutions live up to the trust we place in them as protectors and promoters of the rights of Canadians.

Finally, we must define a role for our courts under the Charter that is consistent with our Canadian system of government. Courts are not, and must not become, the exclusive defenders of the values the Charter seeks to protect.

It has been suggested that the Charter of Rights and Freedoms is causing a legal revolution in our country. Reflecting on a decidedly less metaphorical revolution in eighteenth-century France, Edmund Burke made what I consider to be a genuinely profound comment on the relationship between citizens and their laws. He said, if I may paraphrase, that we should approach the imperfections in our laws as if they were the wounds of a patient.

Burke's idea resonates with a sense of proprietorship, of membership, of a kind of citizenly solicitude for the laws of the community. I am painfully aware that it may seem arcane and otherworldly to us from the standpoint of a modern cynicism. But Burke was – and still is, I am convinced – absolutely right. The Charter is *one* of the instruments that we have fashioned to help ensure that our governance is more principled and humane. It is part of, an element of, a system of government. It cannot replace the other functions with which it must, ultimately, form a working, living, resilient whole. We cannot simply follow other nations in achieving this integration and balance. We must find our own way, a Canadian way, to provide for a complementary and mutually supportive relationship between our commitment to individual rights and our need for a vital and responsive political culture. This is a tremendous challenge that will require both political leadership and a special kind of understanding and sophistication on the part of Canadian citizens. It forms the great challenge and promise of the next ten years of the Charter.

The Political Purposes of the Charter: Have They Been Fulfilled?
An Agnostic's Report Card

Ten years into charterland, the one clear consequence of the Charter is that it has produced an awful lot of Charter chatter by the chattering classes. In case you were wondering who belongs to this group, you need only look at the people attending this conference – those who have the time, the money, and the inclination to attend a decennial anniversary of an event which they must believe was significant for Canada, the adoption of a constitutional bill of rights.

As a charter member of the chattering classes I do not mean to sound ungrateful. For whatever the Charter has done for our fellow citizens, it has surely given us members of Canada's chattering classes a lot more to talk about, to write about, and, yes, to litigate about. Life for us has been much more interesting in charterland than it was in Canada without the Charter.

Still, grateful though we should be to the folks who brought us the Charter, I do not think they had the chattering classes in mind as its principal beneficiary. No, I believe that they had larger goals in mind. Unity, liberty, and equality – these were the larger purposes that animated the Charter's sponsors and supporters. It is in terms of those larger purposes that I wish to examine the first decade of life in the Canadian charterland.

Let me begin with the purpose of the Charter's political sponsors. By political sponsors I have in mind the politicians who took the lead in making the Charter a priority for constitutional reform in Canada. These sponsors were primarily the federal Liberals and above all their leader, Pierre Elliott Trudeau. There were other leaders and other parties who backed the project – in particular, the national NDP and its predecessor, the CCF, right back to the days of M.J. Coldwell and Frank Scott. But it was the Trudeau Liberals who, from the late 1960s on, made it their number one constitutional cause. They, more than any other politicians, are responsible for the birth of charterland ten years ago.

In making the Charter the first plank in their constitutional platform, the Trudeau Liberals aimed to counter the decentralizing thrust of Quebec's constitutional aspirations.[1] If constitutional reform was to take place, it should be directed towards changes that would pull the country together rather than demands emanating from Quebec and other provinces that threatened to pull it apart. Pre-eminent among such unifying proposals was a Charter of Rights crystallizing in Canada's highest law the common values of its people. For Trudeau's own people, the Québécois, such a Charter was designed to reorient their sense of national destiny: instead of remaining cooped up on a provincial reserve they would become citizens bearing equal rights, with full access to a bilingual and multicultural continental state.[2]

Trudeau, in his first public speech on the Charter (to the Canadian Bar Association in 1967), emphasized its unifying potential. In making a Charter of Rights the first priority of constitutional reform, he explained, "Essentially we will be testing – and hopefully, establishing – the unity of Canada."[3] Again in his final speech in the parliamentary debate on the Charter in 1981, he summed up his case for the Charter with these words: "Lest the forces of self-interest tear us apart, we must now define the common thread that binds us together."[4]

So now, after ten years of the Charter, what can be said about its consequences for national unity? Has it become "the common thread that binds us together"?

Undoubtedly the Charter has had a profound effect on how many Canadians think about the constitution and their participation in Canadian citizenship. The Charter's impact on civic consciousness is probably more significant than any of its more direct effects on public policy. No one has described this dimension of the Charter more insightfully than my political science colleague, Alan Cairns. In his writings, Cairns has shown how the Charter, by shifting the focus of Canadian constitutionalism from the powers of governments to the rights of citizens, tends to convert "a government's constitution to a citizen's constitution."[5] That the Charter has given citizens a greater stake in the constitution – indeed, a greater sense of constitutional proprietorship – is most evident in the demand for a more democratic form of constitution-making. A constitution that inscribes the rights of the people belongs to the people and is not to be altered by eleven first ministers meeting behind closed doors.

However profound the Charter's influence has been on how some Canadians think about their country and its constitution, that influence has not been felt evenly in all parts of Canada. To put the matter bluntly, as Cairns and all of us must observe in the aftermath of the Meech Lake debacle, the Charter did not "take" in Quebec the way it did in the rest of Canada.[6] The majority of French Quebeckers did not make Charter rights their fundamental constitutional value. The Trudeau vision of a Canada – composed of citizens bearing equal rights who resided in equal provinces with their prime allegiance to a bilingual/multicultural nation-state – did not capture the hearts and minds of the Québécois. Trudeau may be a constitutional hero in English Canada, but ironically he is not a constitutional hero for the majority in his home province, Quebec.

We should be clear about the asymmetry of charterphilia. It is not a case of Quebeckers being less civil libertarian, less supportive of fundamental Charter values than the rest of Canada. In 1987, four of us carried out a survey of Canadian attitudes to the Charter of Rights and its values. The survey was conducted through in-depth interviews with a representative sample of 2,000 Canadians and 500 of their elected politicians, including 85 members of the Parti Québécois. At that time, we found in both English and French Canada (including Péquiste politicians) a high level of support for the Charter and its fundamental values of political freedom, due process of law, and social equality. Our conclusion, in a nutshell, was that so far as civil liberties are concerned, Quebec is not a distinct society.[7]

The Charter became divisive only when it became involved as a contentious symbol in our constitutional politics. This occurred in the Meech Lake round, which began just as we were completing our survey. During the Meech round, for many citizens and politicians in English-speaking Canada, the Charter became an icon, a symbol of constitutional first principles.

This tendency came to a head in December 1988 when Quebec, in the wake of the Supreme Court's decision overturning its French-only sign law,[8] invoked the Charter's override clause to enact legislation re-establishing the French-only rule for outdoor advertising. In the hue and cry which then arose outside Quebec we could hear how the rhetoric of constitutional rights invests political discourse with a deep sense of moral rectitude. English-speaking Canadians who in the past simply disliked Quebec's language policy could now, as Roger Gibbons has observed, "wrap themselves in the flag of the Charter and come charging forward in defence of universal human rights."[9] There was no need to give any heed to French Quebeckers' beliefs about what was necessary for the survival of their culture. Clifford Lincoln's words, "Rights are rights and will always be rights," brought tears to his own and to English Canada's eyes. Freedom to advertise in the language of one's choice was now elevated to the status of a fundamental human right that must override any other human right or social interest. The Meech Lake Accord must die because its recognition of Quebec's distinct culture posed too severe a threat to fundamental rights.

The message the rest of Canada sent to Quebec – and Newfoundland's premier, Clyde Wells, was the chief messenger – was essentially this: "Quebec, you must choose: either our Charter or your distinct society. Show us that your first allegiance is to a Canadian nation defined by its Charter of Rights and Freedoms and not to a province in which the French majority have the power to preserve and promote their distinct culture."[10] Given that choice, it was clear which option the majority of Quebeckers would choose. They would stick with the original bargain of Confederation. A jurisdiction in which the French majority could maintain and develop its distinct identity would remain their fundamental constitutional value. And if that condition appeared unobtainable under a constitution shared with other Canadians, the majority of Quebeckers would prefer to be a separate people with their own constitution.

And so the Charter, at this moment of Canadian history, rather than realizing its political sponsors' aim of serving as an instrument of national unity, had become a major source, arguably the major source, of disunity. I say "at this moment" because the divisive effect of the Charter need not be a permanent condition. It is not the actual Charter but the Charter as political icon and Charter worship as a misguided political fundamentalism that render the Charter a source of disunity in Canada.

The actual Charter is a complex and highly textured document. It recognizes collective as well as individual rights. Its first section recognizes the need to balance Charter rights against other important concerns of a free and democratic society. Its legislative override clause wisely acknowledges that judges as well as legislators are fallible and that neither should have the last word in making decisions about the balance to be struck among competing rights and freedoms.[11] Section 23 of the Charter even provides for Quebec's distinctiveness by leaving discretion over the language régime for the schooling of Quebec immigrants to the government and legislature of Quebec.

The multidimensional, balanced nature of the Canadian Charter is equally evident in its interpretation by the courts. This is particularly true of the Supreme Court of Canada's jurisprudence, which is so crucial in fleshing out the Charter's meaning in concrete situations. In its decision on Quebec's sign law, for instance, the Court held that a law requiring predominantly (although not exclusively) French signs could be justified as a reasonable limit on freedom of expression in order to achieve the legitimate objective of maintaining Quebec's "visage linguistique." Bill 178's indoor/outdoor compromise may actually satisfy the Supreme Court's ruling.

In the present post-Meech "Canada Round" of constitutional politics, English-speaking Canadians seem much more willing to recognize Quebec's distinctness and incorporate it as a consideration that, like multiculturalism and aboriginal tradition, is to be given weight in interpreting the Charter. So I remain optimistic that we can have our Charter and our country too – provided that we abandon Charter patriotism for Charter realism.

The Canadian Charter of Rights and Freedoms does not owe its existence solely to politicians. The Charter's political sponsors were aided and abetted by a phalanx of academics and lawyers who believed a Charter was needed to enhance our freedom and secure our liberty. These civil libertarian advocates of a Charter I will call "the believers." Has the believers' faith in the Charter as a bastion against oppressive government been borne out by results?

On this front I cannot detect a great deal of change resulting from the Charter. However, I must confess that I am not well qualified to report in this area, as I do not think we Canadians were exactly in chains before the Charter, nor that the quality of freedom enjoyed by citizens in the great republic to the south through two centuries of living with a constitutional bill of rights was distinctly superior to our own.

Most of the laws limiting free expression have survived the first decade in charterland. In considering the challenges to these laws the courts have generally (and for the most part wisely) favoured the rights of those who can be seriously injured by various forms of communication – complainants in sexual assault cases,[12] the targets of publications intended to arouse race hatred,[13] children manipulated by television advertising[14] and those who are vulnerable to consumers of pornography celebrating sexual violence.[15] The main exception, it would seem, is the Supreme Court's decision in the *Edmonton Journal* case [16] permitting journalists to report the smutty details of divorce proceedings – hardly a great blow for freedom.

It is possible that the Charter's impact on the quality of political freedom may not be felt primarily through the courts' striking down oppressive laws but in its influence on public attitudes. The Charter's most emancipating effect could very well be its tendency, earlier noted, to foster expectations of a less élitist, more democratic form of constitution-making. While such a tendency may provide a civic culture more susceptible to genuine constitutional self-determination, it does not necessarily enhance the prospects of Canadian unity.[17] Canadians are learning in the post-Meech round that it is easier to use their political freedom to defeat an élitist accord than to negotiate a popular accord.

On this matter of popular attitudes, I must add, on a personal note, that as a university professor I do not find that ten years in charterland have made my working environment more tolerant or free from oppression. On the contrary, in thirty-five years of university teaching, I have never sensed as much pressure to conform to certain political positions as I do at the present time, particularly when objection is made to the expression of ideas that are offensive to certain groups. As this very presentation may all too clearly show, professors of political science cannot really function if they are not permitted to be offensive.

It is in the field of criminal justice that the Charter has its greatest potential for enhancing liberty and resisting state oppression. Most of the laws struck down by the courts on Charter grounds have been part of

Canada's criminal law.[18] Most of these have been anachronistic elements of criminal law which no one should miss.[19] Most of the activities of the executive branch of government struck down or modified through Charter review in the courts are the practices and policies of prosecutors and the police.

It is also in the field of criminal justice that the Charter is most accessible to the individual Canadian. The Charter gives those who come under police surveillance or are charged with a criminal offence (provided that they retain legal counsel) an extra line of defence. Through legal aid, hundreds of thousands of Canadians have made effective use of professional legal advice and representation. The trench warfare of the criminal justice system is the everyday arena of Charter combat. Important victories have been recorded there. Laws that criminalized abortion[20] and imposed a seven-year mandatory prison term for drug importing have been struck down.[21] Judges have shown that they will throw out evidence obtained through an interrogation in which the police did not afford suspects a real opportunity to exercise their right to legal counsel.[22]

There have been losses in this arena too. The judiciary have on occasion, as for instance with impaired driving[23] and gun control laws,[24] given the nod to crime prevention and social order over individual liberty. For the avid civil libertarian, a single loss is one loss too many. Still, my impression is that, on balance, court decisions on the criminal justice dimension of the Charter have been relatively liberal. Indeed, a comparison with American jurisprudence in this area indicates that on a number of issues the contemporary Canadian Supreme Court has been more liberal than the U.S. Supreme Court even in the Warren court era.[25] As a result, Canada's criminal law and the rules governing its application are more sensitive to the claims of individual liberty than was the case before the Charter.

Even if this is so, it does not necessarily follow that Canada's criminal justice system is actually functioning in a more liberal and less oppressive manner. Jurisprudential triumphs do not automatically change the behaviour of the police and justice officials to whom they theoretically apply. Empirical research in the United States demonstrated that the police in several American cities coped with the Warren court's civil liberty decisions by avoiding the courts and administering their own brand of justice in the back alleys.[26] We simply do not know the extent of police compliance with the Supreme Court's Charter rulings because we have not looked. The answer is not to be found in the law reports but through independent social science surveillance of the police and justice officials.

Even if we were to find out that Charter rulings have actually changed the behaviour of those who administer the criminal justice system, that in itself would not mean that the system as a whole has become much less oppressive. We know that the Americans with their hoary old Bill of Rights and we Canadians with our shiny new Charter continue to incarcerate a higher proportion of our populations than virtually any other liberal democracy.[27] Charters of rights do not change that condition, nor do they do much for the people in the prisons, aside from giving them the right to vote. If in the criminal justice field the Charter does no more than line the path to prison with procedural safeguards, it will indeed be a shallow victory for civil liberty.

There was another cluster of interest groups and ideologues besides the civil libertarians who were strong advocates of the Charter. These I would call "the hopers": the egalitarians on the left who hoped the Charter would be an instrument for reforming society. Whereas the civil libertarians believed the Charter was essential for preserving liberty, the egalitarians hoped it would bring about social equality.

The egalitarian hopers must be much more disappointed with the results of the Charter than the civil libertarian believers. They ought to be more disappointed for the very good reason that a constitutional charter of rights is an ill-conceived instrument for promoting equality in civil society.[28] The Charter's aim is to restrain government, to protect the negative freedom of citizens – freedom from the strong arm of the state. The Charter is used to attack legislation and government programs for what they do – not what they fail to do. But those who seek equality of social and economic condition need a strong state that can and will intervene in civil society to redistribute power and wealth and enhance the welfare of those most vulnerable to the free play of market forces. Government is to be attacked not for its sins of commission but for its sins of omission. For persons of this persuasion, particularly for those who flail about in the courts, the Charter of Rights was bound to be a disappointment.

And of course it has been: the Charter has done little to alter power relations, redistribute wealth, or promote social welfare within the Canadian version of welfare capitalism. The Supreme Court's interpretation of the Charter has minimized its impact on social and economic relations. I refer, in particular, to its decision in *Dolphin Delivery*[29] to exclude from the Charter's reach court enforcement of the common law in so-called private disputes, including labour disputes, in which government is not a party, as well as to the Court's interpretation of the Charter in a series of cases that have the effect of largely excluding from the Charter's ambit both the collective bargaining rights of labour[30] and the corporate economic rights of business.[31] A majority of Supreme Court justices have shown a determination to remain in the middle of the political spectrum on socio-economic issues – a pattern that must be more objectionable to those who want social change than to those content with the status quo.

The Charter's limited scope has not deterred lawyers representing social action groups from trying to use the Charter as a vehicle for social change. Their efforts have aroused the ire of critics on the right who fear that a "court party" led by charterphile lawyers will use Charter advocacy as an undemocratic means of advancing the interests of special interest groups.[32] Some left-wing critics have been equally aroused by the "court party" on the grounds that Charter litigation will fritter away the energy and resources of progressive social forces.[33]

There is little evidence thus far to support the concerns of charterphobes on the right or left.[34] Right-wing critics of the court party can point to few instances where judicial review under the Charter has forced elected politicians to initiate policies or spend money against their wishes. Nor is there any evidence that feminists, anti-racists, the labour movement, environmentalists, or other groups working for social reform in Canada have decided to forsake direct political action for Charter litigation. Most interest groups are smart enough to work both sides of the street.

If the Charter is to have a fundamental effect on the distribution of wealth and power and the level of social welfare in Canada, it will not be through its application in the courts but through its influence on the political consciousness of citizens. If Charter idolatry were to persuade the vast majority of Canadians that the Charter really does embody their most fundamental rights and freedoms and that the key to social progress is restricting government activity, then indeed the Charter would have contributed mightily to a shift of the entire political spectrum to the right.

So let us add up my score card: for the political sponsors, up to now more disunity than unity; for the civil libertarian believers, a wee bit of liberty; for the egalitarian hopers, not much, if any, equality.

Personally, I remain doubtful about whether the Charter is a good or bad thing for Canada. The one feature of charterland I find difficult to stomach is Charter worship. I believe the country might choke on Charter patriotism too. The Charter has done little good for anything I care much about except to enrich the intellectual life of the chattering classes. For that, I know, I should be exceedingly thankful.

NOTES

1 See Peter H. Russell, "The Political Purposes of the Canadian Charter of Rights and Freedoms," (1983) 61 *Canadian Bar Review* 30.

2 For an analysis of Trudeau's ideological use of the Charter and its failure, see Kenneth McRoberts, *English Canada and Quebec: Avoiding the Issue* (North York: York University Centre for Canadian Studies 1992).

3 Pierre Elliott Trudeau, *Federalism and the French Canadians* (Toronto: Macmillan, 1968) 54.

4 House of Commons Debates, 23 March 1981, 8519.

5 See, in particular, Alan C. Cairns, *Disruptions: Constitutional Struggles from the Charter to Meech Lake* (Toronto: McClelland and Stewart 1990).

6 See Alan C. Cairns, *The Charter Versus Federalism: The Dilemmas of Constitutional Reform* (Montreal: McGill-Queen's University Press 1992) chapter 4.

7 Paul Sniderman, Joseph Fletcher, Peter Russell, and Philip Tetlock, "Liberty, Authority and Community: Civil Liberties and the Canadian Political Community," paper presented at the Annual Meeting of the Canadian Political Science Association, Windsor, Ontario, 9 June 1988.

8 *Ford v. A.-G. Quebec* , [1988] 2 SCR 712.

9 Roger Gibbons, "Constitutional Politics in the West and the Rest," in Robert Young, ed., *Confederation in Crisis* (Toronto: James Lorimer 1991), 23.

10 For an analysis of this ideological conflict see Charles Taylor, "Shared and Divergent Values," in Ronald L. Watts and Douglas M. Brown, eds., *Options for a New Canada* (Toronto: University of Toronto Press 1991), 53.

11 For an account of the wisdom of the override, see Peter H. Russell, "Standing Up for Notwithstanding," (1991) 29 *Alberta Law Review* 293.

12 *Canadian Newspapers Co. v. A.-G. Canada*, [1988] 2 SCR 112.

13 *R. v. Keegstra*, [1990] 3 SCR 697.

14 *Irwin Toy Ltd. v. A.-G. Quebec*, [1989] 1 SCR 927.

15 *R. v. Butler*, [1992] 1 SCR 452.

16 *Edmonton Journal v. A.-G. Alberta*, [1989] 2 SCR 1326.

17 This argument is more fully developed in Peter H. Russell, *Constitutional Odyssey: Can Canadians Become a Sovereign People?* (Toronto: University of Toronto Press 1992).

18 For a statistical analysis of the Supreme Court of Canada's first hundred Charter decisions, see F.L. Morton, Peter H. Russell, and Michael J. Withey, "Judging the Judges: The Supreme Court's First One Hundred Charter Decisions," in Paul Fox and Graham White, eds., *Politics: Canada*, 7th ed. (Toronto: McGraw-Hill Ryerson 1991).

19 For instance, the section of the Criminal Code making constructive murder culpable homicide which was struck down in *R. v. Vaillancourt*, [1987] 2 SCR 636.

20 *R. v. Morgentaler. Smoling and Scott*, [1988] 1 SCR 30.

21 *R. v. Smith*, [1987] 1 SCR 1045.

22 See, for instance, *R. v. Manninen*, [1987] 1 SCR 1233.

23 *R. v. Hufsky*, [1988] 1 SCR 621 and *R. v. Thomsen*, [1988] 1 SCR 640.

24 *R. v. Schwartz*, [1988] 1 SCR 640.

25 Robert Harvie and Hamer Foster, "Ties That Bind? The Supreme Court of Canada, American Jurisprudence and the Revision of Canadian Criminal Law Under the Charter," (1990) 28 *Osgoode Hall Law Journal* 729.

26 Jerome H. Skolnick, *Justice Without Trial* (New York: John Wiley 1967).

27 For Canada's high imprisonment rate among Western countries, see Curt T. Griffiths and Simon N. Verdun-Jones, *Canadian Criminal Justice* (Toronto: Butterworths 1989) 313.

28 For an elaboration of this argument, see Alan C. Hutchinson and Andrew Petter, "Private Rights/Public Wrongs: The Liberal Lie of the Charter," (1988) 38 *University of Toronto Law Journal* 270.

29 *Dolphin Delivery Ltd. v. Retail, Wholesale & Department Store Union*, [1986] 1 SCR 573.

30 The leading case is *Reference Re Public Service Employees Relation Act and Police Officers Collective Bargaining Act of Alberta*, [1987] 1 SCR 313.

31 See, in particular, *Irwin Toy Ltd. v. A.-G. Quebec*, supra note 14.

32 See Rainer Knopff and F.L. Morton, *Charter Politics* (Toronto: Nelson 1992), chapter 4.

33 See Michael Mandel, *The Charter of Rights and the Legalization of Politics in Canada* (Toronto: Wall & Thompson 1989).
34 See Richard Sigurdson, "Left and Right-wing Charterphobia in Canada," paper presented at the annual meeting of the Canadian Political Science Association, Charlottetown, 31 May 1992.

The Charter and Quebec

Let's begin with a paradox. The Charter of Rights is a concept borrowed from the United States' political culture; it has no basis in the British parliamentary system. It is often said that the Charter is now a major part of Canadian identity – at least as far as English Canadian intellectuals are concerned. So it is that this import from the United States is now hailed as a vital part of Canadian identity by precisely the same Canadian nationalists whose sense of collective identity has always been staunchly driven by anti-Americanism. Let's continue with another paradox. In Quebec, where anti-Americanism is much less prevalent than in English Canada, the Charter was received with mixed feelings. Which brings us to a question: why these reservations, since the French Canadian minority was the major reason for the Charter's being enshrined in the constitution?

It is widely known that when Pierre Trudeau started to push for a constitutionalized Charter, his main objective was to grant linguistic rights to French Canadians outside Quebec. This was one of his long-held objectives – even one of the main reason for his going into politics. He talked and wrote about it many times, years before he joined the Pearson government. It is not a coincidence that the linguistic rights are the only ones – apart from voting rights and mobility – that are not subject to the notwithstanding clause. (At the very end of the constitutional negotiations of 1981, when at least two premiers expressed serious reservations about the Charter, Prime Minister Trudeau had to compromise. He grudgingly accepted a notwithstanding clause – on the condition that linguistic rights would be exempted.) Needless to say, Trudeau, being a strong civil libertarian, believed in other rights as well. Still, the recognition of the right to schools in the minority language where numbers warrant was what he thought most important – if only because other, classical fundamental rights – right to life, a free press, a fair trial, and so on – are not and probably will never be controversial matters in Canada. Linguistic minority rights, by contrast, are clearly controversial. The protection of these rights could not, in Trudeau's mind, be left to the provinces and the federal political parties.

It must be remembered that at the heart of Pierre Trudeau's involvement in politics was the desire to make Canada a country wherein both French and English could flourish. Thus the need to grant to the francophone minorities some of the public services the anglophone minority was enjoying in Quebec – and thus the need to allow French-speaking Quebeckers to move anywhere in Canada without having to abandon their language and culture. Trudeau's views ran against the prevalent tendency of most Quebeckers to stay in Quebec – the only province in Canada where they could live and work in French. Trudeau knew that if this tendency was reinforced, Quebec would gradually become a "separate" country, whether by fact or by law. French would gradually disappear from the rest of Canada. Quebeckers would lose a vital part of their historical heritage and end up with diminished perspectives. In Trudeau's mind, the guarantee of French schools provided in the Charter would help French Canadians feel at home outside Quebec and help maintain a strong francophone presence in other provinces.

But Trudeau's move – the patriation of the constitution and the inclusion of the Charter in the constitution – gave way to a power struggle between the Quebec government and Ottawa. The Quebec government was excluded from the final agreement, and didn't sign the accord. For this reason, in Quebec the Charter could not be seen as a breakthrough or a progressivist initative. It was seen as part of a package that had been brutally imposed on Quebec without its consent.

This was another episode in the long antagonism between two schools of thought. One, embodied by Trudeau, focused on the rights of French Canadian individuals; given equal chances and a decent degree of protection for their language, they should be able to affirm themselves throughout the country. The second school of thought focused on the collective rights of Quebeckers to develop the institutions and increase the powers of the province that was their only true homeland – the only place where they formed a majority.

Polls taken at the time of the patriation of the constitution, in 1981-82, show that, generally speaking, Trudeau enjoyed a great deal of popular support in Quebec – basically, what a majority really wanted was for their leaders at both levels of government to come to an agreement and make peace. But as far as the fine print of the constitution is concerned, in Quebec, as elsewhere in the country, it is the political class and the opinion leaders who set the tone when these kinds of issues are discussed. Senate reform, for instance, has recently been seen as a crucial topic, but you'll never hear anyone talk about it on Vancouver city buses or in Calgary's pubs. This is another one of those issues that become popular, albeit vague, symbols after academics and political junkies have pushed them to the top of the political agenda. Most people don't know what it is really about, but they know it must be important since all the politicians talk about it.

On the whole, Quebec's political class does not accept Trudeau's views on linguistic rights, and the enshrinement of these rights in the Charter was seen as too little, too late, as another trick of the Trudeau government to thwart the sovereigntist movement – something that looks good on paper but has no real effect in day-to-day reality. These critics might have a point. A local French school, which actually might not even be a very good school, academically speaking, is certainly not enough to attract a French-speaking family to an area where it will be unable to live and work in French. The sad truth is that the type of culture transmitted by such a marginal school might be quite impoverished, because the critical mass needed to develop vibrant cultural institutions is not present in most areas outside Quebec and parts of Ontario and New Brunswick.

As for the rest of the Charter, it was received with some reluctance in Quebec – not because of its content, but because of the political circumstances surrounding it. First, the Charter was part of the fierce battle for power that had been going on for two decades between the Trudeau government and Quebec nationalists. The patriation of the constitution was Trudeau's second victory in less than two years. Bitter memories of the lost referendum on sovereignty were still very fresh, and emotions were running high. Second, it was not felt that there was a need for a federal Charter, since Quebec already had a Charter of Rights, and an older one to boot. The Quebec Charter was promulgated in 1975, seven years before the federal Charter. Its impact has not been as great as the federal Charter because it is not constitutionalized, but it is actually more comprehensive and progressive. For instance, it includes the rights of the gay minority. And, of course, all other basic rights are protected. (The Supreme Court judgment that struck down Bill 101's provision on language was based on the Quebec Charter as well as on the federal Charter.)

Excluding the issue of linguistic rights (I'll return to this later), Quebec holds the same views about rights as the rest of Canada. Quebec's legislative assembly is the oldest continuously sitting democratic parliament in the world outside Great Britain. Quebeckers believe in and live by the same democratic rules as the average Canadian – actually, owing to their long-rooted parliamentary tradition, they might even be fonder of liberal democracy's basic values than many English-speaking Canadians who have not lived for so many generations in a democracy – let alone the aboriginals, whose spokesmen – whose male spokesmen, I should say – want their communities to be exempted from the Charter of Rights.

In Quebec, as elsewhere, it is a given that even in a democratic system, minorities – and individuals – cannot rely on majorities for the protection of some of their rights. In contemporary Canada, simple majority rule would probably bring back capital punishment. Members of visible minorities, lesbian artists, dissident writers – anyone out of the mainstream cannot hope for justice if justice is in the hands of the majority with no checks on its powers. Majority rule is often equivalent to mob rule. As for linguistic minorities, they certainly would be at considerable risk if they had to live under the system proposed by those who advocate exclusive provincial jurisdiction over language and linguistic rights. Nevertheless – and this is a widespread concern in Quebec – the Charter brought us into another world, a world in which unelected people, often influenced by special interest groups and lobbies, can strike down laws voted by duly elected governments. In Quebec as in other provinces, pressure groups have jumped on the federal Charter's train to push for self-serving laws which they cannot obtain otherwise, since they never manage to get elected and do not bother to work within political parties to push for their views. In Quebec as in other provinces, the "court party," as a political scientist calls it, is thriving. The Commission on Human Rights established by the Quebec government after the Quebec Charter was adopted is a large bureaucratic affair, entirely financed by public funds, which leaves little room for grassroots and voluntary organizations like the B.C. Civil Liberties Association. Its guarantee of independence lies in the fact that board nominations must be approved by two-thirds of the National Assembly. Its staff is unionized. Two years ago a separate court was created to deal with human rights. Its decisions have forced publicly financed institutions to change their policies. For instance, the human rights tribunal forced the admission of an autistic child into a regular class on the ground that it was better for his development and that he needed to make friends. The court granted him the right to be accompanied at public expense by a personal teaching assistant. This is, to say the least, a debatable decision and an issue that could have gained from some public discussion among educators and taxpayers.

Precisely because they are attached to the British parliamentary system, many Quebeckers are sensitive to the risk of having non-elected judges interfere with the democratic process of government. But should the judges be elected? Wouldn't that lead to the politicization of the judiciary? Aren't the excesses brought about by the American system worse than the problem it was supposed to cure? As we've seen in recent years, the American way of choosing judges on ideological grounds and checking into their personal life is overly politicized and can lead to thoroughly disgraceful and circus-like scenes such as those we saw during the Robert Bork and Clarence Thomas hearings.

To sum up briefly: in Quebec, the fact that judges infringe on the power of duly elected governments raises more doubts and draws more criticism than elsewhere in Canada – where most critics of the Charter come from the right. This is not the case in Quebec, where people on the left are among the most vocal critics of the excesses brought about by the Charter, because they believe that most public interest issues should be dealt with in the political arena. The court party too is thriving in Quebec, as elsewhere; Quebec's pressure groups raise the same kinds of issues and try to obtain the same benefits. In Quebec, as elsewhere, those who really benefit from the Charter are well-organized pressure groups; individuals do not have the financial means to bring forward their cases. This makes the so-called dichotomy between individual rights and collective rights a bit fuzzy. Which brings us to the famous, or infamous, law 178, which forbids English – or any other language other than French – on public commercial signs in Quebec.

First, let's remember that Quebec never asked for a notwithstanding clause in the Charter. A New Democratic premier, Allan Blakeney, and a Conservatice premier, Sterling Lyon, demanded it. Pierre Trudeau reluctantly acccepted it as a final compromise. Actually, the clause is not as silly as some portray it. The notwithstanding clause protects elected governments – the only institutions directly accountable to the people – against arbitrary judgments. It could be invoked on very sound grounds. One can imagine this clause being invoked to protect society against a judge who strikes down a law on gun control or compulsary seatbelts or higher auto insurance premiums for younger men who are responsible for most accidents, or against a judge who would opt for the Irish way of dealing with women who want access to abortions.

The supporters of the notwithstanding clause argued that a government would pay a very heavy price if they used it against a minority. They were right. The Bourassa government paid a very heavy price when it used the notwithstanding clause after the Supreme Court ruled that banning English from commercial signs was an infringement on freedom of expression. This was the main factor that led to the failure of the Meech Lake Accord. Bill 178 was a godsend for those – like Premier Filmon in Manitoba – who were looking for a pretext to renege on the signatures of their predecessors.

Of course, because this happened in Quebec and because the minority involved was English, not French-speaking, it drew a lot of attention, and raised more outrage than the recent blatant denial of French Canadians' school rights in Alberta and Saskatchewan. Law 178 crystallized the common prejudices already existing against Quebec. Nobody in English Canada paid much attention to the fact that Quebec's English minority has a comprehensive, publicly financed network of schools, universities, hospitals, and institutions for which there is no equivalent in any other province. One can spend his or her entire life in Montreal without bothering to learn a single word of French. And notwithstanding law 178, one can still see quite a lot of bilingual, even unilingal, English signs in the Montreal area.

I personally think that law 178 was a political mistake. (It probably will be repealed next year, when the five-year period for the notwithstanding clause comes to an end.) What needs to be pointed out, however, is that most people who were opposed to the Supreme Court judgment on commercial signs were convinced that they were not going against a fundamental right. They thought the judges were wrong in assimilating the language of commerce to freedom of expression. Freedom of expression, they argued, had to do with political action, ideas, newspapers, radio, public meetings, books, publishing and so on – not with printing the word "shoes" over a shop that sells shoes. Commercial signs and advertising, they argued, have always been regulated by municipalities, for aesthetic, historical, or security reasons. In old Quebec, for instance, signs must conform to a series of criteria to preserve the area's historical character. But of course, I realize that banning a language from public view is not the same as banning neon from historical districts.

My presentation, unfortunately, has no definitive conclusion – only a modest footnote: on the complex issue of the Charter of Rights, most Quebeckers do not react very differently from other Canadians, except on issues dealing with language. In this area also, language is the major dividing line in Canadian politics.

JEFFREY SIMPSON

Rights Talk: The Effect of the Charter on Canadian Political Discourse

A journalist may be forgiven for beginning with a reference to today's news. This morning, we read of the federal government's plans for a referendum bill. Two reactions immediately ensued, both illustrative of contemporary political discourse, one traditional, the other rather new. First, the opposition parties, as is typical, healthy, and traditional in a parliamentary democracy, immediately raised questions about this or that aspect of the proposed legislation. Second, third-party actors – so-called interest groups – threatened to bring a Charter challenge against the legislation, alleging that its provisions infringed, among other possibilities, on the rights of free speech and free association. That interest groups should condemn all or part of government legislation is a traditional part of parliamentary democracy; that they should threaten a Charter challenge is a decade-old twist.

One day's news on the referendum front illustrates the Charter's impact on Canadian affairs in two ways. The government indicated that it could not allow spending limits and umbrella groups because its lawyers had indicated such a bill would not be "Charter-proof" – that is, it would not withstand a court challenge on Charter grounds. This illustrates what all close observers of government now realize: that almost every move any government makes these days, especially in the field of legislation, is reviewed and reviewed again for its charter implications. Departments of Justice in Ottawa and the provinces have become like treasury boards: new central agencies. Whether this has made for better legislation is a moot point; that it has added another complication to governing is not.

Similarly, the immediate threat of a Charter challenge took what I would argue is a profoundly political question – the holding and organizing of a referendum on the country's future constitutional arrangements – and partly deformed it into a legal one. The terms of the debate – what was important, and which side stood where – were transformed from consideration of the essence of the bill into narrower matters concerning the details of the referendum's organization. Such is the almost inevitable impact of the legalization of political debate, a legacy of the Charter.

The Charter, in the space of a decade, has become the country's most important symbol. Polls have their limitations, so I offer these results with due modesty. But consider the results of a November 1991 Focus Canada survey by Environics Research of Toronto. Eighty-nine percent of respondents were aware of the Charter, a very high number given the appalling ignorance of so many Canadians about the basic institutions of their country. Seven in ten respondents – six of ten in Quebec – considered it a "very important" part of the Canadian identity, higher than for any other symbol.

Just how important the Charter has become as a national symbol can be seen from these Environics results. Outside Quebec, 75 percent of respondents considered the Charter a "very important" symbol, compared to 71 percent for the flag, 69 percent for the anthem, 38 percent for multiculturalism, 31 percent for the CBC, 25 percent for the monarchy and 22 percent for bilingualism. Inside Quebec, the Charter still topped the list of national symbols: 64 percent for the Charter, followed by bilingualism (52 percent), anthem (39 percent), flag (38 percent), Radio Canada (31 percent), multiculturalism (29 percent), monarchy (5 percent). The same poll pointed to another intriguing impact of the Charter: the degree to which it is seen as advancing the cause of minorities. Twenty-eight percent believed their personal rights had improved under the Charter, 18 percent believed they had deteriorated, and 53 percent had seen no change. Thirty-nine percent believed the "rights of the average citizen" had improved, 16 percent thought they had deteriorated, and 38 percent thought that there had been no change. But when respondents were asked whether minorities' rights had improved, 56 percent said yes, 9 percent said no, and 26 percent believed there had been no effect.

No one can be definitive in interpreting these numbers. It may be that Canadians are proud of their country's treatment of minorities, or pleased that the Charter is protecting minorities, there being so many of them in Canada, and therefore the Charter will grow in popularity and legitimacy if it continues to be perceived as principally a shield and sword for minorities. It may also be, however, that a Charter whose principal beneficiaries are minorities will begin to lose appeal among the majority, or at least among those on whom the Charter has had little direct effect, and that eventually a backlash against either the Charter or its interpretation by activist judges may set in. It is obviously too soon to draw any conclusions.

The Charter is part of a worldwide concern for human rights, a concern that was once used in the moral battle against Communism, but that even without the Communist "threat" still evokes an emotional appeal beyond the liberal democracies. Next year, for example, the United Nations will be sponsoring a large international conference – like the Rio conference on the environment – dedicated to human rights. Countries from Czechoslovakia to Australia are giving themselves written charters, or thinking about such a move. To be for human rights is apparently to be for written charters which can be used against state infringement of rights or to promote more respect by states of those rights. Even Great Britain, which has managed to struggle along without a Charter yet still be considered among the world's democracies, has found itself bound by certain European rights codes to which it had to subscribe upon joining the European Community. Canada is therefore part of a worldwide trend, a point repeatedly made by Charter proponents in the debates of 1980-1981.

The Charter reflects and encourages the broader trend towards the "Americanization" of politics in Canada. In particular, the Charter is inspired by the suspicions of state power which find their logical expression in the U.S. balance-of-power, or checks-and-balances, system of government, which allocates to the courts a wide latitude for checking or reversing government decisions that found no echo in Canadian courts. Such is the distaste for what government has wrought in recent years in Canada that a series of proposals – some constitutional, others political – have been advanced, which have as their common thread the curtailment of the power of the prime minister and Cabinet through the control of a parliamentary majority. An elected Senate, the devolution of powers to provinces, the creation of aboriginal self-government, referenda, direct recall of members, free votes in the Commons, and, of course, the Charter are all part of this trend. In the same Environics poll quoted above, Canadians were asked in 1986 and 1991 which institutions they considered superior to those in the United States. Of fourteen categories, in only one – system of government – had respect for Canadian institutions sharply fallen. In 1986, 52 percent of Canadians believed Canada had the better system of government; by 1991, only 32 percent of Canadians so believed.

Third, but related to the "Americanization" of Canadian politics, has been the breakdown of the old élite accommodation model of governing Canada. The Charter has played an important role here, in abetting the creation of strengthening of interest groups, in judicializing many political decisions, in increasing the amount of "rights talk" in political discourse, and in making compromises more difficult.

Why has there been more "rights talk" in recent years? In part, this increase reflects the worldwide trends noted above. But there are far more profound domestic reasons. The old élite accommodation model disintegrated because it could not reflect adequately the desire to be represented by a plethora of new groups, which themselves reflected social, economic, and demographic trends. The changes to Canada's immigration policies in 1976-1977, for example, opened the doors to many more immigrants from Third World countries, thereby increasing the number of "visible minorities" who found themselves severely underrepresented among the "élites" who made the country's political decisions. The huge entry of women into the workforce both changed the nature of the family, and propelled many of them against the glass barriers that existed in all walks of Canadian life. Women, too, found themselves underrepresented in the "élite groups," and therefore some of them rejected the model whereby élites made the decisions, then "sold" them to the public. Aboriginals, of course, continued to reject all models of assimilation. They were not going to be "sold" anything by élites other than their own. The Charter, with its clauses specifically directed to each of these groups, became an instrument for their affirmation as distinct entities in the Canadian body politic.

Government scrambled to keep up with these social, economic, and demographic changes, but the political system was unable to produce policy outputs or become sufficiently representative to satisfy these groups. This failure sent groups searching outside government for redress and help, and the Charter provided one such avenue through court challenges to government sins of omission or commission. The Charter, too, was given life by lawyers, who are always disproportionately represented in politics. They were, to use Professor Peter Russell's term, represented heavily among the early "hopers" and "believers" in the Charter. And, of course, there were some historical grievances involving linguistic minorities, Japanese-Canadians and the like, which it was argued would not have occurred had a Charter been in place. Finally, a yearning for something durable and pan-Canadian emerged from the constitutional impasses of the 1960s and 1970s. A desire grew from the interminable federal-provincial bickering, and from the apparent lack of cohesion in Canada, for something unifying, ennobling, and enduring, a desire perfectly met by the Charter, which spoke to rights, values, and principles. That the Charter has not produced the unity so fervently desired, at least in English-speaking Canada, and may even have contributed to widening the existing gaps, is just one of the document's many ironies.

The governance of a heterogeneous society such as Canada has always been a supreme challenge, and that challenge is now more difficult than ever with the multiplication of groups clamouring for attention. It is also a time when respect for government and elected officials has never been lower. The political culture of Canada these days, within which public policy must be conceived and executed, reflects the increasingly self-evident facts that judges are considered more trustworthy, capable, and desirous of advancing the public interest than politicians; courts more appropriate institutions for the rectification of wrongs and the elaboration of solutions than parliaments; the Charter a surer guide to respect for and expansion of human liberties than parliaments; legal cases a better vehicle for confrontations from which will flow ringing affirmations of rights than messy compromises required by parliamentary debates, party politics, and national elections.

At a minimum, the Charter has influenced a generation of Canadians who look upon it as a supplement to parliamentary and political institutions. As the Canadian Advisory Council on the Status of Women said in its report *One Step Forward; Two Steps Back?*, "The full support of both government and the courts is needed for women to take their rightful place in Canadian society. Women must press for changes in both arenas." At worst, the Charter is seen as a surrogate for these institutions. Courts are now immersing themselves in, or being asked to concern themselves with, issues that I would argue are largely if not exclusively political. I say "political" in the non-partisan sense of questions in which all members of civil society in their capacity as citizens might be interested and affected. These would include Sunday shopping, street soliciting, mandatory retirement, tobacco advertising, tax law, spousal benefits, unemployment insurance, and abortion, among others.

Any innocent observer of public discourse in contemporary Canada must be aware, if not amazed, at the escalation of "rights talk," a phrase used by Harvard Professor Mary Ann Glendon in her book of the same name. "In its simple American form, the language of rights is the language of no compromise," she writes. "By indulging in excessively simple forms of rights talk in our pluralistic society, we needlessly multiply occasions for civil discord. We make it difficult for persons and groups with conflicting interests and views to build coalitions and achieve compromise, or even to acquire that minimal degree of mutual forbearance and understanding that promotes peaceful coexistence and keeps the door open to further communication." What Professor Glendon observes about her own excessively litigious society is creeping into Canadian discourse and infecting the political culture.

Let me offer a few contemporary Canadian examples of Professor Glendon's observation about the elevation of issues to ones of rights. When the government cut Via Rail services, those opposed to the cuts insisted that Canadians had a "right" to a national rail service. When Air Canada, even before the Crown corporation was privatized, stopped flying to certain Canadian cities, mayors and others opposed to the decision said their cities had a "right" to air service. When the government announced changes to the unemployment insurance program, taking $800 million from the fund and using it for training, opponents said recipients had a "right" to UI payments. On the east coast it was argued that Canadian fishermen had a "right" to stocks. The fish themselves became bearers of rights. In the *Singh* case, non-citizens, non-landed immigrants, were given "rights" as outlined in the Charter even though they had not been accepted as legitimate entrants into Canada. And the *Singh* case precedent is now being used in lower court appeals to argue that anyone who appears at a Canadian mission abroad has a "right" to the full protection of the Charter, including a face-to-face meeting. Smokers lobby their case in terms of their "right" to smoke; those who oppose them insist upon their "right" to enjoy a smoke-free environment. I could go on.

A distinguishing characteristic of this "rights talk" is the degree to which discretionary decisions of government and the normal and sometimes healthy tensions in a pluralistic, democratic society are elevated to those of apparently fundamental human rights. Of course, when issues are so elevated, compromise and accommodation become more difficult because rights are involved. These rights, by virtue of being rights, cannot easily be compromised. They can only be defended to the maximum. These rights also seldom have obligations or responsibilities attached to them. They "exist," therefore they "are": political statements whose underpinnings are apparently immune from examination because the use of the language of rights has raised the moral stakes. This "rights talk" can gravely deform the nature of political discourse, and, as such, can be considered the particular contribution of lawyers to our politics. Like economists, social workers, sociologists, political scientists, or other intellectual species, lawyers frame issues in terms most familiar to them. Certainly, no self-respecting interest group, labour union, or business association would make a move these days without first vetting everything with a lawyer. "Rights talk," like the fascination with the constitution itself, pleases lawyers and puts public debate within a framework where lawyers can shine. Whether this produces an appropriate framework for resolving disputes, determining priorities, and conveying a realistic sense of what can be expected from public policy is quite another matter.

What the Supreme Court and other courts cannot do effectively is consider the costs of decisions and whether the extension of benefits or the elaboration of new rights are the most urgent matters requiring governmental and societal attention in an age of straitened fiscal circumstances and inevitably jostling priorities. Judges deal with the case at court; cabinets must balance dozens of simultaneous claims. Judges try to find the balance within a case; politicians look for balances among many dossiers. Judges may have the interests of two, three, or four parties to a case to consider; politicians often must take account of the interests of a multiplicity of groups. The weakness of the judiciary in balancing competing claims, especially on the public purse, is perhaps of little con-

sequence in an age of munificence. It can become increasingly burden-
some in an age of distinctly limited government resources.

The battle over the Charter was fought a decade ago, and won by the
proponents. The Charter has changed, for better and worse, the political
culture of Canada. It is the single most Americanizing influence on our
country's political life; yet, in a curious way, it is the hardening glue defining English Canada's sense of community.

Of all the changes wrought by the tempestuous 1980s in Canada, the
Charter has been the most consequential. I am sceptical, however, that in
contributing to smashing the old political order, the Charter and the
"rights talk" it has spawned produced anything cohesive with which to
replace the old order, which, whatever its sins and deficiencies, was based
on a recognition of compromise and accommodation and balance – albeit often imperfectly – of competing claims and regional interests inherent in a geographically immense, linguistically divided, and culturally
heterogeneous country. On my more optimistic days, I believe we are
groping towards something, including new institutions, that can accommodate the new pressures in our society, including the impact of the
Charter. On my pessimistic days, I wonder if we have not imposed upon
ourselves Procrustean institutions that cannot fit the kind of country we
are, and that only by shrinking Canada's size can the country be made to
fit the institutions we are giving to it.

Have the Equality Rights Made Any Difference?

INTRODUCTION

Although this year marks the tenth anniversary of the Canadian Charter of Rights and Freedoms, it is only the seventh anniversary of the effective date of the section 15 equality rights.[1] Still, enough time has passed to make it worthwhile to be retrospective.

In the context of this conference, which included a good sampling of Charter scepticism and even Charter phobia, as well as a warning from the minister of justice about the dangers of over-empowering the courts, I fear that if I say a good word for the Charter I will be seen as contrarian, or, worse still, as a "hoper," "liberal individualist," "court party member," practitioner of "minoritarian politics," member of a "special interest group," or advocate of the Americanization of Canadian political and legal culture. But as the debate over the Charlottetown Accord illustrates, support for compromise arrangements can attract serious and, of course, sometimes quite inconsistent criticism from both ends of a spectrum.

I have three major reasons for arguing that the equality rights have done more good than harm for less advantaged persons and groups in Canadian society, and for the Canadian democratic system as a whole.[2] First, a review of the jurisprudence under section 15, and an analysis of the impact of section 15 in a wider context, leads me to that conclusion. On the basis of that review, I will argue that there have been some clearly good outcomes, a number of promising statements, and indications of rather substantial indirect impact. Second, for the purposes of this discussion I accept the Charter and judicial review of government action under its provisions as a fait accompli – whether or not we would have been better off without the Charter, it is now a part of our legal and constitutional world. In the world as it is, the practical question is whether there is some good reason to refrain from using the Charter to attempt to produce outcomes assessed to be for the benefit of less advantaged persons and groups. I think that, on balance, a boycott of the Charter would be highly counterproductive, and that it is sensible to attempt to continue to use the Charter in addition to (not in substitution for) ordinary political work designed to bring about legislative or administrative policy change in furtherance of egalitarian goals. Third, I think that when we are looking at the comparative merits of assertion of rights in the courts and assertion of claims or interests through political institutions, we should look at the strengths and weaknesses of both alternatives. However, in my view there has been a regrettable tendency in some[3] of the anti-Charter literature to set up a scathing, sometimes over-generalized and under-evidenced picture of what goes on in the courts (focused almost exclusively on the judiciary rather than the process as a whole) as against an idealized vision of what goes on in our legislatures (focused almost exclusively on elected politicians rather than governments as a whole.) I hasten to add that I will not be attempting to correct that deficiency in this paper, but wish to flag the fact that I am not sufficiently persuaded by the evidence to conclude that the courts are institutionally incapable of playing an important role in achieving the objectives embodied in the equality rights of the Charter. (To the extent that there can be found a corresponding tendency to idealize the legal system and denigrate the political one in some of the pro-Charter works, such a tendency is equally problematic.)

REVIEW OF THE IMPACT OF THE EQUALITY RIGHTS

How the Record Might Be Reviewed

First, then, a review of the section 15 jurisprudence and of the impact of section 15. The crucial question to ask is whether the Charter equality rights have done anything to remedy inequalities affecting members of the most disadvantaged groups in our society. This question is the crucial one because section 15 is aimed at counterbalancing certain kinds of inequalities between people – in other words, at disadvantage based upon the kinds of personal or socially attributed characteristics listed in the section, rather than at generic or abstract inequality.[4] As the Supreme Court of Canada concluded in *Andrews v. Law Society of British Columbia*,[5] the purpose of the section 15 rights is connected with the purpose behind human rights legislation, that is, the removal of discrimination caused by characteristics such as race, sex, age, religion, colour, ethnic or national origin, and physical or mental disability[6] (all of which are listed in section 15, and are often referred to as the "enumerated grounds").[7]

Proceeding on that premise, the Supreme Court in *Andrews* and subsequent cases[8] in effect constricted the entrance into the equality rights section, precluding cases not based upon some enumerated ground or one analogous to it. What counts as analogous? In *Andrews*, a requirement that lawyers be Canadian citizens was struck down; citizenship status therefore was analogous in that context. Presumably, illegitimacy is analogous – at least, governments seemed to consider it so in that several moved to remove the legal status of illegitimacy in the three-year hiatus between the effective date of the Charter and the effective date of the equality rights.[9] Some courts have held that sexual orientation amounts to an analogous ground,[10] though the Supreme Court has not yet decided this point.[11] In *Schachter v. A.G. (Canada)*,[12] the federal government conceded that a legislative distinction between natural and adopting parents raised an analogous ground, but the Supreme Court of Canada, giving extensive reasons on another important issue about remedies, was at pains to indicate that its decision was based only upon that concession.[13]

Thus, according to the Supreme Court, when someone is disadvantaged by law or government action on the basis of an enumerated or analogous ground, section 15 is violated. However, what follows at the stage of considering the effects of section 1 of the Charter (where there is a determination of whether the violation nevertheless constitutes a reasonable limit prescribed by law and demonstrably justified in a free and democratic society) is another matter. In general, beyond cases involving rights of the criminally accused, a fairly lenient standard is applied, leaving governments considerable latitude to make judgment calls about, for example, the scope of their programs and the need to restrict individual rights in order to protect important community interests.[14]

The constriction on entrance into section 15 has been a matter of some controversy. It marks a significant departure from a traditional Aristotelian approach to equality, the approach that is often called "formal equality," seen for example in the U.S. Constitutional jurisprudence.[15] I think the *Andrews* approach was the preferable one for the Court to take[16] because it enables, in two ways, more effective use of section 15 than would otherwise be the case. First, this approach means that section 15 can cover unintended discrimination. By way of contrast, under the equal protection clause of the Fourteenth Amendment to the U.S. Constitution, there must be some evidence of an *intention* to discriminate against the group affected.[17] It is now clear from our courts that proof of intention to discriminate is not going to be required under section 15.[18] This is particularly important for persons with disabilities, for religious minorities, and for women, because of the nature of the discrimination that most affects members of these groups (for example, the failure to build a ramp that has the unintended effect of excluding some persons with physical disabilities from a building). Second, the Supreme Court decisions show that the operative understanding of equality does not always require same treatment. Indeed, and this is very eloquently expressed in the Reasons of McIntyre J. in *Andrews*,[19] sometimes equality requires different treatment.[20] Correspondingly, the approach is asymmetrical, as is best illustrated by reference to the reasons of Madame Justice Bertha Wilson in *Turpin*:

> A finding that there is discrimination will, I think, in most but perhaps not all cases, necessarily entail a search for disadvantage that exists apart from and independent of the particular legal disadvantage being challenged. Similarly, I suggested in my reasons in *Andrews* that the determination of whether a group falls into an analogous category to those specifically enumerated in s. 15 is "not to be made only in the context of the law which is subject to challenge ..."[21]

The asymmetrical approach is seen to follow from the limitation to enumerated and analogous grounds, and from the focus on alleviating disadvantage independent of to the governmental provision. Clearly inconsistent with the ideology of formal equality, this asymmetrical approach requires a serious reconceptualization of equality in order to take root and survive.[22]

To this point I have addressed the question in terms of what the Supreme Court of Canada has said the equality rights mean. The important questions, however, are what the courts as a whole have actually done when equality issues have come before them, and what impact, if any, the equality rights have had on Canadian society (whether as a result of judicial decisions or otherwise.)

Specifically, has section 15 made a positive difference for what have come to be called "equality-seeking groups" (overlapping categories of people such as those differently abled, women, people subjected to racism, the aged, religious minorities, gays and lesbians?) There is, of course, a lively debate about this issue in the academic community. One popular view at the moment is that the Charter rights, including the equality rights, have not (and perhaps inherently cannot) be used to attain progressive goals. It is argued that by holding out an empty promise the Charter rights lead to wasted efforts, that by permitting the assertion of individual rights against state or other collective goals they reinforce a retrogressive rights-based analysis of law, that by requiring enforcement through an expensive and élitist process (the judicial system) they prejudice the disadvantaged, that by their orientation against the state they reinforce false dichotomies between "public" and "private" and between state action and inaction, and that by empowering judges to determine the legitimacy of legislation or government action without effective constraints they undermine democracy and progressive political processes.[23]

There are other Charter critics (political scientists rather than legal academics) who tend to come from the other end of the political spectrum, from the right rather than the left. From that different perspective they express grave concerns about the way the Charter permits, in their terms, "interest groups" to assert Charter rights that could defeat the will of duly elected governments.[24] These critiques sometimes carry a certain tone of indignation at the notion that some people might choose to identify with other Canadians on a basis that is not regional, and dismay at the Charter's potential to encourage such heretical forms of non-regional identification. But in some ways,[25] there are common features in the criticism from the left and from the right: "Both left- and right-wing Charterphobes assail the Charter in the way best calculated to evoke shock and horror in a society like ours – that is, they accuse it of generating anti-democratic political consequences."[26]

So far as I am aware, however, no one has taken much of an empirical look at the actual record, at least since the *Andrews* case was decided.[27] And I do not purport to do that in more than a very modest way here. I have not assembled, counted, and analysed all of the section 15 equality cases since *Andrews*, although I have tried to be comprehensive in my search for them.[28] A serious and precise study would have to be very carefully designed. A simple count of successful and failing claims would not really tell us much, even if some means were devised for weighting the initial merit of the cases. One great unknown is whether, with the successful cases, there would have been legal change in any event, and as quickly, through political action alone. If so, then the wasted efforts argument is a strong one. If not, then a victory in court truly marks an advance in the law that would not have been possible without the Charter. Another great unknown is the extent to which the unsuccessful cases rouse political activity, which in turn leads to victory through legislative change. Certainly there have been some examples of that, as in the chronology of the treatment of equality or human rights claims based on pregnancy discrimination between 1978 and the present:

1978 – the *Bliss* case, in which the Supreme Court of Canada held, in a challenge to the Unemployment Insurance Act based on the right to "equality before the law" under the Canadian Bill of Rights section 1(b), that discrimination based on pregnancy was not sex discrimination (because, among other reasons, any discrimination was created by "nature," not the statute);[29]

1978–80 – considerable public outcry and expressions of concern from women's organizations, along with strong criticism of the *Bliss* decision in the academic literature;

1978–92 – legislative reform in several jurisdictions to define "sex discrimination" in human rights statutes to include pregnancy[30] and in the Unemployment Insurance Act to remove the provision that had disentitled Ms. Bliss;[31]

1980–82 – frequent reference to the *Bliss* case in the submissions from women's and civil liberties organizations about the proposed wording of equality provisions in the Canadian Charter of Rights and Freedoms, culminating in Charter wording that seems designed, in several respects, to contradict the *Bliss* reasoning;[32]

1985 – founding of the Women's Legal Education and Action Fund (LEAF), with the objective to promote equality for all women through strategic litigation and public education;

1989 – the *Andrews* decision[33] under the Charter, in which the Supreme Court adopted an approach to equality quite inconsistent with that taken in *Bliss* (LEAF intervening);

1989 – the *Brooks* case,[34] in which the Supreme Court reversed its own previous decision in *Bliss*, relying in part on the *Andrews* approach to equality (and in which LEAF again intervened.) The Court held in *Brooks* that, under the Manitoba Human Rights Act, sex discrimination included discrimination based on pregnancy, such that an employer's sickness and accident benefits plan could not exclude employees during pregnancy. The Court said:

> In terms of the economic consequences to the employee resulting from the inability to perform employment duties, pregnancy is no different from any other health-related reason for absence from the work place.
>
> Furthermore, to not view pregnancy in this way goes against one of the purposes of anti-discrimination legislation. This purpose ... is the removal of unfair disadvantages which have been imposed on individuals or groups in society. Such an unfair disadvantage may result when the costs of an activity from which all of society benefits are placed upon a single group of persons. This is the effect of the Safeway plan. It cannot be disputed that everyone in society benefits from procreation. The Safeway plan, however, places one of the major costs of procreation entirely upon one group in society: pregnant women. Thus in distinguishing pregnancy from all other health-related reasons for not working, the plan imposes unfair disadvantages on pregnant women ... . Removal of such unfair impositions upon women and other groups in society is a key purpose of anti-discrimination legislation. Finding that the Safeway plan is discriminatory furthers that purpose.[35]

The change in approach over the decade between *Bliss* and *Brooks* was dramatic, and in my view was attributable to a kind of synergy between social and legal change; the social change involved the increased numbers of women in the paid work force (a fact referred to by the Supreme Court in *Brooks*), a climate in which organizations such as LEAF could obtain enough funding (from private sources and governments) to be effective, and a changing legal profession with increasing numbers of women and more women in relatively senior positions. In the society of the late 1980s an approach to pregnancy that took it as a necessary and appropriate part of a working person's life, to be accommodated rather than penalized, was, if not mainstream, at least understandable within the bounds of rational thinking. In the society of the late 1970s it had not been, and there was no legal discourse in which to frame such an approach.[36] The legal changes evident in the amendments to human rights legislation, the wording of the Charter and the language used by the Supreme Court in the *Brooks* case, built upon but also provided momentum for the social change.

Although Elizabeth Schneider focuses on gender equality, her comments are relevant to what may be observed in the context of the struggles of many equality-seeking groups:

> The women's movement's experience with rights shows how rights emerge from political struggle. The legal formulation of the rights grew out of and reflected feminist experience and vision and culminated in a political demand for power. The articulation of feminist theory in practice in turn heightened feminist consciousness of theoretical dilemmas and at the same time advanced feminist theoretical development. This experience, reflecting the dynamic interrelationship of theory and practice, mirrored the experience of the women's movement in general.[37]

However, a final unknown is the extent to which even dramatic legal changes, such as the one from *Bliss* to *Brooks*, lead to actual improvement in the lives of members of the groups allegedly benefited, beyond the kind of general social change and changed discourse referred to above. It is likely that some employee benefit plans similar to the one at issue in *Brooks* have been changed as a result of the decision, and that some women employees have therefore received payments during pregnancy that they would not have received before. One Alberta judicial decision following *Brooks* has implemented its principles in a way that leads to material improvement in an employee benefit plan.[38] But court decisions are not self-enforcing. It seems that although some employers respond in a responsible way, others remain unaware of the change in the law or decide to wait for someone to complain before changing their benefit programs. And when one considers the impact of the wider statements in *Brooks*, for example, of the way in which it seems to push back the wall between "public" and "private" responsibilities in its discussion of pregnancy, it is apparent that such statements, though important, will not necessarily have much impact outside their immediate factual context (i.e., benefit programs already in existence relating to women in full-time employment in the paid workforce.)

Concluding this discussion of how one would review the record, I observe that in any event, some of the commonly articulated arguments do not really turn on the record, but on the alleged *inherent* failings of the Charter. There is the shared view from the left and the right that Charter use leads to anti-democratic political consequences. But in addition, there is an interesting contradiction in the views of the critics. To put it somewhat simplistically, for the "left" critics the problem is that the Charter fails to do anything real for the disadvantaged, and may lure them into wasting time and effort on litigation: for the "right" critics the problem is that the Charter encourages the disadvantaged to identify with other Canadians on the basis of characteristics such as gender and may lead them to actually *succeed* in challenging governments.

Assessment of the Record to Date

My review of the record of the impact of the Charter equality rights will focus on this question: to what extent, if any, have the equality rights provided the basis for, or amounted to a causative factor in, legal change that benefits minorities and women? I make the assumption that legal change sometimes leads to or at least assists social or economic change, as when pregnancy discrimination is held to be sex discrimination under law: there is ensuing social change in the meaning of pregnancy in a woman's life, and economic change through the payment of increased benefits to some women. But these are never simple questions. Does the change in law lead to the hiring of fewer women and thus to net deterioration of women's position in the workforce? Does it reinforce the view that child-rearing is "women's work"? Acknowledging these complexities, I do not attempt to go beyond the stage of legal change in this discussion.

The assessment is in two parts; first, litigation and law reform directly affected by section 15; second, the more indirect effects of section 15.

Litigation and Law Reform Directly
Affected by Equality Rights Claims

In section 15 case law, or legislative reform clearly caused by section 15 litigation, one can point to more than a few (though fewer than many) positive outcomes from the perspective of equality-seeking groups. With some exceptions, these outcomes tend to be in areas that do not require large expenditure of funds and that involve an attack on government action rather than inaction.

Beginning with the case law, the right to vote has been extended to persons with some mental disabilities[39] and to some prisoners,[40] and the criminal trial procedures regarding persons found not guilty by reason of insanity have been reformed to ensure that the accused can control and direct his or her own defence.[41] In *Tétreault-Gadoury v. Canada (Employment and Immigration)*[42] the Supreme Court held that excluding otherwise qualified persons over the age of 65 from unemployment insurance benefits was unjustified discrimination. Persons discriminated against on the basis of their sexual orientation have successfully claimed statutory benefits and human rights protection.[43] In a recent British Columbia case it was determined that treatment facilities in psychiatric institutions must be made available equally to women and men;[44] and in *Manitoba Health Care Unions v. Bethseda Hospital*[45] the court held that a legislated arbitrary cap on amounts payable under a pay equity plan should be removed. (Both of those cases are exceptional in that they may require the expenditure of significant sums by government.)[46] The issue in *R. v. Bob*[47] was whether the registrar could refuse to grant a bingo licence to members of First Nations bands who refused to pay the usual licence fee, but who were normally tax-exempt. The Saskatchewan Court of Appeal held that the refusal violated section 15. *Speerin and Whitehead v. Corporation of the City of North Bay*[48] came before the Ontario General Division, which upheld a claim that section 15 required that a person with a physical disability should be able to avail herself of the exemption in the

Limitation Act from the Municipal Act's seven-day notice provision on the same basis as minors or persons with a mental disability. And in *Re Hines and Registrar of Motor Vehicles et al; Canadian Diabetes Association, Intervenor*[49] Motor Vehicle Act regulations that created a blanket prohibition against issuing Class 1 or 2 licences to insulin-dependent diabetics were struck down.

In the realm of legislative change, in the three-year moratorium period between the effective date of the Charter and the effective date of section 15 (17 April 1982–17 April 1985), most governments took the opportunity to do some minor cleaning up of the most obviously discriminatory provisions. (For example, in British Columbia the legal stigmatization of illegitimacy was removed,[50] as was spousal immunity in tort.)[51] Nevertheless, there were still some relatively easy targets left on the legislative books after the Charter came into effect. In several cases, these were removed after litigation was commenced challenging them.[52] In general, however, it is difficult to ascertain the extent to which legislative change has been moved by pending or contemplated litigation. Litigation that is settled before trial leaves limited traces in court records, and changes resulting from government's knowledge of contemplated (never commenced) litigation leave none. More important, the public records do not disclose the extent to which new legislative provisions and reviews of existing legislation, policy, and practices are shaped by a watchful eye on the Charter. As Brian Slattery points out, the Charter belongs at least as much to the governments as it does to the courts.[53] Governments should be taking the Charter's statements of fundamental norms and values into account in policy formation and in the drafting of legislation and regulations. After all, the duly elected governments of the country brought the Charter into effect. Therefore, governments should resist the temptation to offload responsibility for implementing and observing Charter guarantees onto the courts, perforce requiring the courts to serve a policing function, awaiting complaints from citizens that may never come or never succeed. To what extent are governments resisting that temptation, and with what variations from government to government? That is an important question, and would provide the basis for some interesting future research. One recent example of a government paying attention to the equality rights in section 15 and section 28[54] of the Charter may be found in the 1992 federal sexual assault legislation.[55]

There, the Charter rights of persons accused of sexual assault (a largely male group) to a fair trial had to be balanced against the Charter rights of victims and potential victims of sexual assault (largely women and children) to equality and security of the person. The consultation process explicitly included those with real expertise on both sides of that equation. Perhaps this example shines so brightly because of its rarity. (An area in which there has been significant Charter-driven change, though not necessarily linked to section 15, is electoral laws and practices.)

Simultaneously with the judicial decisions and legislative reforms that I have described, there have been not only many unsuccessful attempts to invoke the equality rights (whether for the benefit of enumerated or analogous groups, or others outside those categories) but also a substantial number of cases in which Charter rights (rarely the equality rights, but frequently the legal rights, such as the right to make full answer and defence) have been used to attack provisions designed to remedy inequality. In some of these cases, groups such as the Canadian Disability Rights Council and the Women's Legal Education and Action Fund have intervened to support the existing legislation. The number of times in which this has occurred provides support for both Charter critics (if the Charter did not exist, disadvantaged groups would not have to spend scarce time and resources in defending progressive legislation against this kind of attack) and Charter supporters (providing support for government legislation and programs in this way belies the contention that the combination of the Charter and groups such as LEAF is inherently anti-democratic.)[56]

In this context, it is impossible to ignore the issue of access to the courts. Charter litigation is expensive and, since the cancellation of the federal Court Challenges Program, there is no legal aid available for it.[57] There is clearly differential access to the courts when one compares governments and corporate interests with members of disadvantaged groups. Further, the access issue has several dimensions. It is not simply that financial means enable litigation to be conducted in pursuit of specific claims. It is also that financial resources permit litigation and law reform strategies to be formulated and pursued.[58]

My conclusion, then, with respect to the direct use of section 15 is that it has led to a small number of positive outcomes, either through litigation or through law reform initiatives. There have been one or two instances in which its direct use has brought about what I would consider to be negative or doubtful outcomes.[59] On the whole, however, most of what has been accomplished through the assertion of section 15 has improved the legal position of women, persons with disabilities, non-citizens in Canada, gays and lesbians, and other disadvantaged groups.

Indirect Impact of Equality Rights in Litigation and Law Reform

The second way to assess the effectiveness of section 15 is to examine its impact outside section 15 cases. I think it has had considerable importance in the courts and outside them, simply as an authoritative normative statement about fundamental values of equality. More specifically, it has shaped the interpretation of other parts of the Charter, federal and provincial statutes (particularly human rights legislation), and some areas of common law doctrine.

It is worthy of note that section 15, setting out that every individual is equal before and under the law and entitled to the equal protection and equal benefit of the law without discrimination based on the list of grounds and those analogous to them, states a fundamental norm of equality between Canada's two founding genders, among racial groups, religious groups, and others, that was not previously present in our law. This statement in part fulfils Canada's obligations under various international conventions, such as the Convention on Elimination of all Forms of Discrimination against Women[60] and the International Covenant on Civil and Political Rights.[61] Invocation of this statement can be significant in a number of contexts. For example, it supports the legitimacy and necessity of continuing judicial education programs on gender and race issues. It provides an authoritative basis for moves that it does not compel, such as those recently taken by the Law Society of British Columbia to make it a disciplinary offence for members to discriminate on bases such as race, sex, and sexual orientation.[62] Further, the wording of section 15, in particular the inclusion of subsection 15(2), shows that the Canadian understanding of equality includes measures designed to ameliorate disadvantage such as affirmative action programs, and this is important in a number of contexts.

The equality rights have assisted the court in shaping other Charter rights. For example, the equality rights helped in determining the scope of freedom of expression in both *Keegstra*[63] and *Butler*,[64] and the meaning of freedom of religion in *R. v. Big M Drug Mart Ltd.*[65] and *R. v. Edwards Books and Art Ltd.*[66] The debate about the extent to which this should occur is illustrated in the recent Supreme Court of Canada decision in *R. v. Zundel.*[67] However, it is now clearly accepted that the equality rights, as understood in *Andrews v. Law Society,*[68] are to be taken into account where appropriate in interpreting other Charter provisions and determining their application in particular contexts. (This flows from the general proposition that where there is an interpretation consistent with the Charter and one inconsistent with it, the former should be chosen.)[69] Implicitly, the existence of sections 15 and 28 of the Charter assisted the court in determining the scope of the section 7 right to security of the person and liberty in *R. v. Morgentaler.*[70] And explicitly, in *Native Women's Association of Canada v. Canada,*[71] the Federal Court held that freedom of expression applied equally to men and women – thus, the federal government violated aboriginal women's right to freedom of expression when it funded male-dominated aboriginal peoples' organizations (but not the Native Women's Association of Canada) to participate in the constitutional discussions leading to the Charlottetown Accord, which concerned, among other things, the Charter rights of aboriginal women.

With respect to statutes and common law doctrine, the most obvious impact of the Charter equality rights has probably been in the area of human rights legislation (although it would be much more accurate to describe what has happened there as cross-fertilization rather than one-way impact.) *Brooks v. Canada Safeway Ltd.*[72] and *Janzen v. Platy Enterprises Ltd.*[73] both involved interpretation of the Manitoba Human Rights Act. The Supreme Court of Canada referred to its own decision in *Andrews* and approached the equality claims by women facing discrimination in sex-specific contexts in a very different way from, for example, the American courts.[74] Another example of a case in which the interpretation of a statute was shaped by Charter guarantees is *Re Baby R,*[75] in which the British Columbia Supreme Court held that the provincial Family and Child Service Act, permitting apprehension of a child in need of protection, does not permit the apprehension of a foetus in utero, even when the pregnant woman refuses medical advice (in the case at issue, advice to undergo a Caesarean section because of the assessment of high risk to the foetus through a vaginal delivery). The Criminal Code itself was up for interpretation in *R. v. Sullivan*,[76] and the Supreme Court there said that the provisions of the Code should not be interpreted in a way that afforded legal personhood to a foetus. From the tenor of the decision, it is a fair inference that the Court's decision was influenced by the Charter rights of the women wherein foetuses are located.

In addition, the equality rights may make a difference in interpreting common law principles, particularly in tort law and family law. For example, in *Norberg v. Wynrib*[77] the Supreme Court of Canada overruled the Court of Appeal for British Columbia and the trial court to hold that a physician who took advantage of his patient's addiction to painkillers to obtain her "consent" to sex with him was civilly liable to her. While Charter equality rights are not mentioned in the decision, it seems a fair inference that they informed the analysis and the conclusion.[78] To the extent that this occurs, of course, there is some answer to the criticism that the Charter targets only state action and reinforces an invidious and mythical distinction between "public" and "private." Should principles of gender equality, for example, come to play an important role in the development of private law principles, the limitations imposed by section 32 of the Charter and the *Dolphin Delivery* case[79] will be less significant.

SOME BENEFITS, BUT AT WHAT COST?

Having reviewed these ways in which the Charter equality rights have led to legal change and may have been making a positive difference in economic and social terms for historically disadvantaged groups, do these gains come at a cost to our democratic process? If so, is the cost too high?

I think that sometimes the Charter critics have proceeded on too much of an a priori basis about the costs, and that they have failed to take into consideration the absence of better alternatives. But of course they are right that there are costs. I would identify the following: reinforcement of a rights-based and legalistic analysis of political issues, and correspondingly, inappropriate dominance by lawyers of political discourse; emphasis on top-down rather than bottom-up change (thus creating the potential that there will be change only in the words on paper); reinforcement of distrust of politicians and cynicism about our political process; and (by building up the role of the judiciary) distraction from discussion about fundamental changes in the legal system. I think that those costs can be mitigated or avoided by developing litigation strategies (meaning selection of cases, approaches, assembly of evidence, and arguments) in concert with the community meant to be served;[80] by remaining conscious of the fact that judicial statements even in authoritative decisions are not self-enforcing, and that the achievement of a "victory" in court is only one step in the process of bringing about change;[81] by deciding that democratic institutions should first be looked to for the desired change and that sometimes litigation may be inappropriate even if the change fails to occur; and by working in ways that support or are at least consistent with more fundamental kinds of change. (I cannot resist commenting that one of the striking features of some of the Charter critics' writing is the extent to which it seems to assume that those who conduct Charter litigation are naive believers in the legal system, blind to these issues. My perspective is that the organized groups such as LEAF and the Canadian Disability Rights Council are at least as familiar with the issues as are these writers.)

The point about alternatives is this: when the political process has failed to produce change, litigation provides a way to (1) force a decision one way or the other (and an adverse decision may become a rallying-point for further political activity); (2) focus public attention on the issue in an extremely cost-effective way; (3) focus the attention of the relevant community on a specific objective and the means of achieving it. To my mind, the Charter critics fail to explain why a group, such as gays and lesbians, should refrain from utilizing a litigation strategy when there appears to be no alternative means of achieving a resolution of their concrete claims. Consider the issue of including sexual orientation as a ground of discrimination under the Canadian Human Rights Act.[82] Prior to 1985, responding to arguments from lesbian and gay organizations, the Canadian Human Rights Commission called for this amendment. The Canadian Bar Association supported the change.[83] Despite federal announcements of an intention to change the Act on numerous occasions, this has not yet occurred. It is not surprising that those who support equality rights for gays and lesbians have resorted to the courts, nor that they are meeting with some success.[84] The claim for human rights protection for lesbians and gay men is a meritorious one. It may be that the courts, insulated from the political process, are the branch of government best situated not only to see the merits and accept that point, but to act upon it. To the extent that the Charter, as applied by the courts, can increase the full and free participation of all Canadians, whatever their racial or gender characteristics, sexual preference, age, disability, or religion, in the political process in its widest sense, it does not hinder the democratic process. It improves it.

To address briefly the third argument I identified at the beginning, our political institutions suffer from imperfections such as a lack of representativeness[85] and a lack of responsiveness, especially to issues where there are political costs to be paid. Further, we should not lose sight of the fact that the Charter applies to legislature *and government;* to a considerable extent, when discussing Charter violations, we are looking at the actions of unelected civil servants or officials. In short, the simple dichotomy between democratically elected legislator and appointed (and essentially unaccountable) judge is a false one. We could equally compare a powerful bureaucrat or police officer, making decisions affecting people's lives in a manner oblivious to fundamental human rights and freedoms but sensitive to local political concerns, with a judge, trained in principled decision-making and knowledgeable about rights and freedoms, immune from political winds, reviewing that decision.

CONCLUSION

One's opinion about the effectiveness of the Charter equality rights obviously depends to some extent upon one's political views, and the realism of expectations and degree of pragmatism with which one approaches the issue. Undeniably, the risk of fixation upon rights is real; as is the risk that rights as interpreted by the courts will become both the floor and the ceiling of what is possible.

But on balance, I say that the equality rights have done more good than harm, and show clear potential for further development. In addition, and perhaps this point is most acutely felt by those who have experienced discrimination and inequality, Charter rights provide a powerful and concrete bulwark against backsliding into the kind of government-sponsored discrimination that has so recently been part of Canadian law and practice. Government measures to remove the franchise from women, to reinstate the anti-Oriental measures in provincial legislation, to restore the stigma of illegitimacy, are unlikely events given today's political map. But as Atwood's *The Handmaid's Tale* presents the nightmare, current threads of political discourse present the possibility. While I am the first to agree that the Charter will not in itself prevent reprehensible measures by a government powerful enough to persist with them, it is a deterrent. It is a rallying-point around which citizens would gather. It creates expectations about equality of opportunity, treatment, and outcome in all citizens that governments must now strive to fulfil. I somehow can't see that as a bad thing.

NOTES

An earlier version of this paper was presented at the Canadian Bar Association Conference on *The Charter: Ten Years Later,* Ottawa, 15 April 1992, and appears in Gerald A. Beaudoin, ed., *The Charter Ten Years Later: Proceedings of the April 1992 Colloquium of the Canadian Bar Association and the Department of Justice of Canada in Ottawa* (Cowansville, Que.: Les Éditions Yvon Blais 1992).

I would like to acknowledge and thank my research assistants, Catherine Dauvergne and Sarah Levine, and my colleagues Joel Bakan, Christine Boyle, and Phil Bryden, all of whom read and made extremely helpful comments on this paper. I also gratefully acknowledge my debt to my former colleagues in LEAF, particularly Mary Eberts, Elizabeth Shilton, Catharine MacKinnon, and Helena Orton, with whom I have discussed many of these ideas from time to time. The responsibility for errors is of course mine alone.

1 The equality rights are:
     15(1) Every individual is equal before and under the law and has the right to the equal protection and equal benefit of the law without discrimination and, in particular, without discrimination based on race, national or ethnic origin, colour, religion, sex, age or mental or physical disability.
     (2) Subsection (1) does not preclude any law, program or activity that has as its object the amelioration of conditions of disadvantaged

individuals or groups including those that are disadvantaged because of race, national or ethnic origin, colour, religion, sex, age or mental or physical disability.

Their delayed application resulted from section 32(2) of the Charter, which brought section 15 into effect three years later than the other rights and freedoms.

2 I should acknowledge that I have two somewhat different sets of experience from which I draw these comments – first as a legal academic, and second as the former national president and chair of the Legal Committee of the Women's Legal Education and Action Fund (LEAF) and occasional counsel for LEAF. Prior to the existence of LEAF, as a member of a Vancouver law firm, I carried on some equality rights litigation for women as part of an unorganized diffuse series of attempts by individual practitioners to use provisions such as section 2(b) of the Canadian Bill of Rights for their clients (described in M.E. Atcheson, M. Eberts, and B. Symes, *Women and Legal Action: Precedents, Resources and Strategies for the Future* (Ottawa: Canadian Advisory Council on the Status of Women 1984.) Obviously, I purport to speak only for myself here, not for the LEAF organization, past or present.

3 Though not all – some Charter critics are careful to point out that our democratic system functions far from perfectly, and to avoid the assumption that judicial deference to legislatures is a priori desirable.

4 For the wording of section 15, see note 1 supra. This assertion about the purpose of the equality rights is based upon their wording, their place in the Charter as a whole, and the historical record of the context in which they came to exist. For a more detailed exposition of this argument, see William Black and Lynn Smith, "The Equality Rights," G.-A.Beaudoin and E. Ratushny, eds., *The Canadian Charter of Rights and Freedoms*, 2d ed. (Toronto: Carswell 1989), 557.

5 [1989] 1 SCR 143. The issue in *Andrews* was a statutory requirement that lawyers be Canadian citizens; it was struck down by the court.

6 Ibid. at 174, McIntyre J. defined discrimination as: " ... a distinction, whether intentional or not but based on grounds relating to personal characteristics of the individual or group, which has the effect of imposing burdens, obligations, or disadvantages on such individual or group not imposed upon others, or which withholds or limits access to opportunities, benefits, and advantages available to other members of society. Distinctions based on personal characteristics attributed to an individual solely on the

basis of association with a group will rarely escape the charge of discrimination, while those based on an individual's merits and capacities will rarely be so classified."

7 Wilson J. put it this way (ibid., at 154): "Given that s. 15 is designed to protect those groups who suffer social, political and legal disadvantage in our society, the burden resting on our government to justify the type of discrimination against such groups is appropriately an onerous one."

8 *R. v. Turpin*, [1989] 1 SCR 1296; *Ref. Re: s. 32 and s. 34 of the Newfoundland Workers' Compensation Act* (1989), 44 DLR (4th) 501 (SCC).

9 See, for example, the Charter of Rights Amendment Act, SBC 1985, c. 68, s. 56.

10 See *Haig v. Canada* (1992), 94 DLR (4th) 1 (Ont. CA); *Knodel v. British Columbia (Medical Service Commission)* (1991), 58 BCLR (2d) 356 (SC); *Veysey v. Canada (Commissioner of Correctional Services* (1990), 109 NR 300 (Fed. CA)

11 It again refrained from doing so in the appeal from *Canada (Attorney General) v. Mossop* (1990), 71 DLR (4th) 661 (FCA), reported at [1993] 1 SCR 554.

12 (1992), 93 DLR (4th) 1 (SCC).

13 Ibid., at 10–11. The decision thus may have little precedential value on the issue of criteria for identifying analogous grounds, although it gives a signal that the method of attaining parenthood (that is, through adoption as opposed to birth) would not have been seen as analogous to race, etc.

14 For example, see *McKinney v. University of Guelph*, [1990] 3 SCR 229, (1990), 76 DLR (4th) 545, where human rights legislation permitting mandatory retirement was held to violate section 15 but, at least in the context of universities, to constitute a reasonable limit on the Charter rights, within the meaning of section 1. For trenchant criticism of the *McKinney* decision, see M. David Lepofsky, "The Canadian Judicial Approach to Equality Rights: Freedom Ride or Roller Coaster?" (1992) 55 *Law and Contemporary Problems* 167–99. For a review of the Supreme Court's approach to section 1, see Robin Elliot, "The Supreme Court of Canada and Section 1: The Erosion of the Common Front," (1987) 12 *Queen's Law Journal* 277–340.

15 For more detailed discussion of this point, see Black and Smith, supra note 4, Diana Majury, "Equality and Discrimination According to the Supreme Court of Canada," 4 *Canadian Journal of Women and the Law* 407–39, and L. Smith, "Adding a Third Dimension: The Canadian Approach to Equal-

ity Guarantees" (1992) 55 *Law and Contemporary Problems* 211–33. The term "formal equality" is used in several different ways. First, in a procedural sense, it refers to a method for assessing equality claims, illustrated by the Ontario Court of Appeal decision in *R. v. Ertel* (1987), 35 CCC (3d) 398 (leave to appeal to the SCC refused (1987), 24 OAC 320) – equality claims are assessed according to whether similarly situated persons are receiving similar treatment. That approach is a cousin to the American one under the equal protection clause and suffers from the flaw that it is tautological: "treat likes alike and unlikes unalike in proportion to their unalikeness" (the Aristotelian formulation) is meaningless without further direction as to what counts as "alike" with respect to both persons and treatment. "Formal equality" in this sense was clearly rejected by the Supreme Court of Canada in *Andrews*. However, there is a basic pattern of reasoning, whether legal or otherwise, in which (applying criteria for likeness) we examine situations for similarities and differences in order to reach reasoned and principled conclusions about them. Any approach, including the one the Supreme Court adopted in *Andrews*, involves this kind of reasoning. What *Andrews* did was provide criteria and direction for it.

The criteria and direction that are chosen are important. A second sense in which "formal equality" is used refers in effect to one particular set of criteria and direction – the ideology that legal equality is realized when all individuals are treated as equals by the law, in the sense that all may own property, enter into contracts, be tried in the same courts, and so on, despite the fact that they lead radically different lives owing to uneven distribution of material conditions. The ideology of formal equality is indeed strong in Canada, and the *Andrews* approach runs against it, insofar as it requires assessment of asymmetrical material conditions in determining whether or not a claim involves a "disadvantaged group." Joel Bakan points out in "Constitutional Interpretation and Social Change: You Can't Always Get What You Want (Nor What You Need)," (1991) 70 *Canadian Bar Review* 307–28, that formal equality in this sense can lead to real problems of overinclusion and underinclusion – Procrustean beds of "same treatment" – commonly illustrated by the majestic equality of the law forbidding both the rich and the poor to sleep under bridges. By constricting the entrance into section 15 and by indicating that the approach will be asymmetrical, the Supreme Court reduces the risk that majestic equality will be the paradigm. But the *Andrews* approach is finding difficulty in taking hold in courts, because of the extent to which it runs against this ideology of formal equality. And the ideology is reinforced by certain features of the Charter itself – the limitation to governmental action imposed by section 32, and the negative focus (preventing governments from acting) rather than a positive one (requiring governments to act).

16 It was the approach for which LEAF and some other intervenors argued. For a description of the positions taken by the various parties in the *Andrews* case, see W. Black and L. Smith, "Case Comment: *Andrews v. Law Society of B.C.*," (1989) 68 *Canadian Bar Review* 591–615.

17 Thus, for example, in *Washington v. Davis*, 426 U.S. 299 (1976), the court held that a police test that blacks disproportionately failed did not violate the equal protection clause without proof that the police department had a discriminatory purpose in administering the test. Similarly, in *Village of Arlington Heights v. Metro Housing Development Corp.*, 429 U.S. 252 (1977), although denial of the zoning necessary for Metro to build racially integrated multiple-housing had a racially discriminatory effect, the village could not be held in violation of the equal protection clause without proof of a racially discriminatory purpose.

18 See *McKinney v. University of Guelph*, supra note 14 at SCR 279, and *Tétreault-Gadoury v. Canada (Employment & Immigration Commission)* (1991), 81 DLR (4th) 358, at 370 (SCC). For an application of the principles set out in these cases, see *Dartmouth/Halifax (County) Regional Housing Authority v. Sparks*, NSCA, 2 March 1993, as yet unreported.

19 See supra note 5, at 164–5.

20 This point was reinforced in the *Ref. Re Provincial Boundaries*, [1991] 2 SCR 158, 81 DLR (4th) 16, where section 15 was not at issue, but the approach to equality that it embodies was used in the context of the democratic rights and the issue of permissible departures from "one-person one-vote."

21 Supra note 8, at 1332.

22 Few examples of courts' applying an asymmetrical approach can be found, although it is articulated in the Supreme Court decisions referred to *(Andrews* and *Turpin).* One is a British Columbia Supreme Court decision, *Williams v. Canada (Attorney General)* (1990), 61 CCC (3d) 198, in which the court dismissed a claim that section 718(10) of the Criminal Code, which allowed more lenient treatment for defaulters of fines when they were between the ages of 16 and 21, violated the equality rights of a person over the age of 21. The court said at 206: "In the case at bar an advantage is conferred by s. 718(10) on that section of the population between the

ages of sixteen and twenty-two. The petitioner is not one of that group. She is a member of the majority and complains because a smaller group has the advantage of an additional hearing that she does not possess. She is not a member of a 'discrete and insular minority' as that term is used in *Andrews* and *Turpin*. It is obvious to me that s. 718(10) was passed in the context of the place of the group defined by age in the 'social, political and legal fabric of our society.' The legislators were obviously aware as a matter of common sense that persons falling in the age group embraced by s. 718(10) were generally speaking persons who had not reached real earning capacity and accordingly would be less likely to be able to pay a fine than would adults. It goes without saying that there are also impecunious adults but the law cannot be 'all things to all people.'"

On one reading, the Supreme Court's decision in *R. v. Hess*, [1990] 2 SCR 906, may point in a different direction. The issue was the constitutional validity of the now-repealed statutory rape section in the Criminal Code. Wilson J. (for the majority of the Court) seemed to suggest (in obiter dicta) that where an offence, as a matter of biological fact, could only be committed by one sex, this would not give rise to a section 15 violation. This is probably not precisely what the court intended to say, since it is inconsistent with its own previous decision in *Brooks v. Canada Safeway Ltd.*, [1989] 1 SCR 1219, (1989), 59 DLR (4th) 321. There, discrimination based on pregnancy was found to constitute sex discrimination. Pregnancy occurs only to women, yet the Court held that it is sex discrimination to disadvantage women because of it. *Brooks* thus stands for the proposition that there may be sex discrimination through the creation of rules applying to only one sex, for example where they have the effect of disadvantaging women. In *Hess* (as McLachlin J. discussed in her dissenting reasons at the section 1 stage) it was arguable that the statutory rape offence was designed to promote women's equality through protecting young women against sexual exploitation, unwanted pregnancy, and other consequences of premature sexual activity with older males. Thus, it was not *necessarily* a violation of section 15 to create a sex-specific offence. *Hess* makes the most sense if understood to stand for that proposition alone.

23 A sampling of the writing to which I refer would include Joel Bakan, "Strange Expectations: A Review of Two Theories of Judicial Review," (1990) 35 *McGill Law Journal* 439–58, and "Constitutional Interpretation and Social Change," supra note 15; Andrew Petter and Allan C. Hutchinson, "Rights in Conflict: The Dilemma of Charter Legitimacy," (1989) 23

U.B.C. Law Review 531–548, and "Day Dream Believing: Visionary Formalism and the Constitution," (1990) 22 *Ottawa Law Review* 365–85;
Judy Fudge, "The Effect of Entrenching a Bill of Rights upon Political Discourse: Feminist Demands and Sexual Violence in Canada," (1989) 17 *International Journal of the Sociology of Law* 445–63, and "The Privatization
of the Costs of Social Reproduction: Some Recent Charter Cases," (1989)
3 *Canadian Journal of Women and the Law* 246–55; Michael Mandel, *The
Charter of Rights and the Legalization of Politics in Canada* (Toronto: Wall
and Thompson 1989); and Robert Martin, "The Charter and the Crisis in
Canada," in David E. Smith, Peter MacKinnon and John C. Courtney eds.,
After Meech Lake: Lessons for the Future (Saskatoon : Fifth House 1991.) I
do not intend to suggest that all of these authors support all of the views I
have summarized in the text, but that they share a critical and sceptical view
about the Charter as a means to the end of social change.

24 Most notably, F.L. Morton and Rainer Knopff, *Charter Politics* (Scarbor-
ough: Nelson Canada 1992).

25 "Left- and Right-Wing Charterphobia in Canada: A Critique of the Critics," (1993) 7–8 *International Journal of Canadian Studies* 95–115.

26 Ibid., 96.

27 Shelagh Day and Gwen Brodsky, *Canadian Charter Equality Rights for
Women: One Step Forward or Two Steps Back?* (Ottawa: Canadian Advisory
Council on the Status of Women 1989), counted cases pre-*Andrews* and
concluded that the equality rights were being used much more extensively
by non-disadvantaged persons than otherwise. That trend has begun to re-
verse, of course, as a result of *Andrews*.

28 On the basis of an informal survey, my impression is that the number of
claims based upon non-enumerated grounds has decreased dramatically,
that the ratio of successful cases to unsuccessful ones is highest among the
enumerated grounds claims, and lower when analogous grounds are at issue. However, even when enumerated grounds are claimed, there seem to
be at least as many unsuccessful claims as successful ones, and among the
unsuccessful lot are cases which arguably should have succeeded.

29 *Bliss v. Canada (Attorney General)*, [1979] 1 SCR 183. For a history of the
Bliss case and its political consequences up to 1985, see Leslie A. Pal and
F.L. Morton, "*Bliss v. Attorney General of Canada:* From Legal Defeat to Po-
litical Victory," (1986) 24 *Osgoode Hall Law Journal* 141–60.

30 For example, Human Rights Act, SY 1987, c. 3, s. 6(f); Human Rights
Code, SS 1979, c. L-24, s. 2(o); Human Rights Code, CCSM, c. H175,

enacted by SM 1987, c. 45, s. 9(2)(f); Human Rights Code, RSO 1990, c. H.19, s. 10(2); Charter of Human Rights and Freedoms, RSQ 1977, c. C-12 (as amended), s. 10; Human Rights Act, RSNS 1989, c. 214, s. 3.

31 SC 1980–81–82–83, c. 150, s. 4.

32 In particular, "equality before *and under* the law," and "equal protection *and equal benefit* of the law," in section 15(1), and section 28, which reads: "Notwithstanding anything in this Charter, the rights and freedoms referred to in it are guaranteed equally to male and female persons."

33 Supra note 5.

34 *Brooks v. Canada Safeway Ltd.*, supra note 22.

35 Ibid., at SCR 1237–8.

36 There is an interesting contrast between the *Bliss* and the *Brooks* cases. In *Bliss*, efforts were concentrated on showing how Ms. Bliss was denied regular Unemployment Insurance benefits even though she was similar in all relevant respects (ready, willing, and able to work) to hypothetical male comparators. The Court held, however, that it was appropriate for the legislature to create a special category of benefits for pregnant women with higher eligibility requirements and restrict all pregnant women to that category. The statement that the discrimination was created by nature, not the statute, illustrated the way in which equality arguments based upon treating likes alike fall apart when it comes to conditions that are seen as dramatically "unlike," such as pregnancy. In *Brooks*, counsel concentrated on arguments that emphasized the ways in which the social treatment of pregnancy disadvantaged women as a group; there was discrimination in creating a benefit program that excluded pregnant women even though there were no pregnant male comparators. The arguments referred to the context of inequality in which women become pregnant, give birth, and raise children, and were able to draw upon the recognition in the *Andrews* case that the purpose of equality rights is to assist in alleviating disadvantage. The arguments also attacked directly the assumption that pregnancy is "voluntary" (therefore, "private" and beyond the realm of public responsibility).

37 Elizabeth Schneider, "The Dialectic of Rights and Politics: Perspectives from the Women's Movement," (1986) 61 *New York University Law Review* 589, at 648–52.

38 *Alberta Hospital Assn. v. Parcels* (1992), 90 DLR (4th) 703 (Alta. QB).

39 *Canadian Disability Rights Council v. Canada*, [1988] 3 FC 622.

40 *Sauvé v. Canada (Attorney General); Belczowski v. Canada* (SCC), 27 May 1993, as yet unreported.

41 *R. v. Swain*, [1991] 1 SCR 933.

42 Supra note 18.

43 See the cases cited supra note 10 for examples.

44 *J.C. v. Forensic Psychiatric Services* (1992), 65 BCLR (2d) 386 (SC).

45 (1992), 88 DLR (4th) 60 (Man. QB).

46 I am not in a position to report whether or not such sums have been required or, in fact, whether the remedies ordered in these cases have been implemented.

47 (1991), 3 CR (4th) 348, [1991] 2 CNLR 104, 88 Sask.R. 302 (C.A.).

48 (1991), 5 OR (3d) 492 (Ont. Gen. Div.).

49 (1990), 73 DLR (4th) 491 (NSSC).

50 Charter of Rights Amendment Act, supra note 9.

51 Ibid., s. 55. Spousal immunity in tort meant that neither husband nor wife could sue the other for damages for personal injuries, whether caused by negligence or intentional assault. This prevented battered wives from suing for damages, and it also benefited insurance companies when spouses were injured in motor vehicle accidents in which one spouse was driving.

52 Examples I am aware of include the B.C. Name Act, which prevented giving a child the hyphenated surname of both parents, and the Yukon's Change of Name Ordinance, which required that married women adopt their husbands' names. See M. Eberts and G. Brodsky, *Leaf Litigation Year One* (Toronto: LEAF 1986).

53 Brian Slattery "A Theory of the Charter," (1987) 25 *Osgoode Hall Law Journal* 701–47.

54 Quoted supra note 1 and note 32 respectively.

55 Following the Supreme Court of Canada decision in *R. v. Seaboyer* [1991] 2 SCR 577, after thorough consultations with feminist organizations as well as civil liberties groups and the organized bar, the minister of justice brought forward An Act to Amend the Criminal Code (Sexual Assault), SC 1992, c. 38, which came into effect 21 August 1992.

56 Thus, in *R. v. Keegstra*, [1990] 3 SCR 697, [1991] 2 WWR 1 (hate propaganda), *R. v. Butler* (1991), 70 CCC (3d) 129 (SCC) (pornography), *R. v. Seaboyer*, id. (restrictions on cross-examination of complainants about their previous sexual history in sexual assault cases), and other cases, interventions brought points of view before the court that were not otherwise available, supporting the choices that democratically elected governments had made.

57 All of the cases referred to in note 56, supra, were supported by the Court

Challenges program. Governments (federal and provincial) and private sources have provided some funding to the Women's Legal Education and Action Fund and to other organizations such as the Canadian Disability Rights Council. However, the funding permits only a very small number of cases to be funded, and depends upon a great deal of volunteer work from the lawyers who argue the cases and the other professionals and experts who assist in conceiving and preparing them.

58 With very limited resources, groups such as LEAF have managed to do only a small amount of that kind of work, already commonly done by business interests, the labour movement, and other true special interest groups. I argue that the terminology "special interest groups" should be reserved for organizations representing special interests, such as the textile industry, small business, organized labour, organized religion, or the like. It should not be used to refer to subsets of the population seeking to have a voice as citizens – such as women's organizations, the disabled, aboriginal peoples, and the like. I find support for this approach in the work of the political scientist Iris Young, who, with other feminist political scientists, points out that the notion of generalized universal citizenship assumes common features in its citizens based upon norms that have excluded women, racial minorities, and the poor. See, for example, "Polity and Group Difference: A Critique of the Ideal of Group Difference," in C. Sunstein, ed., *Feminism and Political Theory* (Chicago: University of Chicago Press 1990.) When members of historically excluded groups are attempting to improve the notion and practice of citizenship by making it inclusive, they are not acting as special interest groups simply lobbying for the furtherance of measures that will benefit them or their organizations. Instead, they are acting in the public interest.

59 For example, *Re MacVicar and Superintendent of Family and Child Services et al.* (1987), 34 DLR 488 (BCSC), in which the court held that natural fathers must have rights in the adoption process, on the premise that biological fathers and mothers were similarly situated having regard to the purpose of the Act. Given that the decision was pre-*Andrews*, it may be that it would now be decided differently. The problematic aspect of the decision is that identical treatment of biological fathers and mothers in this context fails to recognize the circumstances in which biological mothers make, and must be able to implement, decisions about the adoption of children they have borne. See, by way of contrast, *T. (D.) v. Children's Aid Society and Family Services of Colchester County* (1992), 91 DLR (4th) 231 (NSSC),

aff'd (1992), 92 DLR (4th) 289 (CA).

60 CTS 1982/31.

61 CTS 1976/47.

62 See Law Society of British Columbia, *Benchers Bulletin,* October 1992, announcing the ruling now embodied in *Professional Conduct Handbook,* ruling G13.

63 Supra note 56.

64 Supra note 56.

65 [1985] 1 SCR 295; [1985] 3 WWR 481.

66 [1986] 2 SCR 713, 35 DLR (4th) 1.

67 (1992), 95 DLR (4th) 202. The Supreme Court (by a 4–3 majority) struck down section 181 of the Criminal Code, which made it a crime to wilfully publish a statement, tale, or news that the person publishing it knew was false and that caused or was likely to cause injury or mischief to a public interest. The decision in *Keegstra,* supra note 56, which involved a different Criminal Code section (prohibiting the dissemination of hate propaganda against certain identifiable groups) was distinguished by the majority in *Zundel.* McLachlin J., for the majority, pointed out the very different legislative history of the two sections, with the one at issue in *Keegstra* having its origins in concern about the protection of racial and religious minorities, and the one at issue in *Zundel* having its origins in the thirteenth-century Statute of Westminster offence De Scandalis Magnatum, which provided that "from henceforth none be so hardy to tell or publish any false News or Tales, whereby discord, or occasion of discord or slander may grow between the King and his People, or the Great Men of the Realm." Cory and Iacobucci JJ., dissenting, said that the rights recognized in the Charter as being fundamental to Canadian democracy should be considered in defining a public interest under the section, and (at 227): "If the wilful publication of statements which are known to be false seriously injures a group identifiable under s. 15, such an act would tear at the very fabric of Canadian society. It follows that the wilful publication of such lies would be contrary to the public interest." The majority rejected this approach as tantamount to writing a new piece of legislation rather than interpreting an existing one.

68 Supra note 5.

69 *Hills v. Canada (Attorney General),* [1988] 1 SCR 513; *Slaight Communications Inc. v. Davidson,* [1989] 1 SCR 1038; *R. v. Salituro,* [1991] 3 SCR 154.

70 [1988] 1 SCR 30; see especially 171–2.

71 (1992), 95 DLR (4th) 106 (Fed. CA) However, NWAC was unable to obtain any remedy for this violation.
72 Supra note 22, holding that pregnancy discrimination is sex discrimination.
73 [1989] 1 SCR 1252, holding that sexual harassment is sexual discrimination.
74 For a discussion of the comparison, see Smith, supra note 15.
75 (1988) 53 DLR (4th) 69, 30 BCLR (2d) 237.
76 [1991] 1 SCR 489, 63 CCC (3d) 97.
77 [1992] 2 SCR 318, (1992), 92 DLR (4th) 449, [1992] 4 WWR 577, 68 BCLR (2d) 29.
78 The LEAF intervention in the case centred on the implications of a commitment to gender equality in the Charter for transformation of traditional legal doctrine regarding consent, and the defence of *ex turpi causa non oritur actio* (from an immoral act no cause of action may arise – used to bar the claim of the young woman in this case). I would suggest that, similarly, considerations of gender equality were important in *Moge v. Moge* (1992), 99 DLR (4th) 396 (SCC), in which the Court rejected the notion that women should, whatever the real social and economic circumstances in which they found themselves after the termination of a long marriage, be presumed able to become financially self-sufficient and therefore disentitled to maintenance.
79 *Dolphin Delivery Ltd. v. R.W.D.S.U., Local 580*, [1986] 2 SCR 573, holding that the Charter applies only to governments and not to private actors, even when private actors are invoking state enforcement of their objectives through the courts.
80 Thus, in the way that the best lawyers do for their best clients. To some extent, the LEAF process for case development reflects this objective.
81 This is highlighted in Sherene Razack's book *Canadian Feminism and the Law: The Women's Legal Education and Action Fund and the Pursuit of Equality* (Toronto: Second Story Press 1991.)
82 SC 1976–77, c. 33, and amendments.
83 In a 1985 paper entitled *A Blueprint for Implementation of Constitutional Equality Right* (submission to the Parliamentary Special Committee on Equality Rights, 17 June1985).
84 See for example, *Knodel v. British Columbia (Medical Services Commission)*, supra note 10, holding that regulations under the Medical Services Act defining "spouse" as limited to heterosexual couples violate section 15 of the

Charter; *Haig v. Canada,* supra note 10, holding that the absence of sexual orientation from the list of proscribed grounds of discrimination under the Canadian Human Rights Act is a section 15 violation. On the other hand, in *Egan v. Canada* (1991), 87 DLR (4th) 320 (Fed. TD) a complaint based on the definition of "spouse" in the Old Age Security Act was dismissed, as was a similar complaint in *Vogel v. Manitoba,* (1992), 90 DLR (4th) 84 (Man. QB)

85 In its report, *Reforming Electoral Democracy* (1991), the Canadian Royal Commission on Electoral Reform and Party Financing said (at vol. I, p. 93), "An examination of membership in the House of Commons reveals that major segments of Canadian society are underrepresented." "Women are the most underrepresented segment of Canadian society" (p. 94), but visible minorities, aboriginal people, and people with disabilities are also severely underrepresented (pp. 95–6.) As the royal commission points out, at 93: "The issue of representation takes on an important symbolic aspect since it contributes to the extent to which Canadians identify with their representative institutions; people who are consistently underrepresented may feel alienated and reject institutions that do not allow for the accommodation of their identity (Breton 1986). The composition of the representative body also affects the type of issues that receive public attention, the priority attached to them on the public agenda, and how and when they receive consideration."

II

THE CHARTER
IN THE COURTS

The Supreme Court Judges' Views of the Role of the Courts in the Application of the Charter

Given the many open concepts that puncture its fabric, the Charter provides the courts with several channels through which to define their role in its application. These include the distance the courts are ready to travel towards the delimitation of the content and the scope of the entrenched rights themselves – such as, in particular, freedom of expression or equality; they also include the definition of the principles of fundamental justice, or the determination of what will bring justice into disrepute as mere examples of signals at which we can look to decipher the courts' concept of their role. But nowhere is this more transparent than in the Supreme Court's treatment of the application of section 1, by which the courts were entrusted with the gatekeeping of the legislative limitations on rights, through the application of a text that encompasses not one but three of the most open-ended concepts in any language: "reasonable limits," "demonstrably justifiable," and "free and democratic society."

It is precisely with the expression "free and democratic society" that our research has dealt in the past two years. With a grant from the Social Sciences and Humanities Research Council and a team of graduate students, we have tried to compare the Dickson Court judges, pre-Charter images and post-Charter interpretations of that expression, through methods derived from linguistic and rhetoric analysis.[1]

In this context the meanings given by judges for the word "democracy" have yielded interesting material for this paper, since, of course, the respective roles of the legislature and the judiciary are important components of the definition of democracy. But another element is equally relevant. We are referring to how far the judges are ready to extend the Court's intervention in matters of constitutional control under the Charter. Some of them are explicitly on the record as recognizing the political role of the Court in such matters. For instance, before her accession to the Court, Justice McLachlin wrote:

> This requires the Court to weigh the significance of the infringement of the individual right against the collective interest of the State in continuing the infringement. This is essentially a judgement of a political rather than judicial nature. The answer cannot be determined by logic or stare decisis, even assuming precedents were available; the answer resides ultimately in the values of the court deciding the case.[2]

And both Justices Beetz and Lamer have commented that judges have not arrogated that power for themselves: it has been handed to them – some would say forced upon them – by elected assemblies in which they did not take part. To this, the chief justice has added the less frequent acknowledgment that this role is not entirely new to the Court: "The novel feature of the Constitutional Act 1982 however is not that it has suddenly empowered courts to consider the content of legislation. This the courts have done for a good many years when adjudicating on ultra vires legislation."[3]

Yet it is not so much the explicit utterances of judges that reveal their exact stance on the role of the judiciary as what can be inferred from their own practice on the bench: when they consider intervention legitimate, and the reasons advanced for intervening or not intervening. It is mainly through this last prism, then, that we have looked at the role some of its judges have designed for the Supreme Court in the application of the Charter. Our comments will focus on the writings of some of the judges, past and present, of the Court: Wilson, LaForest, and Dickson. We must explain why as well as justify our "sample" – if that is the right expression.

First, it would have been very difficult to ascertain the view of the Court as a whole on its role in applying the Charter, because the Court has been so evolutionary in its composition, and so obviously divided on key issues since the inception of the Charter, that it would be misleading at this time, with so many new members not yet fully on the record on that point as on many others, to describe any one viewpoint as "the Court's." As for our choice of judges, it was limited by the advancement of our research on the judges' images and interpretations of the word "democracy" on which it is based, and it is reflective of the main trends of the Court – as represented so far in its decisions – in the definition of its role.

JUSTICE WILSON

No one interested in the application of the Charter will ignore the fact that Justice Wilson has been its most fervent enforcer on the Court, and that her position throughout her tenure on the bench was the most interventionist, although this has come not as an end in itself but as a consequence of the importance she bestowed upon constitutionalized rights. No one (but the Court itself, unfortunately) has forgotten her opinion in *Singh*, the high water mark of decisions bearing on the standard derived from article 1. The standard she was setting for accepting legislative measures impinging on a constitutionalized right summarized all the components of the liberal discourse on the Charter that the Court had held in its pre-*Oakes* days: the importance of rights "which are fundamental to the political structure of Canada" and constitutionalized "as a part of the supreme law of our nation"; the seriousness of an infringement of the constitution, and the correlative importance consequently required of the governmental measure that implements it, if it is to be justified.[4] It also encompassed other elements that were to be found only in opinions that she signed,[5] such as the legitimacy of the Court's intervention in matters attributed by the constitution to exclusive legislative jurisdiction, when executive policy constitutes a violation of a constitutionalized right;[6] the impossibility of a measure's being at the same time "in violation of principles of fundamental justice" and "reasonable and justified", concepts she found "mutually exclusive";[7] and, especially, the irrelevance of the argument derived from administrative convenience. She wrote:

> Seen in this light, I have considerable doubt that the type of utilitarian consideration brought forward by M. Bowie can constitute a justification for a limitation on the rights set out in the Charter. Certainly the

guarantees of the Charter would be illusory if they could be ignored because it was convenient to do so. No doubt considerable time and money can be saved by adopting administrative procedures which ignore the principles of fundamental justice, but such an argument, in my view, misses the point of the exercise under s. 1. The principles of natural justice and procedural fairness which have long been espoused by our courts, and the entrenchment of the principles of fundamental justice in s. 7, implicitly recognize that a balance of administrative convenience does not override the need to adhere to these principles.[8]

From this high standard, established at the onset, she did not waiver, except in cases relating to social policies promoting the interests of the less advantaged, where "less than a straightforward denial of a right is involved,"[9] or where "competing constitutional claims to fixed resources are at stake."[10] These were the ultimate concessions she would agree to. For her, the *Oakes* standard, already less stringent than her own, was to be applied as a matter of principle and not on a contingent basis. She adamantly refused to lower the standard of minimal impairment when the measures considered were not drafted in favour of a disadvantaged minority, such as in *McKinney*,[11] or for the reasons advanced by Justices LaForest[12] and Dickson,[13] who held that the right involved assumed a different value depending on the circumstances of the case, or placed certain elements of a right at its core and others only at its periphery. Thus, in Cotroni, she states:

Given this focus, governmental limits on protected rights and freedoms can only be legitimized in the clearest cases. It is simply not enough to override a constitutionally protected right or freedom for the legislation to be designed to serve a particular state objective. Rather, the state objective must take cognizance of and be tailored to the rights and freedoms on which it impinges.[14]

In this context, distinctions between core and peripheral elements of rights have no place:

I may say that I view with some alarm my colleague's characterization of the proposed extradition of the respondents as a "peripheral" violation of s. 6(1). If one characterizes a complete denial of the citizen's right to remain in Canada under s. 6(1) as a "peripheral" violation, then, of course, one has already pre-judged the s. 1 issue. I would, however, respectfully suggest that such an approach represents a novel departure from the Court's traditional approach to the balancing process called for under s. 1 and one that could pose a very serious threat to the protection for the citizen which the Charter was intended to provide.[15]

In criminal matters, where the Court, in spite of its reputation for maintaining a stringent test, has made some exceptions to its strict standard, especially but not only in cases involving impaired driving,[16] Justice Wilson holds the same position, reacting to the chief justice's claim that "Parliament is not required to seek and adopt the absolutely least intrusive means of attaining its objectives" in both *Swain*[17] and *Chaulk,* where she states:

> In my view, this is not a situation calling for a departure from the strict standard of review set forth in Oakes. On the contrary, the issue on appeal seems to be the quintessential case of the state acting as the "singular antagonist" of a very basic legal right of the accused rather than in the role of "mediating between different groups" as discussed in Irwin Toy. This is, in my view, an appropriate case in which to apply the stricter standard of review on the "minimal impairment" issue.[18]

This remarkable consistency has suffered but two exceptions, in *Keegstra,*[19] where she yields to the "core-periphery" theory that she had previously opposed in *Cotroni,* and in *Lavigne v. OPSEU,*[20] where she refuses to extend freedom of association to the freedom not to associate. Her position is a principled one, consistent throughout her tenure on the bench, based on the importance of fundamental rights, to which she attributes an intrinsic value, and the exceptional character of the constitutionalized guarantee, which justifies a stringent standard and consequently the active intrusion of the courts in the legislative process and their avowed political role.

JUSTICE LAFOREST

Justice Laforest is no less consistent than Justice Wilson and, at first glance, just as much a realist as she is. It would seem only that the reality about which he is no less consistent is quite different: where she admits a political role for the Court, his avowed trademark is reverence for the legislator:

> While, like the Chief Justice, I favour the making of whatever possible exemptions are possible to accommodate minority groups, I am of the view that the nature of the choices and compromises that must be made in relation to Sunday closing are essentially legislative in nature. In the absence of unreasonableness or discrimination, *courts are simply not in a position to substitute their judgment for that of the legislature.*[21]

The standard he favours is much more lenient than Wilson's and even, as we shall see, Justice Dickson's. In matters of social policy, he will void only the most unreasonable measures, and in other spheres he is very flexible, suggesting an approach where facts and interests are weighed first, refusing any intrinsic value to constitutionalized rights, which he protects only in relation to the values underlying them.

He was the first to refer explicitly to the relationship between the challenged activity and the constitutional right as a precondition for the application of the minimal impairment test, and the first to propose the "contextual analysis" that would later rally the then Chief Justice Dickson in *Keegstra*. In *Cotroni*, he concluded his arguments in this way:

> In the performance of the balancing task under s. 1, it seems to me, a mechanistic approach must be avoided. While the rights guaranteed by the Charter must be given priority in the equation, the underlying values *must be sensitively weighed in a particular context against other values of a free and democratic society sought to be promoted by the legislature.*[22]

Later, in *McKinney* and *Tétrault-Gadoury*, he would bring the standard even lower when, claiming to ground his decision on *Irwin Toy*, he would require only a reasonable basis for a legislative policy that he would validate: "In short, as the Court went on to say, the question is whether the government had a *reasonable basis* for concluding that it impaired the relevant right as little as possible given the government's pressing and substantial objectives."[23]

Without resorting to a complete rhetorical analysis of Justice Laforest's decisions at this point, we must nevertheless examine our opening statement about his realism against the background of his claim to base his decision in *McKinney* on the reasons given by the Court in support of *Irwin Toy*. For it seems that in his eagerness to comfort the legislator in his social policies, whatever they may be, he has stretched to "unreasonable" limits the comparability of the facts in *Irwin Toy*, where a vulnerable minority was involved, to those in *McKinney*, where the young professors constitute no such group, as Justice Wilson has aptly remarked. If such is the case, then, this would be a rare occurrence where the author of *Air Canada v. A.G.B.C.* has written a formalist decision, unless of course he would really have been a formalist in disguise all along, professing reverence for a legislator that a court, applying his standard, could censor at will: depending on the relationship it would define, according to the circumstances of each case, between a right and whatever values would be deemed to underlie it. Intervention may not, after all, be what it appears to be, and chances are that it may never be more serious than when it is not overt.

JUSTICE DICKSON

If most of us think of Chief Justice Dickson as an ardent promoter of the application of the Charter, as the coherent leader of the Court he set on its course in writing the *Oakes* test, and thus identified as a liberal jurist, favouring a high standard of respect for constitutionalized rights enforced by vigilant courts, it is because he took pains to maintain that reputation by theorizing and justifying the Court's unpredictable course. Closer scrutiny will in fact reveal less coherence (especially if we take into account the reasons in which he concurred) and more rhetoric (everywhere) than expected, given his image, and than we have found with Justices Wilson and LaForest.

This theorization and rationalization and its lack of coherence should not surprise us, coming as it does from the chief justice of a supreme court, especially a court as divided as the Supreme Court of Canada has been on Charter issues. For this is the role that is required of judges in general, and even more so from the Chief Justice of a Supreme Court, if the ideology on which is grounded the credibility of the judicial system is to be maintained. That ideology requires that courts present an image of their process that shows legal reasoning as deductive syllogism: facts are given, they are meant to be governed by one definite set of rules and no other, and the principles derived from these rules automatically and logically apply to these facts. All that is left for the judge is to deduce the conclusion. In such a context, the legal process appears clothed in utmost objectivity and, as Montesquieu has pointed out, "judges are only the mouth that voices the sayings of the law, mere interpreters who cannot change its meaning or application." Of course legal realists and their descendants have punctured that myth long ago, but few judges are ready to admit that it is unfounded because they see such an admission as sawing the branch on which they sit, and rightly so in the eyes of an important proportion of justiciables.

Let us be honest: what proportion of the population would keep what respect it has for judges if it became clear to all that no precise line can be drawn between their judicial and political reasoning? But then, how can one believe that the phrase "demonstrably justifiable in a free and democratic society" is susceptible of an unequivocal definition? Is there a principle from which can be derived only one rule that could uniformly apply to all facts and cases?

An ideologically unified Court could have at least made it appear plausible that the interpretation of such an expression was contained in a fixed corridor, if not within a narrow one. But a divided Court renders the task of the believers almost impossible, unless appearances are protected through the shield of formalism. Only a formalist discourse attempting to mask at least mutually exclusive if not diverging legal reasoning will do the task and fulfil the expectations of what Perelman[24] has described as the two main "audiences" of the courts: the general public, including the parties involved, their lawyers, the media, and other justiciables who want the law to be equitable and uniformly and objectively applied, although with regard to the particulars of each case on the one hand, and the legal community on the other: lawyers in general, other courts, administrators, legislators, who want the law to be secure and predictable and whose professional status is also in part linked to its "scientific" character.

The functional role of a chief justice is then to reconcile these expectations with one another, to provide equity and predictability at once, and to harmonize these desired results with whatever reasons and conclusions are reached by individual judges on the Court. When analysed against such a theoretical background, Chief Justice Dickson's discourse on section 1 appears in a different light and his rapid evolution or apparent inconsistencies become desperate attempts intended to maintain at all costs at least the formal appearances of a Court unified in its objective approach to Charter application, even though its members may interpret the same facts differently.

As chief justice until 1990, Dickson presided over a divided Court entrusted with the formidable task of giving the Charter its first interpretations. The first case involving section 1 to reach the Court was *Skapinker* in 1984. It dealt only tangentially with the question, and gave only a hint that the burden of evidence would be heavy. In the two years culminating in the *Oakes*[25] test, Chief Justice Dickson held a definitely interventionist position in *Singh*[26] and *QPBS*,[27] which he then maintained unchanged in *Ford*[28] and *Morgentaler*[29] in the following years. As everyone will remember, he devised a sequential test whereby the importance and the urgency of the governmental measure must first be ascertained before the means to implement it are examined for their proportionality to the end pursued by the legislator. The proportionality test itself has three components; the one most discussed relates to the minimal impairment criterion. Dickson presented the test as logically derived from the text of section 1 and based on universal values, namely: "Respect of the inherent dignity of the human person, commitment to social justice and equality, accommodation for a wide variety of beliefs, respects for cultural and group identity, and faith in social and political institutions which enhance the participation of individual and groups in the society."[30]

This test was to be applied, however, only to legal rights and Dickson is not less formalist when he justifies attenuations of the minimal impairment standard for all other cases. In cases involving social policies, as early as 1986 in *Edwards Books*[31] but mainly in 1989 in *Irwin Toy*[32] and *Slaight Communication*,[33] he invoked the necessity of legislative action to preserve social equality. In other circumstances, outside the purview of legal rights, as in *Reference re Criminal Code (Man.)*[34] and *Keegstra*,[35] the attenuation of the minimal impairment test was based on a negative relationship between the activity involved and the values underlying the guaranteed right or freedom. When he departed from the *Oakes* test in criminal cases, such as in *Whyte*[36] and *Chaulk*,[37] the justification is grounded only in the exceptional importance of the aim of the legislative measure. This is especially so when these decisions are seen against the background of the apparent contradiction between his opinions in *Oakes* and *Keegstra*, or between the diametrically opposite reasons of Justice Wilson in *Singh* and Justice LaForest in *McKinney*, to which he both concurred. Given this, Dickson's views of the role of the judiciary in the application of the Charter might appear quite inconsistent, driven in any direction where the facts of the case will take him. The temptation to see his successive positions in that light is only greater if one refers to what may be seen, in retrospect, as the *Oakes* forecast: "In each case courts will be required to balance the interests of society with those of individuals and groups";[38] and "The nature of the proportionality test will vary depending on the circumstances."[39] However, a chronological reading of the apparent contradictions will show that they can be made to be not so much contradictions as an evolution from a high standard at the inception of the Charter to a much more lenient one from 1986 to the end of the tenure of the chief justice, with a sharp turn downward in 1989.

Although no explanation comes readily to mind about what could have spurred such a change in that particular year, other elements can help create a context for this evolution in Dickson's concept of the role of the Court in the application of the Charter. It must be remembered that our comparative analysis of his pre-Charter images and post-Charter interpretations of a free and democratic society[40] has shown that the only different element between the first and the second was precisely the role of the judiciary as a component of democracy. Before the Charter, Dickson is on the record as having repeatedly stated the preponderance of the legislative power over the judiciary, an opinion later modified by the changes in constitutional law brought about by the advent of the Charter and the concomitant expectations both of the legal community, disappointed in the past by the interpretation of the declaration, and of the Canadian public, who already had invested its identity in the Charter. Can we then hypothesize that in his later years as chief justice Dickson might have been taken back where he started from by the scholarly quality of the conservative prose of Justice LaForest in a Court where majorities had to be achieved rather than enjoyed?

NOTES

1 For a description of these methods, see A. Lajoie, R. Robin, et A. Chitrit, "L'apport de la rhétorique et de la linguistique à l'interprétation des concepts flous," in Daniéle Bourcier and Pierre MacKay, *Lire le droit: Langue, texte, cognition* (Paris: L.G.D.J. 1992), 155 – 63.

2 Beverley McLachlin, "The Charter of Rights and Freedoms: A Judicial Perspective," (1988–9) *University of British Columbia Law Review* 579, at 583–4.

3 Re *B.C. Motor Vehicle Act,* [1985] 2 SCR 486.

4 *Singh v. M.E.I,* [1985] 1 SCR 177, at 218.

5 Although some judges concurred in these reasons when she wrote them, none – to my knowledge – ever used them again in other cases.

6 *Operation Dismantle v. The Queen,* [1985] 1 SCR 441, at 471–2.

7 Re *B.C. Motor Vehicle Act,* supra note 3.

8 *Singh v. M.E.I,* supra note 4, at 218.

9 *McKinney v. University of Guelph,* [1990] 3 SCR 229, at 401.

10 Ibid., at 404. To these, one might add *Edmonton Journal v. Alberta (A.G.),* [1989] 2 SCR 1326, where she develops the contextual approach, but follows the Court in the opposite direction.

11 *McKinney,* at 402.

12 *U.S. v. Cotroni,* [1989] 1 SCR 1469.

13 *Reference Re Criminal Code (Man.),* [1990] 1 SCR 1123, and *R. v. Keegstra,* [1990] 3 SCR 695.

14 Supra note 12, at 1506.

15 Ibid., at 1511.

16 *R. v. Ladouceur,* [1990] 2 SCR 1257, and *R. v. Chaulk,* [1990] 3 SCR 1303.

17 [1991] 2 SCR 933.

18 *Chaulk,* supra note 16, at 1390.

19 Supra note 13.

20 [1991] 2 SCR 211, at 259.

21 *Edwards Books and Art v. R,* [1986] 2 SCR 713, at 806 (emphasis added).

22 *Cotroni,* supra note 12, at 1489–90 (emphasis added).

23 *McKinney,* supra note 9, at 286 (emphasis added).

24 Chaïm Perelman et Paul Foriers, *La motivation des décisions de justice* (Bruxelles: Établissements Émile Bruylant 1978), 422–3.

25 *R. v. Oakes,* [1986] 1 SCR 103.

26 Supra note 5.

27 [1984] 2 SCR 66.

28 *Ford v. Quebec (A.G.),* [1988] 2 SCR 712.

29 *R. v. Morgentaler,* [1988] 1 SCR 30.

30 *Oakes,* supra note 25, at 136.

31 Supra note 21.

32 *Quebec (A.G.) v. Irwin Toy,* [1989] 1 SCR 927.

33 *Slaight Communication v. Davidson,* [1989] 1 SCR 1038.

34 Supra note 13.

35 Supra note 13.

36 *R. v. Whyte,* [1988] 2 SCR 3.

37 *Chaulk,* supra note 17.

38 *Oakes,* supra, note 25, at 139.

39 Ibid.

40 To appear in *The Dickson Years,* edited by Delloyd Guth (forthcoming).

The Charter Then and Now

Constitutions have a persistent habit of confounding and contradicting the fondest wishes of their creators. The idea that constitutions should or do conform to the "intentions of the drafters" may well be one of the most widely assumed but rarely observed features of constitutional politics the world over.

No better example of this phenomenon can be found than the case of Canada itself. The drafters of the 1867 Act thought they were creating a highly centralized federation in which the national government would exercise all the significant powers while the provinces would operate as mere local appendages responsible for matters unworthy of Ottawa's attention. One hundred twenty-five years later, Canada is one of the most decentralized federations in the world, with the pressures for further devolution continuing to mount, despite the failure of the Charlottetown Accord.

What of the Charter of Rights which, along with the 1867 Act, constitutes the foundation of the Canadian constitutional order? How does our experience under the Charter compare to the fears, hopes, and expectations that surrounded its enactment in 1982? To what extent has the Charter conformed to or contradicted these "original understandings"?

This paper is a modest attempt to begin to grapple with these questions. I start with the assumption that any conclusions that one might offer regarding the impact of the Charter must necessarily be tentative and preliminary. The Charter is a mere decade old – still in constitutional infancy – and we are too close to its creation to make any confident predictions about its long-term impact and significance for Canada. Assessing the impact of the Charter in 1992 is like predicting the end of a five-hundred-page novel after reading the first chapter. We know the characters, we have a sense of the main plot lines, we understand the conflicts that will eventually have to be resolved, we even have our theories about how it will all turn out. But we also know that it is too early in the story to be overly confident about our prognostications.

Despite these limitations, I believe it is still possible to offer a number of meaningful generalizations about the impact of the Charter over this first decade. The focus of my analysis, as suggested above, is on what might be termed the "original understanding" of the Charter – the motives, expectations, fears, and aspirations that surrounded the enactment of the document in 1982. I have chosen to proceed in this way because I believe that this "original understanding" provides a useful vantage-point from which to attempt to make sense of our recent experience.

One might have assumed that the ideas and attitudes about the Charter that prevailed in 1982 would have dominated the debates over the document during its first decade. While constitutions have a habit of confounding the fondest hopes of their creators, this dynamic normally requires many decades to develop and unfold. Consider again our experience with the Constitution Act, 1867, as a reference point. While the 1867 constitution eventually led to a far more decentralized federation than had originally been expected, this devolution had hardly commenced in the first ten years of Confederation. Similarly, while the Charter will undoubtedly develop in many unexpected and novel directions, one might have assumed that such developments would not have been apparent for many years to come.

Yet, even bearing this caveat in mind, it is difficult to avoid the conclusion that the Charter's impact has far exceeded what many had predicted just a decade ago. Even at this early stage, it is becoming apparent that the Charter may well be the single most important political development in Canada this century. Supreme Court Chief Justice Antonio Lamer, in commenting on the significance of the Charter on its tenth anniversary, described its enactment as a "legal revolution." Comparing its significance to the introduction of the metric system, the invention of penicillin, or the discovery of the laser, the chief justice described the enactment of the Charter as "a great event" (Lamer 1992).

While many might ponder whether the chief justice's references to the discovery of the laser or the invention of penicillin are overdrawn, few would dispute the landmark political significance of the Charter. This significance, I will suggest, cannot be appreciated merely by looking to the Charter decisions of the courts. Indeed, in my view, the decisions of the courts to this point have been moderate and balanced and have left ample elbow room for Parliament and the legislatures. The fears of many critics to the effect that the Charter would lead to "government by judiciary" have not been realized, at least to this point.

Instead, I will suggest that the broader political effects of the Charter have been at least as significant as its strictly legal ones. In the wider political realm, what the Charter has done is to subtly redefine the way in which we debate and evaluate the merits of various public policies. The Charter has added a new element – a new political good – to the policy mix in Canada. This new element is the ability to make a credible claim that some right, privilege, or other entitlement is "protected by" the Charter.

Of course, the most obvious forum for "Charter-claiming" behaviour is the courts; lawyers attempt to convince judges that a particular entitlement or interest is protected by the Charter and that some law or regulatory action is therefore unconstitutional. But Charter-claiming occurs outside courtrooms as well, in political debates about the merits or disadvantages of proposed policy choices. What is becoming apparent (and what was not appreciated in 1982) is the wide variety of political contexts in which Charter-claiming behaviour can be utilized as a means of advancing a particular political interest. What is also becoming apparent (and was similarly unappreciated a decade ago) is the powerful effect of such Charter-claiming behaviour on political outcomes. If a particular political constituency can credibly argue that its interests are in some way encompassed by the Charter, this appears to constitute a very powerful political instrument with which to influence outcomes in their favour. Perhaps the most obvious (but not the only) example of the potent political potential of Charter-claiming behaviour is provided by our recent experience with the Meech Lake and Charlottetown accords; the claim that the proposed amendments interfered with Charter rights was one of the key arguments raised against those accords. Charter arguments of this type have a potency that extends across a broad range of policy fields.

In this paper I glance backward so that we can fix our sights more clearly on the future. By returning to the debates and arguments which surrounded the enactment of the Charter in 1982, we bring the experience of the past decade into sharper focus. We can identify the extent to which the Charter has conformed to the "original understanding" of its purposes and potential; we can also discern the extent to which the Charter has departed from that original understanding, even in the short space of ten years. We can also, I think, gain insights into the types of effects we can expect the Charter to stimulate or to stymie as Canada approaches the twenty-first century.

THE CHARTER THEN

Reviewing the debates that surrounded the enactment of the Charter, one is struck by the divergence between the attitudes of governments on the one hand, and those of interest groups and activists on the other. Within governmental circles, the emphasis was on the dangers associated with handing over political decision-making to the courts. Perhaps the most articulate critic of the Charter and of the dangers associated with judicial law-making was Premier Allan Blakeney of Saskatchewan.

Blakeney's concerns over the Charter stemmed from his social democratic principles and his belief that the state was a positive instrument for achieving social justice and equality (Greunding 1990: 192-6). For Blakeney, the Charter would expand the authority of unelected, unaccountable, and socially conservative judges to thwart the redistributive goals of the state. Blakeney was particularly troubled by the American experience with the Bill of Rights during the so-called Lochner era in the early twentieth century, in which the U.S. Supreme Court had rolled back a wide variety of socially progressive statutes. For Blakeney, the place to strike the appropriate balance between the interests of the individual and those of the community as a whole was the legislature rather than the courts. Blakeney believed that rights are best protected by Parliament and not by a constitution that is interpreted by the courts (Sheppard and Valpy 1982: 145) In the end, Blakeney was prepared to accept an entrenched Charter only if it included a "notwithstanding" clause, which he believed would permit legislatures to ensure that the courts did not unduly limit the choices made by elected politicians (Romanow, Whyte, and Leeson 1984: 197-214).

Blakeney was not the only first minister to express concerns about the increased judicial power associated with an entrenched Charter. Premier Sterling Lyon of Manitoba was ideologically opposed to the Charter, fearing that it would undermine the doctrine of parliamentary sovereignty and the role of the monarchy in Canada (Sheppard and Valpy 1982: 268). Even the prime minister of Canada, supposedly the Charter's ultimate champion, seemed extremely sensitive to the dangers associated with judicial limits on parliamentary sovereignty. The federal government's original draft of the Charter, tabled in the House of Commons on 2 October 1980, appeared to offer relatively limited protection for individual rights. For example, the limitation clause in the original federal version stated that Charter rights were subject to such "reasonable limits as are generally accepted in a free and democratic society." This appeared to be an attempt to import into the Charter the jurisprudence that had been built up under the Canadian Bill of Rights, to the effect that "established" or "accepted" limits on individual rights would not violate the Charter (Romanow, Whyte, and Leeson 1984: 243).

If governments and first ministers were preoccupied with the appropriate balance between judicial and political power, no such concern surfaced among the interest groups and legal activists who were the other major players in the debate. For these groups, the only concern was to strengthen or expand the guarantees of rights found in the Charter. They mounted a campaign in the parliamentary committee hearings held over the winter of 1980-1 designed to remedy what was described as a "seriously flawed" document (Sheppard and Valpy 1982: 135). Women's groups, civil liberties organizations, ethnic and racial minorities, the disabled community, and even Canada's human rights commissioner all urged the federal government to go back to the drawing-board and produce a Charter that would have real teeth. This grass-roots campaign proved to be remarkably effective, and led to a variety of amendments, particularly to sections 1 and 15 of the Charter, designed to strengthen the rights guarantees.

Amongst these interest groups and activists, there appeared to be remarkably little concern over the potential increase in judicial power associated with an entrenched Charter. To the extent that judicial discretion was regarded as a problem at all, it was apparently seen as a matter that could be dealt with through appropriate drafting of the Charter itself. Thus, the focus of the lobbying efforts of the various interest groups was on securing the "correct" wording of the various rights guarantees so that these matters could be "nailed down" in advance.

These two sets of dynamics – the first associated with governments and first ministers, the second associated with interest groups and activists – dominated the debates over the Charter in the 1980-2 period. But at the same time, it was understood that there were larger, more generalized political considerations and purposes at play in this debate. Many believed that the importance of the Charter lay not so much in the details of this or that clause as in the broader political effects the Charter would have on Canadian society as a whole (Milne 1982: 177). The Charter was seen as a instrument of nation-building. It emphasized common values of citizenship, entrenching rights enjoyed equally by all Canadians. In this sense, it was seen as bridging the regional or provincial particularisms that had historically dominated Canadian politics. The Charter provided a common reference point for all Canadians and gave symbolic expression to the idea that Canadians enjoy a collective political identity (Russell 1983).

These broader political purposes appeared to be central to Prime Minister Trudeau's motivation in entrenching a Charter. Reviewing the patriation experience in later years, Trudeau claimed that the goal of the Charter was to strengthen the country's unity by "basing the sovereignty of the Canadian people on a set of values common to all, and in particular on the notion of equality among all Canadians" (Trudeau 1990: 363). Trudeau believed that the adoption of the Charter was a reflection of the "purest liberalism" in which each individual is regarded as a "human personality" who has absolute dignity and infinite value. It follows that "only the individual is the possessor of rights" and that certain inalienable rights can never be interfered with by any collectivity, whether the collectivity be state, nation, or another group (Trudeau 1990: 363-4).

The theory was that the enactment of the Charter would cause these common values of citizenship to be emphasized, while the particularisms of province, region, or group would be correspondingly diminished. The Charter would serve as an important instrument whereby Canadians would transcend these particularisms and focus on a core set of values common to all.

This brief sketch of the dynamics surrounding the enactment of the Charter undoubtedly fails to capture all the various nuances and subtleties of the debate. But it does highlight the main features of the debate, and it provides us with a reference point for assessing the experience of the first decade. What assessment can we can we make of this initial ten-year period in the light of the original understanding of what the Charter was supposed to accomplish?

THE CHARTER NOW

As we have seen, a major preoccupation of governments in the early 1980s was with the increased judicial power associated with an entrenched Charter. In particular, there was a concern that the Charter would be used by powerful elements in Canadian society in order to roll back progressive social and economic legislation. To what extent has the Charter had this effect? What has been the relative balance of judicial versus political authority in the Charter era?

The jurisprudence of the Supreme Court in the first ten years of the Charter appears to fall into two quite distinct and to some extent conflicting periods. The first period is comprised of the initial wave of Supreme Court Charter decisions beginning with *Skapinker* in 1984 and concluding with *Edwards Books* in December 1986. During this initial period, the Court mandated a "large and liberal" interpretation for the Charter. There were two doctrinal cornerstones underlying the activist approach that emerged during this period. First, the various rights guarantees in the Charter were to be read in an extremely broad manner, so as to maximize the possible scope of the guarantee. Second, limits on rights were to be construed narrowly, with governments required to satisfy an extremely high standard in order to restrict a protected right or freedom.

The high-water mark of this first period of judicial activism was undoubtedly the *Oakes* decision in early 1986. In *Oakes* the Court established the well-known two-part test for determining whether a limitation on rights was permissible under section 1 of the Charter. But the test the

Court established was so rigorous as to call into question a wide variety of previously uncontroversial laws and regulatory actions. Particularly demanding was the requirement that governments demonstrate that there were no "less restrictive means" available to achieve its objectives. As some critics at the time pointed out, there are almost always other alternatives available to government that might involve less restrictions on rights (Monahan and Petter 1987: 102-25). The difficulty is that these less restrictive means usually involve greater costs or a loss in efficiency. But if *Oakes* and other cases decided during this initial period were to be taken literally, governments were always required to adopt the alternative that had the least impact on protected rights and freedoms.

The Supreme Court's activist approach in this early period is confirmed by the outcomes of the cases. In the first twenty Charter decisions of the Supreme Court, the Charter claim was successful on eleven occasions, a "success rate" of 55 percent. This far exceeded the success rate for Charter claims in the lower courts during this period and sent a clear signal to the legal community that the Charter was to be taken seriously (Monahan and Petter 1987: 78).

Having mandated a "large and liberal" interpretation of the Charter, in which rights were to be read broadly and limitations on rights read narrowly, the Court suddenly reversed course. The watershed case that marks the transformation in the Court's approach is undoubtedly *Edwards Books*, handed down in December 1986. In this case, the Court was required to determine whether Ontario's Retail Business Holidays Act violated the guarantee of freedom of religion in section 2(b) of the Charter. A majority of the Court held that the Act's requirement to close on Sunday did constitute a limitation of the religious freedom of those who observed a Sabbath other than Sunday. But the majority of these judges went on to hold that the limitations on religious freedom were a "reasonable limit" that could be demonstrably justified in a free and democratic society under section 1 of the Charter.

The Court's section 1 analysis in *Edwards Books* faithfully reflected the formal categories established in *Oakes*. But the way in which the analysis was actually carried out suggested that the Court had rethought the wisdom of the stringent *Oakes* approach. The first stage of the *Oakes* test was the requirement that limitations on rights be for a purpose that is "pressing and substantial." In *Edwards Books*, Chief Justice Dickson held that the importance of the objective of the legislation – preserving a "common pause day" – was "self evident" and required no serious analysis. As for the second part of the *Oakes* inquiry – whether the means chosen was proportional to the objective sought – the Chief Justice evinced a newfound deference for legislative discretion. The only "evidence" the government had tendered in support of its legislation was a sixteen-year-old Law Reform Commission study. Yet the chief justice was prepared to agree that the legislation infringed religious freedom "as little as possible."

Two key elements were introduced into the section 1 analysis by Chief Justice's Dickson's judgment in *Edwards Books*. The first was the idea that the courts should show deference to legislative choices that involve trade-offs or compromises between the interests of competing social groups. Chief Justice Dickson thought that the Retail Business Holidays Act was legislation of this type, balancing the interests of workers in a common pause day against the interests of non-Sunday observers in religious freedom. The government had made a good-faith effort to strike a compromise between these competing interests. This good-faith effort on the part of the government was all that was required in terms of the section 1 analysis. "The courts," according to Dickson C.J., "are not called upon to substitute judicial opinions for legislative ones as to the place at which to draw a precise line" (*Edwards Books*: 781-2).

The second key element in the chief justice's reasoning was his characterization of the legislation as one designed to assist retail workers, a group that has historically been low-paid and unorganized. The effect of striking down this legislation, therefore, would be to leave this vulnerable group in an even more unprotected position. In a passage that was to be cited frequently in later judgments, the Chief Justice opined that "[i]n interpreting and applying the Charter I believe that the courts must be cautious to ensure that it does not simply become an instrument of better situated individuals to roll back legislation which has as its object the improvement of the condition of less advantaged persons" (*Edwards Books*: 779).

The Chief Justice's judgment in *Edwards Books* was the first signal that the Court's "Charter Express" was about to begin slowing down. The Court had built up an impressive head of steam over the previous two-and-a-half years, suggesting that it would permit limits on individual rights only in exceptional circumstances. But the *Edwards Books* decision was a key turning-point, signalling a new era in which the watchwords would be restraint, moderation, and judicial deference to legislative choices.

The turnabout in the Court's approach is reflected in both the results and the reasoning in the Court's decisions since 1986. In terms of the results in the cases, we noted earlier the fact that the "success rate" for Charter claims in the first two years of the Court's Charter jurisprudence was well over 50 percent. In subsequent years, the "success rate" has dropped off dramatically, averaging somewhere between 25 and 30 percent annually since 1986 (Morton, Russell, and Withey 1992: 9; Elliot 1991: 91). Accompanying this "precipitous" drop in the success rate for Charter claims has been a growing number of dissenting judgments (Morton, Russell, and Withy, 1992: 11), an indication that the Court's initial burst of Charter confidence has given way to greater division and uncertainty.

But what is most revealing about the Court's attitude in this second, deferential period is the reasoning employed in the cases. The Court has taken up the arguments that were initially advanced in *Edwards Books* by Chief Justice Dickson and made them central to its emerging jurisprudence under the Charter. An important refinement of the *Edwards Books* doctrine was the court's decision in *Irwin Toy,* where the Court sought to distinguish between cases in which the government is "mediating between the claims of competing groups" as opposed to those in which the government is "the singular antagonist of the individual whose right has been infringed." (*Irwin Toy:* 993-4).

In the former case – where the legislature is striking a balance between the claims of competing groups – *Irwin Toy* suggests that an extremely deferential standard of review is appropriate. Two considerations led the Court to this conclusion. First, this type of legislation will typically require an assessment of conflicting scientific evidence and differing "justified demands" on scarce resources. The Court suggests that the legislature is far better placed to make the kinds of judgments required in these situations than is the judiciary. Second, this type of legislation is often designed to protect vulnerable groups in society. Citing the passage in *Edwards Books* in which the Court had referred to the importance of taking into account the interests of disadvantaged persons, the Court in *Irwin Toy* concluded that it would not "require legislatures to choose the least ambitious means to protect vulnerable groups" (*Irwin Toy:* 999).[1] The Court contrasts this first type of case with cases in which the government is best characterized as the "singular antagonist" of an individual litigant. The Court offers the example of a criminal case in which the accused is asserting a right protected by sections 7 to 14 of the Charter. In this instance, the government is apparently advancing the interests of the community as a whole against those of an individual, rather than assessing competing claims among different groups. In these "singular antagonist" cases, the Court argues that a more rigorous standard of judicial review is warranted; it is appropriate for the Court to assess "with some certainty" whether the government has selected the "least drastic means" for achieving its purpose. The only justification that is offered for this more exacting standard of judicial review is that the "singular antagonist" case tends to involve the "authority and impartiality of the judicial system," and the courts have an "accumulated experience in dealing with such questions" (*Irwin Toy:* 994).

The distinction between cases involving a "singular antagonist," as opposed to those involving the competing claims of groups for scarce resources, is certainly open to question. For one thing, the distinction is one that is not always easy to draw. Whether a particular law falls into one category or the other will depend to a large extent on the analytical perspective one happens to adopt. For example, the Court in *Irwin Toy* suggests that criminal laws tend to advance the interests of the community as a whole, and involve a "singular antagonist" asserting rights against the state. But many, if not most, criminal laws might also be characterized as designed to advance the competing interests of social groups. Laws against theft might be said to advance the interests of those with greater amounts of property against those with less; hate literature laws restrict those who would foment hate against those who are the objects of such hate; anti-solicitation laws restrict those involved in the practice of prostitution in favour of the interests of local residents directly affected by the practice; drunk-driving laws restrict those who would drive automobiles while intoxicated in favour of those who are endangered by such behaviour. One could offer numerous other examples. The point is simply that the distinction the Court seeks to draw depends to a large extent on judicial perspective; the critical question is whether one views a law from the perspective of the individual accused, as opposed to the perspective of the larger social interests or groups which the law is designed to serve.

Despite the fact that the line between these two categories of cases is to a significant extent discretionary, the court's underlying motivation is clear. The overriding concern is to pay proper respect to the separation of powers between the legislative and the judicial branches of government. Where the legislature is making trade-offs between competing claims for scarce resources, the Court is more likely to take a "hands-off" approach. This will particularly be so where the legislature has acted on the basis of complicated social science evidence or is advancing the interests of some clearly identified "vulnerable group." By contrast, the Court will tend to be more activist in areas where it believes that it has an accumulated body of expertise, notably in the criminal law area. In these cases, the courts appear to regard themselves as having a kind of "comparative advantage" over the legislative branch, thereby justifying a more rigorous standard of review (Beatty 1992: 191-2).

This bifurcated approach provides a powerful framework for explaining and categorizing the Court's Charter jurisprudence over the past few years. In cases where the Court believes that the legislation under review involves trade-offs between competing group claims, it is far more likely to uphold such legislation. Thus, laws designed to restrict advertising aimed at young children *(Irwin Toy)*, laws mandating retirement at a fixed age *(McKinney)*, and laws prohibiting hate propaganda *(Keegstra)* have all been upheld on essentially this basis. In cases where the Court sees itself as having a degree of expertise and experience such that the legislature does not possess any comparative advantage, it has been far more willing to intervene. In the criminal law field, for example, the Court has been particularly activist in cases involving constructive murder *(Vaillancourt)*, abortion *(Morgentaler)*, absolute liability provisions in driving offences *(Motor Vehicle Reference)*, "rape shield" protections for victims of sexual assault *(Seaboyer)*, and a variety of practices employed by the police to investigate crime (see, i.e. *Wong* and *Duarte*). The Court has also demonstrated a relatively activist approach in professional licensing cases involving the regulation of lawyers, dentists, and other professionals *(Andrews v. Law Society of B.C.; Black v. Law Society of Alberta: Rocket v. Royal College of Dental Surgeons)*. In these professional licensing cases, the

Court apparently regards itself as having sufficient first-hand knowledge of the matters involved in order to justify a more rigorous review of government regulation.

AN OVERALL ASSESSMENT

What assessment can we offer of the Supreme Court's first decade of Charter jurisprudence? In general terms, it would appear that the Court is off to a very good start indeed. What is particularly significant is that the Court has successfully avoided two potential difficulties that loomed large back in 1982. On the one hand, the Court very quickly signalled to the legal community and to Canadians generally that the Charter era was not to be a repeat of the unhappy experience with the Canadian Bill of Rights. Particularly in its first wave of Charter judgments between 1984 and 1986, the Court established that the Charter was to be taken seriously and that it was to operate as a significant constraint on the actions of governments and legislatures.

At the same time, the Court has resisted the temptation to install itself as a kind of "super-legislature." Many critics had warned that the Charter would permit the judiciary to roll back the considerable achievements associated with the modern welfare state in favour of a theory of "limited government." Indeed, I should confess that I was one of those voicing precisely this concern (see Monahan 1987). I am happy to report that this fear has not materialized in the first decade of the Charter, and there is little evidence at this point to suggest that things will change for the worse in the future. The Court has evinced a very considerable sensitivity for the difficult trade-offs between competing social interests that most modern regulation requires. Particularly in the field of social and economic regulation, it has been willing to accord to the legislature a "margin of appreciation" in which the legislature is not required to follow the judges' ideas as to the "best possible means" of achieving its objectives. In most cases involving social and economic regulation, all that the Court has tended to require is that the government demonstrate that there is a "reasonable basis" for the choices that it has made. Indeed, the Court's deference in these cases has been such as to provoke complaints that the highest Court has abandoned any semblance of serious judicial review under the Charter (Beatty 1990: chapter 4).

In my view, however, the Court has adopted a fundamentally sound approach, particularly given the relative novelty of the Charter. The Court has chosen to proceed in a deliberately prudent manner, building first in areas where it regards itself as having some particular expertise or knowledge, and the capacity to assess the likely effects of its rulings. The fields of criminal law and of professional regulation have been the clearest examples of areas where the Court has adopted a relatively activist approach. But it has been much more restrained in areas of social or economic regulation, where its understanding of the subject-matter is much more limited and where its calculation of the possible effects of its rulings is more problematic.

By proceeding in this way, the Court has been able to give significant "bite" to the Charter, while at the same time avoiding any large mistakes. In fact, what is remarkable is the near absence of public criticism of the Court's Charter rulings over the past decade. The only significant public criticism has come from the police community, which has complained about Court-imposed restrictions on criminal investigations. But, in contrast to the United States, where restrictions on police practices have emerged as a major political issue, the police complaints in Canada have not resonated in the broader community. This is all the more remarkable given that the Canadian courts have often imposed more stringent rules on police conduct than are applicable in the United States. (Harvie and Foster 1990).

In effect, the Court has conducted itself in a politically astute fashion, intervening in discrete areas where its perceived legitimacy and authority are high, while deferring to the legislature in the broad majority of cases. This approach – which might be described as "selective activism" – helps to explain the fact that Canadian politicians and the broader public seem to have absorbed the Charter into the Canadian political system in an almost effortless fashion. A decade after the enactment of the Charter it remains very popular with the general public, with those who believe the Charter to be "a good thing" outnumbering those who believe it to be "a bad thing" by a three-to-one margin (Angus Reid 1992). Nearly three in five Canadians praise the Charter for permanently protecting individual Canadians from the actions of legislative majorities, with the highest support for the Charter coming from the province of Quebec (Angus Reid 1992: 3-4).

In sum, the warnings about the dangers of an entrenched Charter – warnings voiced mainly by a number of governments during the patriation debate in the 1980-2 period – have not been realized. What of the second major feature we observed during the patriation debate – the political lobbying by various interest groups to amend the Charter to better protect individual rights? Did those lobbying efforts, and the amendments they produced, have a lasting impact on the first decade of Charter review?

My impressionistic conclusion is that the lobbying efforts by interest groups to strengthen the original federal draft have proved to be of critical significance, both for the Court's jurisprudence and for the broader political significance of the document. I describe this conclusion as "impressionistic" because the Court has not been particularly reliant on the legislative history of the Charter during the 1980-2 period as it has gone about the task of interpreting the document. Nor has the Court focused on the precise wording of the legal text of the Charter in more than a handful of its Charter rulings. Instead, the vast bulk of the Court's Charter decisions have tended to turn upon the judges' views as to the purposes of the particular piece of legislation under review, and the "fit" between those purposes and the means chosen to achieve them. As one recent commentator observed, "the real concern of the Court is in assessing the reasonableness of the balance of interests struck by the challenged law rather than in searching after the intention of those who drafted the Charter in choosing the particular words they used" (Beatty 1992: 194).

But the efforts to strengthen the Charter in 1980-2 were nevertheless very important, at least in terms of the general message that was sent to the judiciary about the nature of the document. The process of expanding and strengthening the rights guarantees in the Charter sent a clear message to the judiciary that they were to take the document seriously.

This laid the groundwork for the early judicial activism of the 1984-6 period, by preparing both the courts and the public for what was to follow. It enabled Mr. Justice Lamer to proclaim in the *Motor Vehicle Reference* in 1985 that "[a]djudication under the Charter must be approached without any lingering doubts as to its legitimacy" *(Motor Vehicle Reference:* 497*).* Had the 1980-2 process not taken place, the legitimacy of an activist judicial role under the Charter would have been much more doubtful.

THE BROADER POLITICAL SIGNIFICANCE OF THE CHARTER

I indicated at the outset that the greatest significance of the Charter has been its impact on political debate and political culture in this country. There is little doubt that the drafters of the Charter envisioned the document having these types of broader effects. As noted, Prime Minister Trudeau believed that the Charter would be an instrument of national unity, rallying Canadians around a core set of universal values. The Charter, Trudeau thought, would break down the particularisms of region, province, language, and ethnicity, and highlight the common citizenship possessed by all Canadians.

Trudeau's assumption that the Charter would have political significance is turning out to be absolutely correct. But the precise nature of this political significance may well develop in directions that are quite different from those prophesied by Trudeau. Rather than emphasizing a set of common values associated with citizenship, the Charter may well give rise to a heightened focus on particular characteristics of social groups.

Other commentators have already observed that the Charter has altered the Canadian constitutional order in ways that go beyond the "conventional assertion that the Supreme Court has acquired an enhanced role as a national policymaker" (Cairns 1989: 120). As Alan Cairns has pointed out, an unanticipated consequence of the Charter is that different parts of the Constitution Act 1982, now seem to "psychologically belong" to particular groups: women's groups identify with section 28, the multicultural community and visible minorities with sections 15(1), 15(2), and 27, the disabled community with section 15(1), and aboriginals with section 35 (Cairns 1989: 119-20).

For these and other groups, the Charter has introduced a new kind of political instrument that can be used to advantage in the political arena. This new political instrument is the ability to claim that the interests of the group are constitutionally protected and therefore are deserving of political recognition, status, or advancement.

The important point to notice about this kind of Charter-claiming behaviour is that it is as likely to be advanced outside a courtroom as within one. A court ruling, while authoritative, is difficult and expensive to obtain. Raising a Charter claim in the political arena is far less expensive and time-consuming and may make court action to vindicate one's interests unnecessary.

Consider, as illustrations of the way in which Charter-claiming behaviour can influence political outcomes, the debates over two recent pieces of legislation, Bill C-49, An Act to amend the Criminal Code (sexual assault)2 and Bill C-81, the Referendum Act.[3] In both instances, arguments about possible Charter violations were key factors in the shaping of the legislation. But there were some important differences in the way in which these Charter arguments were utilized, differences that tell us a good deal about the role played by the Charter in political debates.

Bill C-49 was designed to alter the defences available to an accused charged with sexual assault, in the wake of the Supreme Court's decision in *Seaboyer* striking down certain "rape shield" provisions. The first-reading version of the bill provided that an accused must take "all reasonable steps, in the circumstances known to the accused at the time, to ascertain that the complainant was consenting."[4] This provision would have made it possible to convict an accused of sexual assault in circumstances where the accused honestly but mistakenly believed that the complainant had consented. Critics of the bill argued that this attempt to import a "reasonableness" standard into the definition of the offence raised a Charter issue.[5] But the government drafters of the first reading version of the bill came to the conclusion that this risk was not so significant as to preclude this approach.

Contrast this with the government's approach to the Charter in Bill C-81, the Referendum Act. Here, the government argued that it was constitutionally precluded from imposing spending limits in a national referendum campaign. The main obstacle standing in the way of spending limits appeared to be the guarantees of free speech and free association in section 2 of the Charter. According to the government, these Charter rights made it impossible to require that a referendum be fought between a single Yes committee and a single No committee. The inability to provide for two umbrella committees made the imposition of spending limits impracticable.[6]

These Charter arguments continued to feature prominently in the debates over the two pieces of legislation as they worked their way through Parliament. This was particularly the case in relation to Bill C-49. Bill C-49 had been drafted through what the government termed a "democratic, consultative process"[7] in which government officials met with representatives of various interest groups. These representatives argued that the government was under an obligation to bring forward some kind of protection for sexual assault complainants in the wake of the *Seaboyer* case.[8] The first-reading version of the bill reflected the concerns and arguments raised during the consultative process and, in particular, the wish "to encourage the reporting of incidents of sexual violence or abuse ..."[9] However, once the bill was introduced there was widespread criticism of certain of its provisions by the Canadian Bar Association and other legal groups. These legal groups argued that the bill violated the Charter rights of individual accused. In the face of this sustained criticism, the government's legal opinion apparently changed, with the minister agreeing to a number of changes designed to strengthen protections for the accused.

There are a number of important lessons to be gleaned from these two episodes. First, as the debates over Bill C-49 illustrate, Charter arguments and opinions are certainly not carved in stone. Charter considerations that on one occasion are regarded as inconclusive might be said at another point to be absolutely decisive. A critical factor in determining the weight that will attach to a particular Charter argument appears to be who is raising the argument in question. In the Bill C-49 episode, for example, an important factor was the involvement of the Canadian Bar Association, which is regarded as an independent and authoritative legal organization. The fact that the CBA was arguing that the provisions violated the Charter appeared to be a particularly important consideration in persuading the government to amend the legislation. Contrast this with the debate over the Referendum Act, where the most vocal proponents of referendum spending limits were Quebec sovereigntists. Quebec sovereigntists have no political constituency outside the province of Quebec, and their arguments in relation to the Charter were seen as political rather than strictly legal.

This demonstrates that the simple act of claiming that one's interest is protected by the Charter is not sufficient; one must be able to invoke some credible source or authority in support of one's claim. There are a variety of ways in which this credibility can be established. Perhaps one of the most important, as in the Bill C-49 example, is for the claim to be supported by an organization that has received some sort of official sanction or recognition. Organizations that fall into this category include human rights commissions and organizations, independent law reform commissions, university-based organizations, judicial bodies, and the associations of the organized bar. The Court Challenges Program, cancelled in the 1992 federal budget, also provided a form of official sanction and recognition. Indeed, the credibility and recognition the Court Challenges program conferred on funding recipients may well have been as important as the funding itself.

A second lesson to be drawn from the above examples is that it takes resources to establish the kind of credibility that is required to successfully advance Charter arguments in political forums. This suggests that it will be organized interests that stand to gain a comparative political advantage from the existence of the Charter. Established interests, such as governments, large corporations, and trade unions, are obviously well positioned to take advantage of this opportunity and have done so in the first decade of the Charter. But the enactment of the Charter has been the catalyst for a whole series of new organizations, most of them linked in some way with the enumerated grounds in section 15 of the Charter. These organized interests, most of them funded in some way by government, have taken advantage of the new political opportunities provided by the enactment of the Charter.

Beyond these general lessons, is there anything that we can conclude about the kinds of impacts the Charter is likely to have on the substance of political outcomes? While it is obviously still too early to make any confident predictions on this score, there are already clear indications of the kinds of considerations the Charter is likely to highlight.

An emerging focus for debate over the Charter relates to the question whether the rights are guaranteed to individuals or to groups. The text of the Charter tends, on the whole, to use language that refers to individuals. Thus, rights are guaranteed to "everyone" (sections 2, 7), "every citizen" (sections 3,6), "anyone" or "any person" (sections 11, 24), "every individual" (section 15(1)), or "citizens of Canada" (section 23). There are references to groups, particularly in sections 15(2) and 35(1), but these references are relatively exceptional compared with the numerous references to individuals. This, of course, is consistent with the vision of Prime Minister Trudeau, who saw the Charter as reflecting the "purest liberalism," the principle that a collectivity can exercise only those rights it has received by delegation from its members (Trudeau 1990: 364).

But over the past decade, the Charter has been increasingly described and understood as protecting the rights of groups rather than those of individuals. Defenders of the idea of "collective rights" argue that it flows from a vision of democracy that does not make the individual supreme (Day 1992). It is argued that the idea that each of us is an individual first and foremost does not accurately describe the experience of disadvantaged groups; members of those groups experience their solidarity, their "groupness," in large part because of the history of discrimination they have endured (Day 1992).

The idea that the Charter is intended to protect the interests of groups as opposed to those of individuals has already had a powerful impact on discussions of the document. A number of important decisions of the Supreme Court have described the Charter as protecting the rights of "individuals and groups" or, in certain instances, as the rights of groups alone. (Note the subtle differences in the approaches of Mr. Justice McIntyre and Madam Justice Wilson in the *Andrews* case on this issue.) At the same time, the concepts of individual responsibility and individual dignity have been very much at the centre of the Supreme Court's jurisprudence over the first decade of Charter interpretation.[10]

It is in the wider political realm where the idea that the Charter protects "group rights" has attained a greater degree of prominence. This was most obvious in the drafting and debate of the proposed "Canada clause" in the Charlottetown Accord. The proposed Canada clause was primarily organized around concepts of group identity and collective rights. It referred to the fact that aboriginal peoples were the first peoples to govern Canada; to the fact that Quebec constitutes a "distinct society"; to the commitment to the development and vitality of minority language "communities"; to a commitment to racial and ethnic equality; to a respect for "individual and collective human rights and freedoms of all people"; to the equality of female and male persons; and to the principle of the equality of the provinces. What was distinctly lacking in the clause was any countervailing notion of unifying characteristics – of the

Trudeau vision, which holds that all Canadians share certain common values of citizenship.

The emergence of these conflicting visions of the Charter was certainly not anticipated in the debates leading up to its enactment in 1982. But this merely confirms the observation I made at the outset- constitutions rarely develop in the precise manner contemplated by their drafters. In this case, a document that was consciously designed to give effect to Trudeau's vision of "pure liberalism" has instead created competing visions of its purpose and effect.

We cannot predict how these debates will turn out. The rejection of the Charlottetown Accord in the referendum – in part because of the intervention of former Prime Minister Trudeau against a supposed "hierarchy of rights" in the Canada clause, has thrown a wild card into any discussions of Canada's future. What can be confidently predicted is that in the ongoing and ceaseless struggle for political advantage, arguments about the "true meaning" of the Charter of Rights will play an increasingly pivotal role, both in the courtroom and in the broader political arena.

NOTES

1 Note the subtle difference in the two references; whereas *Edwards Books* had referred to "disadvantaged persons" *Irwin* speaks exclusively of "disadvantaged groups." This distinction is an important one, and I will return to it later.

2 Third Session, Thirty-fourth Parliament, First Reading 12 December 1991.

3 Third Session, Thirty-fourth Parliament, First Reading 15 May 1992.

4 See Bill C-49, section 273.2 (b).

5 See Geoffrey York, "Lawyers Wary of Proposed Rape Law: Commons Committee Told New Standards Are Contrary to 'Centuries of Accepted Behaviour,'" *The Globe and Mail*, 15 May 1992, A6. But note the amendments introduced by the government at the committee stage on 2 June 1992 designed to reduce the risk of a Charter challenge. In particular, the government proposed to delete the word "all" in section 273.2(b), requiring the accused to take only "reasonable steps to ascertain that the complainant was consenting."

6 See Graham Fraser, "Fear of Court Case Prompts Looser Law," *The Globe and Mail,* 16 May 1992, A5. Note that on second reading the government introduced amendments to that limit referendum expenditures, but without limiting the number of campaign committees. The amendments do not constitute any real limit on overall expenditures by any particular group or interest.
7 See the Right Honourable Kim Campbell's essay elsewhere in this volume. According to media reports, the bill was drafted after the justice minister held a series of meetings with a coalition of women's groups. See "Lawyers Win Concessions from Ottawa on Rape Bill," *The Toronto Star,* 3 June 1992, A3.
8 *Steven Seaboyer v. The Queen,* [1991] 2 SCR 577.
9 See Bill C-81, supra. This philosophy is reflected in the substantive terms of the bill, which provides that courts shall consider "society's interest in encouraging the reporting of sexual assault offences" in determining whether to allow evidence of a complainant's previous sexual history. See proposed section 276(3)(b).
10 See, in particular, the Court's judgments in cases such as the *Motor Vehicle Reference* and *R. v. Vaillancourt.*

REFERENCES

Beatty, David (1990) *The Canadian Production of Constitutional Review: Talking Heads and the Supremes* (Toronto: Carswell).
Beatty, David (1992) "Human Rights and Constitutional Review in Canada," *13 Human Rights Law Journal* 185–96.
Cairns, Alan (1989) "Citizens and Their Charter: Democratizing the Process of Constitutional Reform," in M. Beheils, ed., *The Meech Lake Primer: Conflicting Views of the 1987 Constitutional Accord* (Ottawa: University of Ottawa Press).
Day, Shelagh (1993) "The Charlottetown Accord and Central Institutions," in K. McRoberts and P. Monahan, eds., *The Charlottetown Accord, the Referendum, and the Future of Canada* (Toronto: University of Toronto Press).
Elliot, Robin (1991) "Developments in Constitutional Law: The 1989–90 Term," in E. Belobaba and E. Gertner, eds., *The Supreme Court Law Review,* vol. 2 (2d Series), 83, 173 (Toronto: Butterworths).
Greunding, Dennis (1990). *Promises to Keep: A Political Biography of Allan*

Blakeney (Saskatoon: Western Producer Prairie Books).

Harvie, Robert, and Foster, Hamar (1990) "Ties That Bind? The Supreme Court of Canada, American Jurisprudence, and the Revision of Canadian Criminal Law Under the Charter," 28 *Osgoode Hall Law Journal* 729–88.

Lamer, Antonio (1992) "How the Charter Changes Justice" (interview transcript) *The Globe and Mail,* 17 April 1992. A11.

Milne, David (1982) *The New Canadian Constitution* (Toronto: James Lorimer).

Monahan, P. (1987) *Politics and the Constitution: The Charter. Federalism and the Supreme Court of Canada* (Toronto: Carswell).

Monahan, P., and Petter, A. (1987) "Developments in Constitutional Law: The 1985–86 Term," in E. Belobaba and E. Gertner, eds., *The Supreme Court Law Review,* vol. 9, 69–181 (Toronto: Butterworths).

Morton, F.L., Russell, P.H., and Withey, M.J. (1992) "The Supreme Court's First One Hundred Charter of Rights Decisions," 30 *Osgoode Hall Law Journal* 1–56.

Reid, Angus (1992) "A Decade With the Canadian Charter of Rights and Freedoms" (National Angus Reid/Southam News Poll, 11 April 1992) (mimeo).

Romanow, R., Whyte, J., and Leeson, H. (1984) *Canada ... Notwithstanding* (Toronto: Carswell /Methuen).

Russell, Peter H. (1983) "The Political Purposes of the Canadian Charter of Rights and Freedoms," 61 *Canadian Bar Review* 30–54.

Sheppard, Robert, and Valpy, Michael (1982) *The National Deal: The Fight for a Canadian Constitution* (Toronto: Fleet Books).

Trudeau, Pierre Elliott (1990) "The Values of a Just Society," in Pierre Trudeau and Tom Axworthy, eds., *Towards a Just Society: The Trudeau Years* 357–85 (Markham, Ontario: Viking Books).

CASE REFERENCES

Andrews v. Law Society of British Columbia, [1989]1 SCR 143.
Black v. Law Society of Alberta, [1989] 1 SCR 591.
Edwards Books and Arts Limited v. the Queen, [1986] 2 SCR 713.
Irwin Toy v. A.G. Quebec, [1989] 1 SCR 927.
McKinney v. University of Guelph, [1990] 3 SCR 229.
R. v. Duarte, [1990]1 SCR 30.
R. v. Keegstra, [1990] 3 SCR 697.

R. v. Morgentaler, [1988] 1 SCR 30.

R. v. Seaboyer, [1991] 2 SCR 577.

R. v. Oakes, [1986]1 SCR 103.

R. v. Vaillancourt, [1987] 2 SCR 636.

R. v. Wong, [1990] 3 SCR 36.

Rocket v. Royal College of Dental Surgeons, [1990] 2 SCR 232.

Skapinker v. Law Society of Upper Canada (1984), 9 DLR (4th) 161.

ROBIN ELLIOT

The Supreme Court's Rethinking of the Charter's Fundamental Questions (Or Why the Charter Keeps Getting More Interesting)

A few days after the Charter's tenth anniversary, I was asked by a member of the judiciary what I now thought of the Charter. I suspect that he was expecting me to tell him whether I thought the Charter had proved itself to be either a positive or a negative force in the life of the Canadian polity. If that was what he was looking for, then I'm sure I disappointed him with my answer. What I said to him was that I thought the Charter was a good deal more interesting now than I thought it was back in the early 1980s when it was first introduced.

What I meant by "more interesting" was that the Charter – through the jurisprudence it has generated, the academic and other commentary that that jurisprudence and the Charter itself has spawned, and my own involvement in litigating Charter cases – had obliged me to rethink my position on a number of fundamental questions raised by a document of this character. Some of these questions fall under the rubric of social and political theory. For example:

1 How should the state be conceived? Must it be conceived only in negative terms (as in the often-used phrase "the tyranny of the majority"), or can we conceive of it in positive terms as well? And if the latter, when do we conceive of it in negative terms and when in positive terms?

2 How should we conceive of freedom? Must it too be conceived only in negative terms (as meaning simply the absence of outside interference, particularly by the state, in our personal lives), or can we not conceive of it too in positive terms (as meaning the ability to realize one's

potential as a human being, if necessary with the assistance of others, including the state)?

3 What are we to make of the public/private distinction, so important to the classical liberal tradition but so offensive to feminists and those on the political left?

4 How are we to conceive of equality – in the purely formal terms favoured by most liberal theorists or in the substantive terms favoured by feminists and the political left?

5 Is it necessarily a good idea to employ the discourse of rights in resolving the difficult issues raised by a document like the Charter – might we not be better off, at least on some occasions, to use the discourse of interests?

Like many early supporters of the Charter, I suspect, I had given very little serious thought to these questions when the Charter was first introduced. By and large, I had simply assumed that the traditional approach to questions of social and political theory taken in the United States, and incorporated into American constitutional jurisprudence, should govern our thinking about those questions in Canada. Hence my conceptions of both the state and freedom were distinctly negative; I accepted the validity of the public/private distinction and of a purely formal conception of equality; and I saw no reason not to use the discourse of rights in resolving the kinds of issues raised by a document like the Charter.

While it would be wrong to say that I have abandoned all of my early views in these areas, I have abandoned many. And I have most definitely abandoned the notion that it is adequate justification for one's views in these areas that they find expression in American constitutional theorizing and jurisprudence. We in Canada must be prepared to engage these issues of social and political theory on our own ground and in the light of our own social, cultural and political traditions and values.

It is also fair to say that I had given very little serious thought to another important question raised by the Charter – the extent to which it is appropriate to give the judiciary what amounts to (apart from the legislative override and the constitutional amendment process) the final say on these difficult questions of social and political theory. For no one can doubt that the Charter requires the judiciary to address these questions – in defining the scope of the Charter's application, for example (where the public/private distinction comes to the fore), in giving content to the rights and freedoms (e.g., the right to equality in section 15, which raises foursquare the conception of equality that we should endorse), and in applying section 1 (where questions about the proper conception of the state and of freedom and the appropriate discourse to use arise for consideration).

Perhaps because I had given the substantive questions themselves such little thought, I tended to view judicial review as not only a good but a necessary thing in the area of basic civil liberties. It is apparent to me now that the matter is far more complex than that. Unless one subscribes to the wholly discredited view that the answers to these questions lie in the text of the Charter itself or in some other text or set of texts upon which the judiciary might choose to rely for guidance, the judiciary – and in particular the nine judges on the Supreme Court of Canada at a given time – will essentially be free to fashion the answers as they see fit. And that is surely something to concern us. The question of the proper scope of judicial review is a real and important one.

My purpose here today is not to explore in detail how and why my thinking on these questions has changed over the last decade. My reason for introducing the paper in this way is to provide a lead into the main thesis I want to develop. That thesis, in simple terms, is this: I am not the only person who has been rethinking his position on these kinds of questions – so, too, have a number of judges, in particular some of the more prominent members of the Supreme Court of Canada.

Time doesn't permit me to develop this thesis with respect to all of the questions in respect of which there is evidence of judicial rethinking (and I should make it clear that this rethinking does not extend to all of the questions), but I can, I think, develop it at least partially with respect to three:

1 how to conceive of the state;
2 how to conceive of freedom; and
3 the proper scope of judicial review

My reason for selecting these three questions is that they permit me to link what might otherwise appear to be a somewhat abstract and perhaps even abstruse theoretical analysis with a critically important empirical observation about the Charter: the fact that the Supreme Court of Canada has been rethinking its position on these three questions goes a long way to explaining the most striking feature of the Court's response to the Charter to this point – the dramatic drop in the frequency with which it has been prepared to check the exercise of governmental power over the last five or six years.

That the exercise of governmental power is checked far less often now than in the early years of the Charter is, I take it, common knowledge. It certainly is on the part of most reputable commentators on the Charter – at least those whom I read, including former Justice Wilson. However, if this proposition comes as a surprise to you, perhaps it will be enough to persuade you of its validity if I recite the following statistics. In the first fifteen cases the Supreme Court decided under the Charter (in 1983 to 1986), the Court sided with the party invoking the Charter in nine (60 percent). In the 1989-90 term (1 September 1989–31 August 1990), the overall success rate for parties invoking the Charter in the Court had dropped to 17.5 percent (seven out of forty); the rate outside the realm of criminal law had dropped even lower, to 11.8 percent.[1]

What is the explanation for this dramatic turnaround in the Court's response to the Charter? Some would argue that it is a function of the changing nature of the cases the Court has been getting – the first few, it is said, were easy ones that cried out for the exercise of the checking function. Others would point to the new appointments that were made in the mid- to late 1980s – the new appointees, it is said, are simply less enthusiastic about the Charter than their predecessors.

I am not prepared to discount entirely explanations like these. But I am also not prepared to accept that they provide a complete answer. I think it is clear that a complete answer would have to include recognition of the fact that the Court has rethought its position on the three questions I have identified. That is especially true, I think, of the first and third of those questions, those relating to the conception of the state and the proper scope of judicial review.

I propose to establish that thesis in a very simple and straightforward manner – by invoking the words of the judges themselves. The judges whom I have selected for this purpose are the former Chief Justice Dickson, the current Chief Justice Lamer and the former Justice Wilson. My reason for selecting these three is that they were on the Supreme Court in the early days of the Charter and remained on it until the end of the 1980s. In fact, they are the only judges of whom that can be said. Moreover, it is clear that during that whole period they were leaders on the

Court insofar as the court's response to the Charter was concerned, both in the sense that they frequently wrote the majority reasons and in the sense that they wrote often and they wrote powerfully. To the extent that they can be said to have rethought their positions on these questions, it is therefore fair, I think, to say that the Court has rethought its position on them.

I begin with the position of these three judges on these questions in the early years, which culminated in the Court's now famous judgment in *R. v. Oakes*,[2] decided in early 1986. It is clear from the judgments written by these judges in those years – and at that time one or other of them almost invariably did write the majority reasons – both that their conceptions of the state and of freedom were strictly negative, and that they were distinctly unimpressed with claims that the court should exercise caution in performing its checking function under the Charter.

Here is Dickson in *Hunter v. Southam*, an unreasonable search and seizure case decided in late 1984, in the context of arguing for a broad and purposive approach to the interpretation of the rights and freedoms in the Charter: "A constitution ...is drafted with an eye to the future. Its function is to provide a continuing framework for the legitimate exercise of governmental power and, when joined by a Bill or a Charter of Rights, for the unremitting protection of individual rights and liberties."[3]

And later on, in discussing the purpose of the Charter: "[The Charter] is intended to constrain governmental action inconsistent with those rights and freedoms; it is not itself an authorization for governmental action."[4]

Dickson does not deal explicitly in these passages with the questions of how to conceive of the state and of freedom, but what he says in them is clearly premised on the assumption that for the purposes of the Charter the state is to be viewed in negative terms – as the enemy of rights and freedoms – and so too is freedom: it is freedom *from* the state that we are to be concerned about.

These assumptions are made more explicit in Dickson's judgment in *R. v. Big M Drug Mart*, the Court's first freedom of religion case – in fact, the first case to involve any of the fundamental freedoms that reached the Supreme Court. Consider the following passage:

> Freedom can primarily be characterized by the absence of coercion or constraint. If a person is compelled by the State or the will of another

to a course of action or inaction which he would not otherwise have chosen, he is not acting of his own volition and he cannot be said to be truly free. One of the major purposes of the Charter is to protect, within reason, from compulsion or restraint. Coercion includes not only such blatant forms of compulsion as direct commands to act or refrain from acting on pain of sanction, coercion includes indirect forms of control which determine or limit alternative courses of conduct available to others. Freedom in a broad sence embraces both the absence of coercion and constraint, and the right to manifest beliefs and practices. *Freedom means that, subject to such limitations as are necessary to protect public safety, order, health or moral or the fundamental rights and freedoms of others, no one is to be forced to act in a way contrary to his beliefs or his conscience.*

What may appear good and true to a majoritarian religious group, or the State acting at their behest, may not, for religious reasons, be imposed upon citizens who take a contrary view. The Charter safeguards religious minorities from the threat of "the tyranny of the majority."[5]

Perhaps the clearest articulation of these conceptions comes in Wilson's judgment in *R. v. Morgentaler*, the case in which the Court struck down the abortion provisions of the Criminal Code. (I realize that that case takes us beyond *Oakes* – it was decided at the beginning of 1988; it is evidence of the fact that Wilson was more tenacious than the other two judges in holding to these conceptions.) I could invoke a number of passages from this judgment, but I will limit myself to one very short one. It reads as follows: "Thus, the rights guaranteed in the Charter erect around each individual, metaphorically speaking, an invisible fence over which the state will not be allowed to trespass. The role of the courts is to map out piece by piece, the parameters of the fence."[6]

At the same time that these three judges were viewing the state in negative terms and conceiving of freedom strictly as "freedom from," they were also refusing to acknowledge, at least explicitly, that growing concerns about the increasing power of judges, grounded in democratic theory and relative institutional competence, had any validity. On the few occasions on which they would deign to speak to those concerns, they quickly discounted them. Here, for example, is Lamer in the *94(2) Reference*, in which the Court struck down mandatory imprisonment for the absolute liability offence of driving a car while one's licence was suspended, responding to concerns grounded in democratic theory:

> This was an argument which was heard countless times prior to the entrenchment of the Charter but which has, in truth, for better or for worse, been settled by the very coming into force of the Constitution Act, 1982. It ought not to be forgotten that the historic decision to entrench the Charter in our Constitution was taken not by the courts but by the elected representatives of the people of Canada. It was those representatives who extended the scope of constitutional adjudication and entrusted the courts with this new and onerous responsibility. *Adjudication under the Charter must be approached free of any lingering doubts as to its legitimacy.*[7]

The combination of these traditional negative conceptions of both the state and freedom, and an unwillingness to acknowledge any merit in arguments favouring judicial restraint, do not *compel* the frequent use of the checking function by the Court, but they are clearly consistent with it. A court that sees the state as the enemy of freedom and has no difficulty with the notion that judges can check the exercise of state power when, in their view, its exercise encroaches unduly on someone's freedom is far more likely to perform that checking function aggressively than a court that is prepared at least sometimes to see the state as the source or promoter of freedom and has a good deal of difficulty with the notion that judges can check the exercise of state power. I am going to attempt to demonstrate that the much less frequent use of the checking function on the part of the Court now is a product at least in part of a shift on the Court's part from a court that fit the first description to one that fits the second.

Evidence of a change of thinking about the nature of the state and of freedom begins to appear in late 1986, particularly with the Court's decision in *Edwards Books*, which, like *Big M*, involved a challenge, based on freedom of religion, to Sunday observance legislation. In the course of his majority judgment upholding the legislation, Dickson makes it clear that he sees the state in this instance in positive terms, as the source or at least the guarantor of the freedom of vulnerable retail workers who would, absent the legislation, be compelled by their employers to work on a day that they would otherwise be free to spend with friends and family. This reconceptualization of both the state and freedom is at least partly captured by a sentence cited in support of the courts staying their hand certain kinds of Charter cases: "In interpreting and applying the Charter I believe that the courts must be cautious to ensure that it does not simply become an instrument of better situated individuals to roll back legislation which has as its object the improvement of the condition of less advantaged persons."[8]

Dickson's willingness to reconceptualize both the state and freedom is also evident in his recent majority judgment in *R. v. Keegstra*, in which the Court upheld the hate propaganda provisions of the Criminal Code in the face of a freedom of expression challenge. Perhaps the most useful passage here is the following, in which he examines the extent to which hate propaganda can be said to promote the purposes underlying our commitment to freedom of expression:

> Another component central to the rationale underlying s. 2(b) concerns the vital role of free expression as a means of ensuring individuals the ability to gain self-fulfillment by developing and articulating thoughts and ideas as they see fit. It is true that s. 319(2) inhibits this process among those individuals whose expression it limits and hence arguably works against the freedom of expression values. *On the other hand, such self-autonomy stems in large part from one's ability to articulate and nurture an identity derived from membership in a cultural or religious group. The message put forth by individuals who fall within the ambit of s. 319(2) represents a most extreme opposition to the idea that members of identifiable groups should enjoy this aspect of the s. 2(b) benefit. The extent to which the unhindered promotion of this message furthers free expression values must therefore be tempered insofar as it advocates with inordinate vitriol an intolerance and prejudice which views as execrable the process of individual self-development and human flourishing among all members of society.*[9]

Ironically, perhaps, given the tenacity with which she appeared to cling to traditional negative conceptions of the state and freedom, it is Wilson who provides the strongest affirmation of the need to move beyond those conceptions and endorse a more positive conception of both.

That affirmation comes in her dissenting judgment in *McKinney v. University of Guelph,* the leading case of four the Court decided on the issue of mandatory retirement at the end of 1990. One of the questions in that case was whether the Charter applied directly to universities. In answering that question, the Court was required to address for the first time the larger question of how the term "government" should be defined for the purposes of the Charter (the Court having already held that the Charter only applies directly to "government"). In the course of her answer to that question, she reviewed the historical development of the role of government in Canada. At the conclusion of that review she said:

> I believe that this historical review demonstrates that Canadians have a somewhat different attitude towards government and its role from our U.S. neighbours. Canadians recognize that government has traditionally had and continues to have an important role to play in the creation and preservation of a just Canadian society. The state has been looked to and has responded to demands that Canadians be guaranteed adequate health care, access to education and a minimum level of financial security to name but a few examples. *It is, in my view, untenable to suggest that freedom is co-extensive with the absence of government. Experience shows the contrary, that freedom has often required the intervention and protection of government against private action.*[10]

Evidence of a rethinking of the Court's early position on the proper scope of judicial review can also be found as early as late 1986. Dickson's judgment in *Edwards Books,* the second Sunday observance case, is full of signals that courts have to be careful not to play their Charter hand too freely. One almost gets the impression from that judgment that so long as the government has made, as he put it, "genuine and serious attempts" to strike a fair balance between the various competing interests, the courts should leave well enough alone.[11]

A particularly striking example of the rethinking that has been occurring in this area is provided by Lamer in his judgment in the *Prostitution Reference.* At issue in that and two related cases decided at the same time (in the spring of 1990) was the validity of the new street soliciting offence in the Criminal Code, which had been challenged on a number of grounds, including section 7 (the right to liberty). Troubled by the fact that the Court had failed to that point to provide much meaningful guidance on the manner in which the term "liberty" was to be defined, Lamer decided to provide such guidance. In the result, he defined the term very narrowly. In support of that narrow definition, he invoked a number of different arguments, one of which was grounded in precisely those concerns about judicial review that he had so summarily discounted in the *94(2) Reference.* To adopt a broad interpretation of "liberty," he said, would take the Court into "the realm of general public policy dealing with broader social, political and moral issues which are much better resolved in the political or legislative forum and not in the courts."[12]

That brings me to the last passage I want to invoke in support of my thesis. It comes from *Irwin Toy Ltd. v. Quebec,* a freedom of expression case decided in 1989. My reason for leaving it until the end is that it captures the essence of, and brings together, the rethinking in which the Court has been engaged in respect of all three of these questions. Fortuitously, although not surprisingly, at least to me, the judgment in which the passage appears was co-authored by the three judges at whom we have been looking – Dickson, Lamer and Wilson. The passage appears in their application of section 1 of the Charter to the legislation at issue in that case, which they had found to infringe on freedom of expression. It reads:

> Thus, in matching means to ends and asking whether rights or freedoms are impaired as little as possible, a legislature mediating between the claims of competing groups will be forced to strike a balance without the benefit of absolute certainty concerning how that balance is best struck. Vulnerable groups will claim the need for protection by the government whereas other groups and individuals will assert that the government should not intrude. In *Edwards Books, supra,* Chief Justice Dickson expressed an important concern about the situation of vulnerable groups (at p. 49):
>
>> In interpreting and applying the Charter I believe that the Courts must be cautious to ensure that it does not simply become an instrument of better situated individuals to roll back legislation which has as its object the improvement of the condition of less advantaged persons.
>
> When striking a balance between the claims of competing groups,

the choice of means, like the choice of ends, frequently will require an assessment of conflicting scientific evidence and differing justified demands on scarce resources. Democratic institutions are meant to let us all share in the responsibility for these difficult choices. Thus, as courts review the results of the legislature's deliberations, particularly with respect to the protection of vulnerable groups, they must be mindful of the legislature's representative function. For example, when "regulating industry or business it is open to the legislature to restrict its legislative reforms to sectors in which there appear to be particularly urgent concerns or to constituencies that seem especially needy" (*Edwards Books, supra*, at p. 44).

In other cases, however, rather than mediating between different groups, the government is best characterized as the singular antagonist of the individual whose right has been infringed. For example, in justifying an infringement of legal rights enshrined in ss. 7 to 14 of the Charter, the state, on behalf of the whole community, typically will assert its responsibility for prosecuting crime whereas the individual will assert the paramountcy of principles of fundamental justice. There might not be any further competing claims among different groups. In such circumstances, and indeed whenever the government's purpose relates to maintaining the authority and impartiality of the judicial system, the courts can assess with some certainty whether the "least drastic means" for achieving the purpose have been chosen, especially given their accumulated experience in dealing with such questions: see *The Sunday Times v. United Kingdom* (1979), 2 E.H.R.R. 245 at p. 276. The same degree of certainty may not be achievable in cases involving the reconciliation of claims of competing individuals or groups or the distribution of scarce government resources.[13]

What emerges from this passage, at least as I read it, is an answer to the question about the proper scope of judicial review that is defined in large part in terms of the competing conceptions of the state and of freedom. When, in the Court's view, the proper conceptions are negative – the state as the enemy of individual freedom – boldness rather than caution on the part of the courts is called for. By contrast, when the proper conceptions are otherwise – when the state is more appropriately viewed in positive terms, which it will be if it is seen to be promoting the interests of vulnerable groups in society – caution rather than boldness is called for. In the former context, the message is that concerns about democratic theory and relative institutional competence are to be given little, if any, credence. In the latter context, those concerns are to be taken seriously and given considerable weight.

As this passage makes clear, rethinking one's positions on these questions need not entail rejecting in their entirety the negative conceptions of the state and of freedom and the checking of governmental power by the courts. It can entail, and in the case of the Supreme Court of Canada it has entailed, limiting the scope of those conceptions and the frequency with which the checking function is exercised. A more positive conception of the state takes its place alongside the negative one; a more positive conception of freedom takes its place alongside the negative one; and judicial restraint takes its place alongside judicial activism.

A number of important and intriguing questions flow from this analysis of the Supreme Court's changing response to the Charter. How does one determine which side of the line a particular case falls on? Why did the Court choose to rethink its position on these questions? Has the Court been right to rethink its original positions on these questions?

Also flowing from this analysis is, I think, the need to recognize that the courts are involved in much more than the checking of governmental power when they are engaged in judicial review under the Charter.[14] In those cases – and the number has been growing – in which the courts decline to check the exercise of governmental power, the effect of their decisions may well be, and often is, to legitimate the particular forms of governmental action that were under attack. That is particularly true in cases in which the courts' refusal to check the exercise of governmental power is based on a finding under section 1 of the Charter that the governmental action is "demonstrably justified in a free and democratic society."

It is also apparent from some of the passages quoted above that the courts are engaged in an important expressive function when they exercise the power of judicial review under the Charter. In addressing questions about the appropriate conceptions of the state and of freedom and the proper scope of judicial review, the courts tell us and the rest of the world important things about the kind of people Canadians are and the kind of values we have. The courts do not, of course, have a monopoly on the ability to tell our story, but because of the legitimacy they continue to have in the minds of most Canadians, they occupy a privileged position in relation to others who offer competing versions. This expressive function of theirs is, therefore, deserving of some attention.

It is also possible to ascribe other functions to judicial review under the Charter. The fact that some of the rights and freedoms operate to impose positive obligations on government – that is, obligations *to act*, rather than to desist from acting – means that on occasion courts are called upon to command the exercise of governmental power. This command function, as it might be termed, is exemplified by decisions enforcing the minority language educational rights under section 23.

Less obvious, perhaps, but no less important, is what I like to call the prompting function of judicial review. Courts will on occasion use the power of judicial review to signal to the elected branches of government that the time has come for them to take up or reconsider an issue that, for one reason or another, they have chosen to avoid for a lengthy period of time. I have always thought of *Morgentaler* as an exercise of this function in relation to the issue of abortion.

To this point, little attention has been given by constitutional scholars to the multiplicity of functions performed by judicial review. The assumption from the beginning has tended to be that judicial review is about nothing more than checking the exercise of governmental power. With the Supreme Court of Canada having made it clear that the power to check is going to be used sparingly now, it is clearly time to pay greater heed to the other functions of judicial review, each of which raises its own set of challenging questions.

That has been the problem with the Charter all along. It just keeps getting more and more interesting.

NOTES

1 For an extended analysis of the non-criminal cases decided in the 1989–90 term, and of the change in the court's attitude towards the Charter reflected in them, see R. Elliot, "Developments in Constitutional Law: The 1989–90 Term," (1991) 2 *Supreme Court Law Review* (2d) 83–173.

2 [1986] 1 SCR 103.

3 [1984] 2 SCR 145, at 155.
4 Ibid., at 156.
5 [1985] 1 SCR 295, at 336–7 (emphasis added).
6 [1988] 1 SCR 30, at 164.
7 [1985] 2 SCR 486, at 497 (emphasis added).
8 [1986] 2 SCR 713, at 779.
9 [1990] 3 SCR 697, at 763 (emphasis added).
10 [1990] 3 SCR 229, at 356 (emphasis added).
11 [1986] 2 SCR 713, at 781.
12 [1990] 1 SCR 1123, at 1177.
13 [1989] 1 SCR 927, at 993–4.
14 These additional functions of judicial review are explored in much greater detail in the article cited supra in note 1, particularly at 154–71.

III

The Charter and Our Intellectual Traditions

Is Democracy a Constitutional Right?

New Turns in an Old Debate

How does the idea of democracy figure in constitutional argument? I offer here a report on current stirrings in American constitutional thought about that question.[1] More precisely, the question is whether constitutional argument as we know it has room for such a notion as a "right to democracy." Does any such notion belong – does it or can it possibly fit – within those parts of our constitutions that we call charters and bills of rights?

It may be that the answers are not exactly the same for our two countries. We shall see that the notion of a right to democracy is in certain respects at odds with mainstream American constitutional understanding. Certainly democracy has a place in standard American constitutional argument, including argument about the Bill of Rights. Democracy has not, however, usually figured in such argument as itself one of the rights. It has rather figured as what we may call a background fact or background value – a consideration that enters into arguments over the scope and content of rights (rights to freedom of speech, for example) that are not themselves rights to democracy as such.

One reason for raising this matter with Canadian friends is the Canadian Charter's express allowance, in section 1, for rights-infringing laws that are "demonstrably justified in a free and democratic society." Two features of that immediately strike an American observer. The first is something that perhaps makes you look a little different from us: that is, the Charter's rhetorical placement of the norm of democracy on a plane of shared primacy with the norm of freedom. In prevailing American constitutional thought, especially in regard to our Bill of Rights, democracy takes a decidedly second place to liberty; and this is one reason why the notion of a right to democracy fits uneasily in American constitutional thought. Another feature of section 1, though, quite echoes American thought and experience. And that is the Charter's placement of this express tribute to democracy in a power-authorizing clause, as distinguished from a rights-naming or rights-granting clause. That suggests that, for Canadians as well as Americans, democracy will figure in constitutional argument as a background fact and value, but perhaps not as a constitutional right.[2]

Explanation is in order. I must first briefly describe the notion I am using of a constitutional right to democracy, and put before you certain arguments that are made in support of the conclusion that we do have or ought to have such a right. Then I have to explain what I mean by saying that, in American constitutional argumentative practice, democracy figures rather as a background fact and value than as a right. Next, I will suggest how this feature of our practice connects with certain other pervasive traits of mainstream American constitutional thought.

The step after that will be to describe, very hastily, a recent venture in academic American constitutional theory – one among several – that does, despite evident difficulties, insist that democracy itself is a right set forth in our Bill of Rights. Finally, I will try briefly, through a specific example, to convey some sense of the possible import of proposals of this kind.

First, then, we need some approximate starting definition for the term "democracy" and the notion of a right to democracy. By democracy, I mean simply collective, popular, political self-government organized on a majoritarian principle. I mean the condition in which laws are made and governments chosen and directed, in and for a state, by the mass of the people in that state,[3] either directly or through elected representatives, by procedures based on voting and majority rule. A right to democracy is simply a right that our laws be made, and our governments chosen and directed, by and only by popular-majoritarian processes.

I have assumed that democracy thus conceived can allow for institutional devices – such as representation, a separation of powers, and various procedural regimens – aimed at supporting due deliberation, fair access, effective administration, and formal justice. It would follow that the exact contours of any constitutional right to democracy as there may be are open to wide variation. For now, I only want to establish that the existence of even a quite radical right of this sort – call it a right to plebiscitary rule – is really quite thinkable.

Suppose we hear someone urge that the people of a state have a constitutional right that any voting majority of them be authorized to alter their state's law – including its constitutional law – in any way they decide to do, simply by voting their decision in a duly publicized, fairly accessible, statewide plebiscite. We may ask: what does it mean to speak here of a "constitutional right?" It means, I take it, that constitutional law, presently in force, places someone under a pertinent duty, to the performance of which someone else is entitled on demand. Of what, then, might the pertinent duty consist? Here is one possibility: Popular majoritarian, direct-democratic law-making really cannot be done without our first having in place a duly prescribed, authoritative, and workable procedure for doing it. Suppose no such specific prescription now exists in state law. In that case, to speak of a constitutional right to plebiscitary rule would mean, among other things, that those in a position to enact state law setting forth the requisite procedures are placed by constitutional law under a duty to do so. If the ordinary legislature possesses the necessary authority, it would be obliged by constitutional law to exercise that authority. If only an extraordinary popular convention would have the authority, then those who can instigate such a convention are bound by constitutional law to do that; and the resulting convention, once in place, will then be similarly bound to legislate procedures that satisfy the right in question.

As must by now be clear, it is not essential to a claim of a constitutional "right" to plebiscitary rule (at least as I am using the term here) that the claimant be saying that some *court* necessarily ought to *order* the duty-bound officials to take the requisite actions. The speaker claims a constitutional right insofar as he says there is constitutional law telling those officials to do so on demand, making their unexcused failure a violation of a positive obligation those officials assumed by accepting their offices.[4]

The next task is to put briefly before you a normative argument in support of a constitutional right to democracy, construed to encompass a popular power to determine the content and meaning of law, including constitutional law, by act of a majority. A main task of such an argument must be to dispel worries that the notion of a constitutional right to democracy, thus conceived, is at war with the very idea of constitutional rights and so is incoherent, at war with itself. For it does initially seem that to assert such a constitutional right as that is to deny that there are or possibly can be any constitutional rights at all, not even this asserted "constitutional right" of popular majorities to rule. It does initially seem that if popular majorities are granted authority to alter and interpret the laws at will, including the laws of the constitution supposed to establish this very authority, then it is idle to speak of any longer of *constitutional* rights. For what is it, after all, that makes a right constitutional, if not legal entrenchment of that right against direct majoritarian alteration?

This is a forceful question. It invites suspicion that conceptual equations of democracy – or, at any rate, constitutional democracy – with majority rule must be mistaken. That is why Ronald Dworkin can use it to support what he presents as a richer and better conception of constitutional democracy, a conception in which substantive limits on popular law-making authority are integral, built in from the start.[5] A persuasive argument in defence of a broad constitutional right to popular-majoritarian rule will have to fend off such potentially devastating objections.

Professor Jeremy Waldron of the University of California at Berkeley has provided the makings for an argument that may do the trick.[6] Waldron's argument contains two basic premises. The first will certainly not be regarded as outlandish by Canadian constitutionalists. It is simply that the commands contained in our constitutions, including those contained in their enumerations of rights, require interpretation.[7] On this view, each text of command may be considered a token – an inevitably partial and incomplete expression – of some more generally apprehended precept or theory of political morality and prudence.[8] Nor may we assume (until, if ever, the fact shall be demonstrated) that all the commands necessarily reflect any one theory, even a complex one, that we shall ever know how to articulate convincingly. Rather, as hard as we may study to reduce the manifest theories to one, they may intractably appear to be several, differentially manifesting themselves through different clauses, adopted in sometimes widely differing times and circumstances. Working them all into one may arguably be the unfinishable task – the regulative idea – of constitutional jurisprudence, but in the meanwhile, determining the application of constitutional commands to particular cases will require not just elucidation but accommodation of an ostensible plurality of underlying normative ideas, not all evidently and fully compatible with each other.[9]

Professor Waldron's second basic premise may strike you as rather more heroic than his first. It is that ordinary citizens not only are capable of addressing such interpretative questions competently and in good faith, but that they can be expected at least sometimes to do just that in ordinary political settings. Good faith here means acting with a view to arriving at publicly reasonable interpretations,[10] and not just with a view to promoting one's own advantage or ideology or otherwise satisfying one's own desires. Waldron assumes that it is entirely possible that ordinary citizens would turn their minds in good faith to pending questions about what rights we have, how they should be balanced, and so forth.[11]

On that assumption, Waldron argues, there is nothing intrinsically "tyrannical" about a popular-majoritarian procedure for resolving interpretative questions, any more than when a majority of the judges of our Supreme Court – or yours --makes such a determination over the dissent of a judicial minority, let alone over the possible disagreement of a popular majority. And, Waldron reminds us, in constitutional regimes that deny to popular majorities the authority to make such determinations (for example, by reserving the last word for a politically insulated judicial élite), there does plainly lie an abdication from self-government.

Waldron's two premises together can support a constitutional right to popular-majoritarian rule that is not conceptually self-defeating or deeply antagonistic to the very idea of constitutional rights. Here is how: Even with our enacted charters and bills of rights, we cannot, in plural societies like ours, regularly expect consensus or publicly certifiable, objective certainty about exactly what our constitutional rights are. Accepting (because we have no honest alternative) this fact of good-faith irreducible uncertainty, we require, says Waldron, constitutional structures that accord respect and honor to people's ability to deliberate morally and transcend a preoccupation with particular or sectional interests.[12] The belief is widespread that "participation in the public realm is ... part of a fulfilling human life," so that denial of such participation amounts to denying people "a part of their essence."[13] At stake here, moreover, is something more than regard for individual human flourish-

ing. Also involved are issues of individual entitlement to political freedom and self-government, and, hence, issues of political legitimacy. The
straightforward argument is that every denial of effective participation in
determinations of the laws one lives under is a clear and direct denial of
freedom. Institutions deny liberty, and they accordingly lack legitimacy,
if they fail to accredit "the capacity of ordinary men and women to govern their own lives on terms that respect the equal capacities of others."[14]
People, writes Waldron, "fought long and hard for the vote and democratic representation. They wanted the right to govern themselves, not
just on trivial issues of policy, but also on high matters of principle."[15]

I hope now to have suggested how the notion of a constitutional
right to popular-majoritarian rule can possibly be reconciled with show-
ings, like Dworkin's,[16] that constitutionalism – the practice of entrenching rights in a bill or charter of rights – essentially involves the idea of
substantive restraints on the powers of rulers. Reconciliation requires belief in possibilities of public reason and good faith in popular-majoritarian determinations of interpretative questions. Insofar as public reason
and good faith did prevail, then constitutional entrenchments would significantly *exist*; they would really and purposively limit or constrain political action, even though the scope and reach of the constraint would
always, in some important respects, remain open to popular interpretation. Understood in this relatively open way, entrenchment of certain
rights is compatible with a coexistent right to democracy understood as
the right of the people at large (acting directly or through elected representatives) to decide at any time upon the interpretations of their entrenched rights or – with due solemnity – to revise occasionally the
instrument of entrenchment. In sum, the argument uses the possibility
of good-faith exercise of public reason to disentangle the question of
whether rulers (including popular-majoritarian rulers) are substantively
restrained from the question of who sets and construes the restraints; it
aims to sever the question of constitutionalism from that of judicial
supremacy.[17]

I must now return to what I meant by saying that in American constitutional argument, democracy has in practice figured not as itself a
constitutional right but as a background fact and background value. Democracy figures as background fact and value when someone argues that

the precise scope and content of some (other) right guaranteed by a clause in a bill or charter of rights ought to be determined, at least partly, in the light of the observation that our political systems *are*, as a matter of fact, by and large both operationally based on democratic processes and normatively committed to them. In the American literature of constitutional-legal theory, two classics in that genre are Alexander Meiklejohn's *Free Speech and Its Relation to Self-Government*[18] and John Hart Ely's *Democracy and Distrust*.[19]

Professor Meiklejohn's work is today often cited for the instrumentalist idea that a chief reason for making freedom of speech a constitutional right is the importance of the free exchange of ideas to sound and responsive democratic deliberation and decision.[20] In such an argument, democracy's status is that of a fact – a very salient one – in our lives. For better or for worse (Meiklejohn plainly thought it was for the better), our governments are chosen and our laws are made democratically. Instrumentally explained, the right of freedom of speech is rooted in this fact – this given value – of democracy.

Such a view can significantly shape and steer debate over various controversial extensions and restrictions of the constitutional right of freedom of speech.[21] On the one hand, the Meiklejohn view can be and has been used in support of arguments that pornography is not "speech" protected by the first amendment because it contributes nothing of value to political debate.[22]

On the other hand, the Meiklejohn view can be and has been used in support of arguments that the first amendment rules out laws forbidding the use of business corporation treasury funds for political advertisements by corporation managements. It's not that anyone dares say that corporations as such have cognizable interests of their own in autonomy or self-expression, in the way that an ordinary person has an interest in expressing her feelings and thoughts. It's not that anyone dares say that managers have personal rights to proselytize or otherwise express themselves by spending funds from the corporate till. Rather, the argument is that what the constitution values is not so much the activity of self-expression as the consequence in getting all the arguments into circulation among the people engaged in democratic political deliberation.[23] Meiklejohn wrote that what is "essential" is not "that everyone shall speak" but that "everything worth saying shall be said."[24] And who can know that one of those things worth saying won' t be especially tellingly said by corporation mangers spending treasury funds?

Now let's spend a moment with John Ely. Dean Ely argued that the fact of democracy provides a basis for principled attribution by judges of specific, substantive content to "open-ended" constitutional clauses such as our due process and equal protection clauses.[25] Of course, Ely's conception of the fact of democracy differs in a basic way from Meiklejohn's – and, one may well add, from Waldron's. Meiklejohn envisioned a collective deliberation among the people and their representatives attempting in good faith to find out together the requirements of both constitutional right and the common good. Waldron's argument is partly based on the claim that this can really happen in politics and does happen at least sometimes. Ely, by contrast, seems to have supposed a more self-servingly strategic interaction among particularistic interests. Whereas Meiklejohn envisioned a prevailingly civically virtuous – republican – political ethos, Ely supposed a prevailingly interest-group pluralist political ethos.

Or, rather, Ely ascribed to the authors of the constitution the intention and expectation of having chartered an interest-group pluralist democratic system. From this ascription, Ely felt able to derive some fairly concrete conclusions regarding, for example, what particular kinds of legally imposed inequalities count as major denials of constitutionally guaranteed equal protection, requiring specially compelling justification in order to withstand a constitutional challenge. One easy derivation was that – although our constitution nowhere says so in concrete terms – laws that impose special franchise qualifications on subsets of residents of a geographically defined electoral unit (for example, by disqualifying new arrivals, non-ratepayers, or members of the armed forces) are highly constitutionally suspect.[26]

Thus, in a way quite different from Meiklejohn's, Ely set himself to defining the contents of the rights in our Bill of Rights by attaching exceptional value to the interests people have in effective participation in democratic processes, given that democratic processes are what we have. His argument requires no supposition that the existence of these democratic processes corresponds to any right we have to their existence. The proposition is simply of an existent fact – democracy – from which existent fact certain rights of participation in that fact, by speech or votes, may be inferred by instrumental reason.[27]

Much of what I have said so far confirms that American constitutional argument is broadly reponsive to norms of democratic governance – is, indeed, geared to controversy over the precise content and implications of such norms. My next point is that this same argumentative practice is somewhat resistant to the idea of democracy as a right. I am about to mention four factors in our constitutional thought that figure in this resistance. (I don't think it much matters whether one calls these factors reasons for the resistance or manifestations of it.) These are not, I believe, a random collage but rather a set of intellectual tendencies that hang together ideologically. We can call them, respectively, (1) judicial review; (2) rule of law; (3) protection of minorities; and (4) attribution of entitlement.

First, *judicial review.* When we speak of constitutional rights, we think immediately of judicial review of government action with a view to judicial enforcement of the putative right. But as we have already noticed, the proposition of a right to democracy looks very much as though it might itself be a broadside attack on judicial review. Jeremy Waldron, for example, deploys the idea specifically in order to question the Supreme Court's arrogation unto itself of final authority over questions of constitutional meaning.[28]

Next, *rule of law.* Here I mean that aspect of the rule-of-law ideal that aspires to a government "of laws" and not "of men." I mean the aspiration to submitting ourselves to rule by reason and steadfast principle, not by passion and happenstance power. A right to democracy encompassing the authority of current popular majorities to determine the meaning of the constitution strikes many as not just contrary but opposite to that ideal, a paradigmatic subversion of it.[29]

Third, *protection of minorities.* Especially when thinking about rights enumerated in those parts of our constitutions that we call bills and charters of rights, we tend strongly to think that the central point of such enumerations is to secure certain exceptionally meritorious interests of persons against majoritarian abuse. Bills and charters of rights, we think, are there to protect the deviant, the dissident, and the downtrodden. They are instruments of protection against that immanent tyrant, the majority. It would, therefore, be an inversion of their purpose – it would be a travesty – to read them as conferring a right of majorities to rule unboundedly.

Fourth, *attribution of entitlement.* The problem here is conceptual, not political or ideological. Yet it echoes the political resistances I have already mentioned. Conceptually, a right is an entitlement. It is an entitlement that someone act differently from how he would choose to act but for deference to the right. A constitutional right is of that kind. As with all such entitlements, there must be someone in particular against whom it runs, and there is: A constitutional right runs against those who hold and wield recognized political power, which it seems under our systems could well mean not just elected officials but electorates, the franchised citizenries who elect the officials. Again, as with all such entitlements, there must be someone in particular who is the entitlement's subject, its holder or (so to speak) owner. But the owner of the entitlement cannot be identical with the ower of the corresponding duty. The idea of someone having a right against herself is incoherent. And this makes the idea of a constitutional right to majority rule look incoherent. To whom, after all, can we attribute ownership (so to speak) of such a right, except to the citizenry at large? And are not the citizenry at large the very folks, ultimately, against whom constitutional rights are meant to run?

None of these factors poses an insuperable intellectual obstacle to the idea of a constitutional right to democracy. We ought briefly to notice why not. First, it is a plain error to say that there is no right there, just because we have trouble imagining or countenancing judicial enforcement. There is no reason why it can't be true that officials are in default of constitutionally imposed duties, corresponding to someone's constitutionally recognized right, although no court will or ought to enforce the duty.[30]

Next, I believe it may be equally mistaken to think that judicial review, in something like the form we know and love, cannot coexist with a right to democracy. I can only sketch here how the full argument to that effect would go. The argument would start from Professor Waldron's reliance, in defending a right to democracy, on the motivational supposition of *good-faith* deliberation by the people or their representatives on questions of constitutional meaning, including questions about exactly what our constitutional rights are. The argument would then build on the intuition that this optimistic assumption can, at best, be true in some but not all cases of constitutionally questionable political action. Agreeing to this extent with Professor Richard Epstein,[31] one might suggest that it's in the space opened by this uncertainty about civic virtue that judicial review can perhaps find a niche even in the presence of a right to democracy. In fact, one might point to section 33 of the Canadian Charter of Rights and Freedoms as a device designed to carve out just such a place for judicial review.[32]

Next, I think we really cannot hold to the view that allowing disputes over constitutional meanings to be resolved by (supposedly) good-faith popular deliberations, ultimately decided by majoritarian processes, violates the rule-of-law ideal. How could we, given that we do not think the rule of law is violated when we allow resolutions of constitutional controversies by the similarly non-unanimous (and perhaps similarly idealized) actions of multimember judicial bodies?[33]

By way of commentary on the last two of my four trouble-making factors, protection of minorities and attribution of entitlement, I offer a reference to recent work by Professor Akhil Reed Amar of Yale University. Professor Amar is a leading contemporary proponent of the idea that our Bill of Rights in fact contains a right – or rights – to democracy.[34] The core of his argument is that the Bill of Rights is not concerned exclusively with protecting minorities against abuse of their rights by popular majorities; it is concerned, as well, with protecting the people – meaning, in practice, the people in their majoritarian disposition – against abuse of the constitution by faithless governments and officers.

Notably, for our purposes here, Amar includes courts and judges among the potentially faithless. His main vehicle for this is his exploration of the three jury clauses in our federal Bill of Rights – one each for grand juries, petit juries in criminal trials, and civil juries.[35] Juries, argues Amar, were very possibly intended by the framers as prime vehicles of popularly based legal, including constitutional, interpretation. We have come to treat juries as law-takers, strictly bound to follow legal instruction from presiding judges. Amar believes this may be a lapse from an original understanding by which juries were expected to ponder questions of constitutional and other legal meaning independently, as organs of the populace at large reviewing and, where necessary, revising official-dom's favoured answers.[36]

For our purposes here, it is useful to spin out Amar's thesis in the following manner: The Bill of Rights does, to be sure, have a minority-protecting aspect. In that aspect, the Bill of Rights creates duties – that is, duties to refrain from certain kinds of political acts – that are owed *by* the citizenry and their representatives (acting by majority rule) *to* particular claimants for protection. The Bill of Rights also has a pro-popular (pro-majoritarian) aspect. In that aspect, it creates duties both to facilitate and to defer to deliberate majority decision. These duties are owed *by* governments and officials *to* the body of the citizenry, the franchised people at large in their deliberate majoritarian disposition.

One can see, then, how Amar's thesis, if correct, directly responds to claims that there cannot be a constitutional right to democracy, either because such a right falls outside the constitutional project of protecting minorities against majorities or because such a right would incoherently fail to differentiate the right's owner from the ower of the pertinent duty. As to the former objection, Amar simply asserts that protection of popular majorities against governments is in fact a historical aim of the Bill of Rights (along with protection of popular minorities against popular majorities). As to the latter difficulty, Amar could simply point out the obvious lack of identity between the people at large (owners of the right he has in mind) and the holders of office (owers of the duty).

Of course, it remains highly controversial whether Amar's thesis is correct – that is, as a reading of our Bill of Rights. Amar elaborates his thesis in various and even wondrous ways as he surveys and explores the texts, and their histories, of the various clauses in our Bill of Rights. Here is one line of development especially worth noting: Our first amendment declares a right of "the people" to assemble and petition for redress of grievances. Our ninth amendment points to retention by "the people" of certain (unspecified) rights not mentioned in the other clauses of the Bill of Rights.[37] Amar urges that the framers understood "the people" in these clauses to be one and the same with that "We the People of the United States" who have already declared themselves the constitution's authors, ultimate lawgivers and popular sovereigns of the country. Thus, Amar argues, chief among the ninth amendment rights retained by the people is their continuing right to determine the content and meaning of the country's laws, including the constitution; and the first amendment right of assembly is, in effect, that very right to provision of a direct-democratic, simple-majoritarian, process of constitutional revision that I first mentioned as the most straightforward concretization of a constitutional right to democracy.[38]

Following Amar, I have now put before you the idea of a constitutional right to democracy in its most astounding form. Astounded, however, is not how I wish to leave you. I would rather leave you somewhere closer to nodding in bored agreement. So I want to finish by briefly showing the idea of a right to democracy at work in a manner that may strike you as more natural and ordinary, in a bit of constitutional debate that is right now taking place in the United States.

Constitutional clauses, we have said, require interpretation: Many clauses are imperfect expressions of animating normative ideas, different clauses express different ideas, and it is not always obvious how best to formulate an inclusive theory that gives its due to each idea demanding recognition.

For example: In American constitutional understanding, the first amendment's prohibition of laws abridging the freedom of speech is widely to taken to express an ideal of personal autonomy, implying a certain scope of virtually absolute freedom from state control of expression.[39] Autonomy here means personal freedom to think and give voice to one's thoughts without external constraint. Accordingly, the correlative notion of liberty is strictly "negative." This means more than that the first amendment imposes no affirmative obligation on the state to assist people's efforts to speak and be heard. It further means (for those who find autonomy to be the first amendment's central, animating value) that the state is *not* even *permitted* to enact speech-restrictive measures that may be found necessary to ensure effective inclusion for all in communicative exchange.

At the same time, our constitution's "reconstruction amendments,"[40] especially as revivified by the country and its courts during our post-*Brown* civil rights "revolution," are widely held to express a principle of opposition to structural, systemic, second-class status for any visible minority of citizens.[41] In the particular context of hate speech regulation, it has been forcefully argued that the private-libertarian principle of the first amendment and the emancipationist principle of the fourteenth collide so as to produce a degree of indeterminacy and a need for interpretation.[42] Such arguments rest on a sociological claim, eloquently summarized by Waldron's Berkeley colleague, Professor Robert C. Post:

> In ordinary life, members of victim groups do not experience a string of distinct disadvantages. Rather, if representations in the current literature are ... true ... groups confront in public discourse [a] ... complex of circumstances in which they are systematically demeaned, stigmatized, ignored; in which the very language of debate resists the articulation of their claims; in which they are harassed, abused, intimidated, and systematically and egregiously injured both individually and collectively. The question is ... whether these liabilities ... when taken together as a complex whole ... render public discourse unfit as an instrument of ... self-determination for members of victim groups, and whether this unacceptable situation would be cured by restraints on racist speech.[43]

Without directly answering Professor Post's "question," American courts have made clear their view that sociological grounds of the kind he cites cannot overcome constitutional objections against government censorship, even of racial hate speech. The courts treat such censorship as a prime example of a content-discriminatory, hence super-suspect, restriction on people's expressions of their views in public discourse, and find the claimed sociological justifications too speculative to satisfy the demand for a strictly "compelling" or "overriding" justification.[44]

It is possible that this curt judicial response reflects active disbelief in the empirical truth of the sociological claim. More likely, it reflects uncertainty or undecidability. Our courts have consistently read the first amendment as containing a strong principle against allowing the "offensiveness" of certain speech to serve as a justification for suppression. On that basis the court has, for example, invalidated laws prohibiting public burnings of American flags.[45] A court lacking any other firm basis for resolving the issue of state censorability of racist speech might be moved by the difficulty of distinguishing this case from that of, say, flag burnings, in a way likely to be convincing to large sections of the public.[46] Uncertain about the sociological basis for censoring racist speech, or feeling that its truth is judicially undecidable, a court may find good reason to rule against censorability in a basic concern for the apparent consistency (at an accessible level of complexity) of the corpus juris.

A constitutional ruling of this kind has, of course, no direct application to non-governmental institutions. However, there is now pending in Congress a bill – known, after its principal sponsor, as the Hyde bill – that would, if enacted, in effect extend the application of these rulings to virtually every private college and university in the country.[47] The bill is clearly aimed at "speech codes" restricting racially stigmatizing expression that have recently blossomed in our universities. The bill has met with strenuous objection on the part of many who share its sponsors' dislike of the campus speech codes and the spirit of "political correctness" the codes are said to represent. Critics see the bill as poised to commit not just a prudential mistake but a constitutional wrong. They see it as a grave insult to basic precepts of American constitutional-structural morality.

It is not clear, however, what precept is offended. One leaps at first to condemn the bill as offensive to some principle of institutional autonomy or privacy, academic freedom, or freedom of association. This, however, will not do. Without the least objection from many who criticize the Hyde bill, American constitutional law has easily welcomed congressional legislation extending to non-governmental organizations, including private colleges and universities, the prohibitions against racial discrimination that the constitution directly imposes only upon governments. The theory, I have argued,[48] must be that the constitution's textual focus on infringements of certain "rights" by *governments* cannot come from nonchalance about infringements by non-governmental power-holders. Rather, it must spring from a sense of the unwisdom of enacting, at the constitutional level, a flat and sweeping legal demand upon every person in all circumstances to defer to the "preferred freedoms" of others. (May parents censor their children? May householders discriminate on ethnic grounds in their selection of dinner guests?) The constitution relies on more concretely situated law-making to extend beyond the domain of governments proper, selectively as circumstances indicate, its mandates to respect people's rights.

But that leaves the Hyde bill resistant to attack on simple grounds of disrespect of private institutional autonomy. For it is apparently judicially resolved that among the American people's constitutional rights are rights against censorship of speech, including racist speech. However troubled may be the arguments leading to this particular conclusion, courts have determined that the constitution means that, all things considered, the correct way for governments to respect people's fundamental interests in freedom of expression is just to forbear from regulatory censorship of speech, including racist speech. And so it seems that the right to be free of such official censorship just is, then, an established fundamental right of persons in the United States. By enacting the Hyde bill, then, Congress would apparently be moving to protect a duly established, fundamental right of persons in the United States against a class of relatively powerful agents positioned to violate the right – just as Congress did when it imposed anti-discrimination law on non-governmental institutions including universities.

Such considerations suggest that perhaps what the Hyde bill is felt to pinch is not so much an institutional autonomy right as a democracy right.[49] Recall the argument that racist speech plays into and reinforces socio-culturally seated, race-based impairments of status, autonomy, influence, and access. We saw how judges hesitant to decide judicially this sociological claim might leave it undecided while still holding against the constitutional-legal permissibility of state censorship of racist speech. Such a holding, we said, might be mainly guided by a judicial preference for evident consistency, without too much complexity, in constitutional-legal doctrine.

Among Americans attentive to such matters, not all are primarily concerned, as conscientious judges may well be when speaking ex cathedra, with transparent consistency in legal doctrine; some are simply citizens concerned to get things right. Some feel strongly both the force of the sociological argument for restricting racist speech and the sting of the resulting normative dilemma. For them, public censorship of racist speech raises a profound question of constitutional meaning: Is formal universal freedom (vis-à-vis the state) precedent to racial desubordination? Is desubordination precedent to abstract, formal liberty? Or is the relation more recalcitrantly plural and contextual? What is the constitutional meaning of the post-New Deal civil rights "revolution?" Is this a sort of question over which we grant judges the last word?[50] Or does it belong ultimately to the people to decide? We find in our law principles of institutional settlement, designed to let society get along with business and life despite disputes about what the law is.[51] A conscientious judicial decision against public censorability of racist speech doubtless merits respect as legally controlling within its domain, that is, as controlling on government censorship. Yet it may be an open question whether that same decision adequately represents the whole of pertinent American political morality respecting fundamental human rights.

Along such lines, an arguable difference appears between the Hyde bill and congressional imposition of anti-discrimination law on non-governmental institutions. In each case, Congress extends to the non-governmental sector a protection of human rights drawn from constitutional law. In the case of anti-discrimination law, the extended human right is that of freedom from invidious race-based discrimination by public official authority. By now, the status of that particular human right as an American constitutional right is unquestionably settled. (To be sure, dispute persists over certain aspects of this constitutional right: what is invidious? what is attributable to official authority? But there is no room for doubt that the right includes protection against official imposition of segregation, exclusion, deprivation, or restriction on non-whites as such. As to that protection, the constitutional meaning of our civil rights "revolution" is crystal clear.)

Arguably different in stage and certainty of resolution are the questions of constitutional meaning raised by official restrictions against racist speech: what do we make of the sociological claim? insofar as we do not or cannot deny it, then how do we give their dues to both formal negative liberty (vis-à-vis the government) and substantive desubordination? These (the argument goes) are questions of constitutional meaning that the People have yet to confront and resolve.

Perhaps these questions might in time be settled by a kind of default – an absence of political challenge to a sustained judicial stance against censorability. How about the Hyde bill itself as a token of settlement? Congress is popularly elected. If the bill is enacted, maybe that would count as the People's endorsement of implicit propositions of specific constitutional meaning: either that the sociological claim is untenable in the constitution's eyes, or that the constitution prefers formal negative liberty of expression (vis-à-vis the government) over substantive racial desubordination. Yet Congress, as Congress, "is not us."[52] Congressional enactment of legislation cannot convey popular endorsement of constitutional meaning-claims unless, at the very least, Americans at large have had their attentions drawn to the pending legislation and its implication of those claims – a condition that has not remotely been met in the case of the Hyde bill.

It is a constant bafflement to explain how the People are actually supposed to address themselves to questions of constitutional meaning. Scholars argue compellingly that the Article V provisions for constitutional amendment, our official arrangements for nationwide "constitutional politics," are neither in good, up-to-date, working order[53] nor otherwise adequate to the need.[54] Perhaps the country right now could use an extended, committed mulling over of the sociological claim and of the post-*Brown* interpretative question it prompts: as between material erasure of racial subordination and formal universality of autonomy or access to public discourse, what is the priority? The country could use, in other words, some sites of proto-constitutional politics.

Enter now private associations to the rescue. They claim for themselves a constitutional function, which is to provide just such staging areas for democracy. Private universities dealing with campus speech codes – debating, rejecting, adopting, experiencing, modifying – are providential sites of the constitutional politics the country could use now. Congress, therefore, does democracy in America a disservice by nipping this process in the bud. Nipping it in the bud is what the Hyde bill is contrived to do. That is what is wrong with the Hyde bill (and is not also wrong with ordinary civil rights law), as a matter of basic constitutional morality. If anything is.

NOTES

1 What I call American constitutional thought is, of course, a branch of what Professor Peter Russell calls constitutional chatter, so I suppose he would call this chatter to the second power. See Russell's essay elsewhere in this volume.

2 It is true that section 3 of the Charter expressly classifies the right to vote as a "democratic" right. This, however, is not clearly a right to democracy as distinct from a right to participate by voting in the democracy that is. Section 5's guarantee of parliamentary sessions is more like what I mean by a right to democracy itself.

3 In the case of our federalisms, that means both our nation-states and their respective provinces and states of the union.

4 There may, I grant you, be a question about the "ownership" (so to speak) of this right – about who is its subject or holder, who is the person or body entitled to demand its fulfilment. That is a question I want to postpone.

5 Professor Dworkin has contended that because (1) "any legal interpretation should aim at a coherent account of the legal order as a whole," then (2) "any interpretation of our democracy must be consistent with the fact that we have [through bills and charters of rights] rejected unconstrained majoritarianism," which drives us to (3) a conception of democracy in which "disabling" constitutional provisions are integral. See Ronald Dworkin, "Equality, Democracy, and Constitution: We The People in Court," (1990) 37 *Alberta Law Review* 324, at 344.

6 Jeremy Waldron, "A Rights-Based Critique of Constitutional Rights," (1993) *Oxford Journal of Legal Studies* 18. As Waldron's title indicates, he does not himself argue to the conclusion that a right to pure-majoritarian democracy is compatible with (other) constitutional rights. He presents a certain problem about squaring the practice of judicial review with a due recognition of people's fundamental (moral) rights to political self-government. My purpose here is to suggest that Waldron's argument is made of ingredients that are capable of supporting a right to majoritarian democracy while allowing room for other rights and for judicial review.

7 See, e.g., Peter Russell, "Standing Up for Not Withstanding," (1991) 29 *Alberta Law Review* 293, at 295–7, pointing out that constitutional cases rarely involve frontal attacks by governments on core values obviously animating constitutional clauses. Rather, they usually involve more debatable issues of constitutional "policy."

8 See, e.g., *Hudson v. McMillian*, 112 S. Ct. 995, 1000–1 (1992) (O'Connor J.) (arguing that because the Eighth Amendment's prohibition against "cruel and unusual punishments" is "animated" by "concepts of dignity … humanity, and decency," its concrete meaning must be drawn from "evolving standards of decency that mark the progress of a civilized society"); *Pennell v. San Jose*, 485 U.S. 1, 19–22 (1987) (Scalia J., dissenting) (arguing that a rent control law requiring landlords to accept reduced rentals from financially needy tenants must be considered to "take" the landlords' "property" in violation of the fifth amendment, because "the purpose" of the amendment is to "keep Government from forcing some people alone to bear burdens which, in all fairness and justice, should be borne by the public as a

whole").

9　Below, I offer a dramatic example from contemporary American debate over the constitutional permissibility of official censorship of racial "hate speech" – the question resolved for Canada by *R. v. Keegstra*, [1990] 3 SCR 697.

10　On "public reason" see John Rawls, *Political Liberalism* (New York: Columbia University Press 1993), chapter 6.

11　See Waldron, supra note 6, at 33–6.This is not necessarily equivalent to a naive assumption that substantive consensuses can always easily be found. The assumption of good faith can allow for the likelihood that divisions of experience, condition, and outlook are often too deep for that. The more cautious assumption is that people may nevertheless listen open-mindedly to one another and genuinely try to find decisions – interpretations – that others can accept as decent or defensible, in the light of reasons that have been offered in their support. See, e.g., Iris Marion Young, "Polity and Group Difference: A Critique of the Ideal of Universal Citizenship," (1989)99 *Ethics* 250, at 256–63 (1989).

12　Waldron, supra note 6, at 51.

13　Ibid., at 37. See also Russell, supra note 7, at 300.

14　Ibid., at 49.

15　Ibid.

16　See supra note 5.

17　Reconciliation of judicial review with a right to popular-majoritarian democracy is discussed below.

18　Alexander Meiklejohn, *Free Speech and its Relation to Self-Government* (New York: Harper 1948).

19　John Hart Ely, *Democracy and Distrust: A Theory of Judicial Renew* (Cambridge: Harvard University Press 1980).

20　See, e.g., Ronald Dworkin, "The Coming Battles over Free Speech," *New York Review of Books*, 11 June 1992, p. 55. In fact, Meiklejohn more deeply argued (in a fashion akin to Dworkin's own: see supra note 5, and accompanying text) that freedom of speech is a conceptual requirement of democracy understood as the form of rule demanded by political justice and legitimacy. See Alexander Meiklejohn, *Political Freedom: The Constitutional Powers of the People* (New York: Harper & Bros. 1960).

21　It is highly controversial how completely such a socially "instrumental" account of entrenched protection for freedom of speech, as distinguished from emphasis on the personally "constitutive" value of such freedom to individuals, ought to govern interpretation of the first amendment. See Ronald Dworkin, supra note 5. In the cited article, Professor Dworkin mainly worries about the ways in which instrumentalist accounts can shave away protection that otherwise would come from strict attention to the personally constitutive values. But Dworkin would probably agree that appeal to a democracy-based view can also, in other ways, enhance the protection that might have been expected from sole reliance on a libertarian approach. See Vincent Blasi, "Learned Hand and the Self-Government Theory of the First Amendment: Masses Publishing Co. v. Patten," (1990) 61 *University of Colorado Law Review* 1.

22 Of course, that may not be a very good argument. Nor is it the only kind that can be offered in defence of the constitutional permissibility of pornography regulation. See *R.v.Butler* (1992), 70 CCC (3d) 129 (SCC).

23 See *First Nat' l Bank v. Bellotti,* 435 U.S. 765 (1978) (Powell J.).

24 See Meiklejohn, *Political Freedom: The Constitutional Powers of the People,* supra note 20, at 26.

25 See U.S. Const. amend. 14 ("No State shall ... deprive any person of life, liberty, or property, without due process of law; nor deny to any person ... the equal protection of the laws.")

26 See Ely, supra note 19, at 116–20. Here is a good place to note that normative theorists of many different stripes have been able to make plausible appeals to democracy as a background fact and value. Some have sought to extend Ely's sort of argument to encompass constitutional rights to be affirmatively provided by the state with the sustenance, health care, and education that a person requires in order effectively to pursue and defend her interests in pluralist politics. You can easily see how that argument goes. Surely – we contended – strength, health, and learning are no less instrumentally prerequisite to effective defence of one's interests through participation in politics than is one's freedom to speak or one's right not to have one's electoral district arithmetically underrepresented in a state legislature. See Frank I. Michelman, "Welfare Rights in a Constitutional Democracy," (1979) *Wash. University Law Quarterly* 659, at 674–9. Such contentions have largely fallen on deaf ears.

Other theorists, most notably Professor Richard Epstein of the University of Chicago, have sought to use the fact of pluralist democracy as a premise in a quite opposite argument – equally unavailing to date – to the effect that all designedly redistributive government action violates our constitutional clause (U.S. Const. amend. 5) prohibiting uncompensated taking of property for public use. Epstein's argument is elegant: Given a democracy driven by a self-serving political ethos, and given various prisoners' and other strategic dilemmas, legislative powers will tend strongly to be used in ways that are privately enriching but socially impoverishing; "rent-seeking" irresistibly becomes the order of the day. The Constitution's inspired device for stopping that is, Epstein says, the clause prohibiting uncompensated takings of property, which is properly (on Epstein's construction) read to contain a prohibition against all lawmaking that leaves anyone worse off than they were before. Law-makers, then, are left with nothing to do except pass laws that make everyone better off, and so that's what they will do. See Richard A. Epstein, "Beyond the Rule of Law: Civic Virtue and Constitutional Structure," (1987) 56 *George Washington Law Review* 149.

27 There is another way in which the notion of democracy can figure in constitutional argument as a background fact and value. I have in mind cases in which a claim that government action violates a constitutional right is met by confession and avoidance, and the avoidance is a plea that the violation is justified by some overriding public value, and the overriding value is closely tied to democracy and its proper functioning. In the lingo of American constitutional law, democracy here figures in the role of a "compelling governmental interest" capable of justifying an infringement of a constitutional right. The Canadian Charter makes explicit this possible rhetorical function for democracy in constitutional argument by its express allowance, in section 1, for infringement of the rights enumerated in the succeeding clauses by laws that are "demonstrably justified in a free and democratic society."

Here is one example of how this works in American constitutional law. In the case of *Buckley v. Valeo*, 424 U.S. 1 (1976), our Supreme Court upheld against first amendment challenge a law restricting the sums that individuals may contribute to the support of other people's candidacies for election to government office. The court did so even as it also held that contributing money to a political election campaign is an exercise of the "freedom of speech" protected by the first amendment. The court said that there is a compelling governmental interest in protecting the system of democracy against the discreditation that may result from either the actuality or the appearance of "corruption" – elected officers having been "bought" by large campaign contributors – that may result if contribution amounts are not subjected to a legislative cap.

28 Our Supreme Court's recent, widely heralded opinion in *Planned Parent-*

hood v. Casey, 112 S. Ct. 2791, 2815, 2816 (1992), exemplifies the arrogation against which Waldron objects. The court declared itself responsible, on occasion, for "call[ing] the contending sides of a national controversy to end their national division by accepting a common mandate rooted in the Constitution." Correspondingly, the court portrayed the American people as bound by their aspiration to a rule of law to grant the court "authority to decide their constitutional cases and speak before all others for their ideals."

29 See *Planned Parenthood v. Casey,* supra, at 2813–15.

30 See, e.g., Guido Calabresi, "Foreword: Antidiscrimination and Constitutional Accountability (What the Bork-Brennan Debate Ignores)," (1991) 105 *Harvard Law Review* 80, 84–5.

31 See supra note 26.

32 See Russell, supra note 7, at 300–1: "[T]he presentation of *Charter* issues before judges and their reasoned decisions on those issues can contribute significantly to public understanding ...But in a democracy that aspires to government by discussion and full participation by its citizens in questions of social and political justice, court decisions should not close off further debate and decision-making in elected and publicly accountable legislatures. Legislatures, it is true may act precipitately and make questionable decisions ...But it is a dreadful distortion to suggest that such impassioned and inconsiderate behaviour is the norm in Canadian legislatures." See also Paul C. Weiler, "Rights and Judges in a Democracy: A New Canadian Version," (1984) 18 *University of Michigan Journal of Law Reform* 51, 82–6 (1984); Calabresi, supra note 30, at 124–5.

33 See Waldron, supra note 6.

34 See Akhil Reed Amar, "The Bill of Rights as a Constitution," (1991) 100 *Yale Law Journal* 1131; "Philadelphia Revisited: Amending the Constitution Outside Article V," (1988) 55 *University of Chicago Law Review* 1043.

35 See U.S. Const. amends.5, 6, 7.

36 See Amar, "The Bill of Rights as a Constitution," supra note 34, at 1191–5.

37 U.S. Const. amend. 9 provides: "The enumeration in the Constitution, of certain rights, shall not be construed to deny or disparage others retained by the People."

38 See Amar, "The Bill of Rights as a Constitution, " supra note 34, 1152–5, 1200; Amar, "Philadelphia Revisited," ibid., at 1044–60. See also James Gray Pope, "Republican Moments: The Role of Direct Popular Power in the American Constitutional Order," (1990) 139 *University of Pennsylvania*

Law Review 287.

39 See, e.g., Charles Fried, "The New First Amendment Jurisprudence: A Threat to Liberty," (1992) *University of Chicago Law Review* 225. But compare democracy-based instrumental accounts of the first amendment described above.

40 U.S. Const. amends. 13, 14, 15.

41 See, e.g., *Brown v. Board of Education,* 347 U.S. 483 (1954); *Loving v. Virginia,* 388 U.S. 1(1967).

42 See, e.g., Charles R. Lawrence III, "If He Hollers Let Him Go: Regulating Racist Speech on Campus," (1990) *Duke Law Journal* 431.

43 Robert C. Post, "Racist Speech, Democracy, and the first amendment," (1991) 32 *William and Mary Law Review* 267, at 312. There is little need to explain this view to an audience familiar with Chief Justice Dixon's reasons in *R. v. Keegstra,* [1990] 3 SCR 697, at 746–8: "Hate propaganda ... [can alter the view of members of society at large, and this alteration] may occur subtly, [without] conscious acceptance of the communicated ideas. Even if the message of hate propaganda is outwardly rejected, there is evidence that its premise of racial inferiority... may persist in a recipient's mind as an idea that holds some truth."

44 See *R.A.V. v. St. Paul,* 112 S. Ct. 2538 (1992); *American Booksellers Ass' n v. Hudnut,* 475 U.S. 1001 (1986), affirming per cur. 771 F.2d 323 (7th Cir. 1985); *Collin v. Smith,* 578 F.2d 1197 (7th Cir. 1978), application for stay denied, 436 U.S. 953 (1978); *Doe v. University of Michigan,* 721 F. Supp. 852 (E.D. Mich. 1989).

45 See, e.g., *United States v. Eichman,* 110 S.Ct. 2404 (1990).

46 "[T]he Court's legitimacy depends on making legally principled decisions under circumstances in which their principled character is sufficiently plausible to be accepted by the Nation." *Planned Parenthood v. Casey,* supra note 28, at 2814. See Toni Marie Massaro, "Equality and Freedom of Expression. The Hate Speech Dilemma," (1991) 32 *William and Mary Law Review* 211, 227 (describing the view that, even if racist speech deserves suppression on the merits, suppression is "too dangerous because we cannot devise a truly distinctive, easily understood, and cabined rationale for censoring" it but not other offensive speech).

47 See H.R. 1380,102d Cong., 1st Sess. (1991). I discuss the Hyde bill in Frank Michelman, "Universities, Racist Speech and Democracy in America An Essay for the ACLU," (1991) 27 *Harvard Civil Rights and Civil Liberties Law Review* 339. The cited article expands at length on various points I

make in summary form in what follows here. It should be consulted for a full statement of my views.

48 See Michelman, supra at 360.

49 See ibid., at 363–6, from which the balance of this essay is drawn.

50 It is the sort of question to which Professor Bruce Ackerman of Yale University has insistently been directing attention through his work on non-formal constitutional amendments. See, e.g., Bruce Ackerman, "Constitutional Politics / Constitutional Law,"(1989) 99 *Yale Law Journal* 453.

51 See Henry M. Hart Jr. and Albert M. Sacks, *The Legal Process 1–9* (tentative. ed. 1958).

52 See Frank I. Michelman, "Foreword: Traces of Self-Government," (1986) 100 *Harvard Law Review* 4, at 75.

53 See Bruce A. Ackerman, "Transformative Appointments," (1988)101 *Harvard Law Review* 1164.

54 See, e.g., Amar, supra note 34.

11 EDGAR Z. FRIEDENBERG

Après Nous la Liberté?

At the time the Constitution Act of 1982 was being drafted, one of the arguments most vigorously advanced against the Charter of Rights was that it would, by its very existence, violate Canada's most fundamental tradition: parliamentary supremacy. Sterling Lyon, then the premier of Manitoba, condemned the proposed Charter as an infernal American device that Canadians, who already knew what their rights were, did not need and should not accept. While many Americans might agree that liberty, like the automobile, the atom, and pizza, was an American invention, that is hardly sufficient reason to shackle it. At an election shortly after he voiced these irascible comments, Sterling was sharply devalued, and the issue became moot.

The argument that adoption of a Charter of Rights and Freedoms would violate the Canadian civic tradition by encroaching on parliamentary supremacy is valid on its face; but it is misleading or, more precisely, distracting. The power of a constitution to limit abuses of liberty is very restricted. It is of crucial value in particular cases, but these are likely to be cases in which public opinion and economic power have already moved beyond the limits set by established law and practice. Until then, constitutional guarantees deliver very little.

Yet, Premier Lyon did have a point. Liberty, automobiles, the atom, and even pizza have indeed assumed the cultural significance with which American enterprise has imbued them; and there is a sense in which a Charter of Rights is a peculiarly American concept that doesn't quite fit the Canadian Way of Life – which is not, of course, a phrase Canadians would use. The Charter is often effective but, like solar panels on an igloo, it doesn't look indigenous and isn't enough to get you through the winter.

What functions would a Charter of Rights designed especially for Canada serve? What rights are to be protected? How does the enumeration of these rights both reflect and affect the culture of the country: what it means by freedom, what it recognizes as constraint? In a multicultural nation, what about conflicts among the rights considered vital or taken for granted in different subcultures? Consider the case of David Thomas, a thirty-five-year-old member of the Lyackson Indian band, who in 1988 was abducted, at the request of his wife, and subjected to a four-day long initiation that was intended to make a "spirit-dancer" of him, but landed him in hospital instead. British Columbia Supreme Court Judge Sherman Hood found that Mr. Thomas's Charter rights had indeed been violated; his decision angered band members, who defended their action as sanctioned by their customs. I think Judge Hood's decision was correct; it is difficult to argue that years of discrimination could be redressed by denying an individual the rights guaranteed to any resident of Canada because he is also an aboriginal person. But that is precisely the issue here.

I would place the question of procedure ahead of that of content because Canadians have learned by experience to ask first of any piece of proposed legislation not "is it just?" but "is it justiciable?" Can you assert and defend its provisions in court? Most such charters have served a liturgical function and lack the force of law. In many countries, attempting to assert the rights they purport to guarantee is the quickest route to prison or a death squad. Even in democratic countries the structure of government may render a charter of rights inoperative. In Canada, the Supreme Court consistently refused to recognize the Diefenbaker Bill of Rights as paramount over other statutes that contravened it.

Canadians have been peculiarly ambivalent towards the rights and freedoms the Charter is designed to protect, and remain wary of establishing liberty beyond the reach of Parliament, though they have guaranteed the equality of "male and female persons" in section 28. Since each of us is, in some degree, a male and female person, this should be conclusive, though it clearly hasn't been as yet. But what of the specific freedoms the Charter does purport to guarantee, subject to such reasonable limitations as are demonstrably necessary in a free and democratic – Canadian, eh? – society?

With one important exception, the list covers essentially the same areas as the first ten amendments to the U.S. constitution – the American Bill of Rights. That exception is property rights, which are protected, equally with life and liberty, in the American Bill of Rights. Conservatives – not all of them Progressive – continue to demand that property rights be constitutionally guaranteed; this omission required courage and tenacity. John Locke who, in a sense, started the discussion, referred to "life, liberty, and property," which was apparently a little too gross for the Founding Fathers to put in the Declaration of Independence. But they knew what they wanted, and lodged "property" securely in the Bill of Rights, where it has jeopardized legislation purporting to control the powers of private corporations ever since.

The Charter, like the U.S. Bill of Rights, creates a subtler danger which the authors of both documents tried to guard against: in the United States by the ninth amendment in the Bill of Rights – the one nobody remembers; and in Canada, more diffusely, in sections 22, 25, and especially section 26. The ninth amendment, the clearest and most succinct of these statements, simply asserts: "The enumeration in the Constitution, of certain rights, shall not be construed to deny or disparage others retained by the people."

Amen? No, at most, modified rapture!

For the enumeration of rights does inevitably disparage others that remain unstated. They lose some of their legitimacy. I have already stated my opinion that in the case of property rights this has been a good thing. The omission of social guarantees like those Ontario's Premier Rae advocates is, however, damaging. It doesn't just fail to provide for social programs; it indicates that they are relatively dispensable and have a lower priority. The omission compromises them.

But even those rights and freedoms that are specifically addressed in the Charter may be subtly compromised. Their meaning becomes limited to the significance legally ascribed to them. And the assumptions about government and society that gave rise to them are both forgotten and reified; they are assumed to be part of the natural moral order rather than political mechanisms that can and do become incompatible with changing operating systems and therefore ineffective and even obstructive. When this occurs, the people who rely on the Charter are misled by the illusion of protection as they struggle to defend the very institutions that now threaten and oppress them.

Consider limitations on freedom of expression, for example. These are conceived as imposed by affirmative government action: censorship, or prosecution for the expression of views that conflict with orthodoxy, or for revealing information the state seeks to conceal.

Now, clearly, official repression is a serious and continuing threat; and section 2(b) of the Charter is intended to protect us against it. But there are other threats to freedom of thought and expression that are equally serious, against which such declarations provide no protection. For some time now, there has been conflict about the meaning of freedom of the press. Third world governments, accused by the Western media of violations of established norms of press freedom, respond that from their point of view these are not freedoms at all, but merely license the media to distort their story to suit primarily American political and economic interests and spread their underlying ideology. What they need is a way of getting their story out that is not subject to the biases built into those media, which are not merely ideological but also determined by Western preferences for violent action or pompous, carefully "balanced" documentaries narrated by well-tailored experts. The legitimacy of the American commitment to media freedom is not enhanced by the compliance – indeed, the complicity – of those media in transmitting an almost totally controlled and misleading account of the Persian Gulf War and the events leading up to it.

And, yet, how misleading – that is, misleading in what ways? As the story of the war later unravelled and its origins and planning were more and more fully revealed, I can remember no moment of astonishment. I, like nearly everyone else in North America, had no source of information whatever except what the media were presenting; yet the pattern had been clear, for whoever cared to observe it, from the moment Defense Secretary Cheney had flown so hastily to instruct the Saudis where their interests lay: from the moment King Hussein of Jordan had been snubbed by Baker and Bush for daring to suggest avenues to peace that might yet be explored. So why, then, all the fuss about controlling the flow of information?

Well, it isn't so much about the flow of information as about the ebb and flow of legitimacy – and that is important. The coverage of politically important events like the Gulf and Vietnam wars or televised congressional committee hearings is not intended to inform, or even, primarily, to disinform. It is designed to persuade rather than to convince. Indeed, it is sometimes most persuasive when it is least convincing. The statements of U.S. administration spokespersons like Marlin Fitzwater or Margaret Tutwiler are not presented plausibly. Their tone is officious and minatory. You are not expected to believe them but to accept them even though you do not; to understand quite clearly that any contradiction will be dismissed as impertinent and either stupid or disloyal.

To the extent that communication functions in this way, the media will not convey information even when they provide it, which renders their freedom more or less meaningless. Information doesn't appear to have much effect until, through some combination of events, a catastrophic shift in the distribution of power occurs, transforming the acceptable picture of events. This may be a scandal or a revelation; but scandals are not usually widely reported until the risks of spreading them have already been weakened by other factors. It is never news that the emperor has no clothes. The news is that it may now be okay to say so; but that fact is not proclaimed in a press release.

I have chosen to make my point by American examples because they are still more blatant than Canadian examples: there are still noticeable differences. These are far from absolute, however. The CBC's television coverage of Meech Lake followed government policy as obsequiously as American commentators did Desert Storm; but the public responded differently. Despite media hostility, Clyde Wells emerged as a much more influential public figure than before. Pollsters report that Canadians reject the prime minister because they cannot trust him and his colleagues: the government lies to them. I think most Americans would find this rather quaint. Political discourse there is hardly supposed to reflect reality; it is a device designed to achieve certain results. Sometimes they blow it; but no process works every time. Its truth or falsity is irrelevant.

Polls have also indicated that many Canadians think well of the Right Honourable Joe Clark because they perceive him to possess integrity. Perhaps he does; he often sounds embarrassed by what he has to say, though he says it anyway. I simply cannot imagine President Bush as embarrassed – only as angry and confused when caught out – but the more important point is that integrity, if attributed to an American president, would not be considered praiseworthy. People used to say that about Jimmy Carter. They usually meant he was too dumb to be president.

The value of freedom of expression depends on the assumption that in a democratic society the people will be guided by and will act on the information they have access to, which should therefore be comprehensive and penetrating. But it will not be, because the selection and distribution of information is extremely expensive and is financed – and hence subject to focus and control – by the interests and the values that dominate the society. Meanwhile, the existence of the Charter lulls us into assuming that we enjoy the rights and freedoms it purports to guarantee.

In this respect, the U.S. Bill of Rights is more misleading than the Charter, beginning as it does with the majestic injunction "Congress shall make no law ... " It places no limits on incursions on liberty by private corporations or interests. The maintenance of the distinction between the public and private sectors of the economy and of society is crucial to such legitimacy as our institutions retain. It is largely a sham. Normally, the government is not only the ally but the instrument of major corporate economic interests. Successful Crown corporations are "privatized" while dubious private enterprises are launched with government grants and loan guarantees; the stockholders and executives reap the fruits of success if there are any. Billions in tax money are used to bail them if they fail, in the interests of protecting jobs. This is no truer of Canada than of other countries; but Canadians seem more prone to assume that the government serves their interests, or should.

Neither the Constitution Act of 1982 nor the American Bill of Rights includes any social charter. These documents purport to guarantee rights, but not the means of access to them.

The values underlying the Charter are derived from classic liberalism and the Protestant ethic. Neither Canadians nor Americans like liberty very much for its own sake. A society that deeply valued rights and freedoms would have come up with a much more inclusive list. It would have included funding for poor litigants who have no access to the guarantees of the Charter without it. In fact, the Government of Canada has now abolished funding for its minuscule Court Challenges Program and has abolished the federal Law Reform Commission. It would include a comprehensive social charter, to permit people to exercise their freedoms and prevent their atrophy. It would demand housing even for those poor people who had not been convicted of any crime. It would require both public and private employers to respect rights enumerated in the Charter. It would require corporations that have received public funding or tax concessions to repay these if they closed down or moved away. It would guarantee juveniles: – no, it wouldn't guarantee juveniles. It would disregard the category and affirm that they, too, are legally and completely persons.

But historically, the concept of political liberty as a natural right shared by all citizens was formulated as a cornerstone of the ethical revolution that brought capitalism into being. To put the matter as clearly and bluntly as possible, I see little evidence that liberty would ever have become popular, despite its implicit threat to order and community, if it were not so damned useful in making money. In a global, post-industrial economy dominated by interlocking corporate interests, it won't be – quite the contrary. And what we call, with a deprecatory smile, "democracy" will seem as quaint as Upper Canada Village compared to EuroDisney.

Freedom of religion already needs to be retargeted if it is to remain relevant in North America. The true and official doctrinal commitment prevailing in the United States, with Canada panting at its heels, is not to God, whoever She may be, but to a Market Economy. In the interests of suppressing the growth of heretical views and institutions, the capitalist nations have committed atrocities that make the religious wars of yesteryear, limited as they were by primitive technology, look like hockey games; which can, of course, get quite fervent. It cannot be necessary or even useful to recapitulate here the story of American involvement in the suppression of socialist movements from Central America to Indonesia – this last with even greater Canadian complicity than usual – or of harassment and imprisonment of alleged Communists and "fellow travelers" in both Canada and the United States.

Many people expect that, with the collapse and discrediting of Communism in Eastern Europe and the Soviet Union, obsession with this heresy will abate. Perhaps. But the collapse of the Soviet Union has led very rapidly to precisely the hardships Marxian theory predicted that a market economy would bring: persistent, catastrophic unemployment, inflation, or both; and to the inability to mobilize resources to meet dire human need. Economic catastrophe, like AIDS, can spread to nations that pride themselves on being absolutely straight.

Economic heresy should be protected under the Charter; it will certainly need it as socialism beckons again from the grave to which it has so hastily been consigned. But whether it can be will depend on whether values that form the basis of a market economy can be invoked to restrain and, as human need may require, replace it. Francis Fukuyama argues that it can and will. It seems to me equally probable the Western, including the Canadian, conception of Liberty will, like the monarchy, continue to be invoked as a rather effective means of convincing potentially conflicting groups that they share more interests than they actually do; and that – again, like the monarchy – this will work only as long as people cannot use it for actual political power or even serious protection.

There seem to be more serious grounds for concern about the vitality of Canada's democratic institutions and the narrowing scope of its sovereignty than about its territorial integrity. In my vision of the future, Prime Minister Bourassa is addressing the question of aboriginal land-claims by adapting a slogan made famous by an eminent anglophone predecessor: "Extinction if necessary, but not necessarily extinction." While along Yonge Street, from Harbourfront to The Bay, throngs of happy young people will disport themselves in T-shirts reading: "Quiconque, quand il meurt, posséde la plupart de cette merde, aura gagné." Then, truly, we will be one nation, with liberty and justice for all.

Multirow Federalism and the Charter

STRANGE MULTIPLICITY

What are the relations of the Charter of Rights and Freedoms to our intellectual traditions? This is a difficult question to address because our aboriginal, Québécois, and English Canadian intellectual traditions are so complex and intertwined after four hundred years of interaction that it would take volumes to understand how the Charter fits into this rich tapestry. This paper addresses one aspect of the question. I will try to clarify the relation of the Charter to our main aboriginal, Québécois, and English Canadian traditions of federalism. This is one of the central issues in Canada today. As Sir Isaiah Berlin has remarked, it is similar to the question raised in many other deeply plural societies around the world. They too are turning to traditions of federalism in order to recognize and affirm cultural and political diversity, and, at the same time, to guarantee rights and freedoms.[1]

In 1991 a black bronze canoe, six metres in length, was placed in the courtyard of the Canadian embassy in Washington as a symbol of Canada as it enters the twenty-first century. Called "the spirit of Haida Gwaii," this magnificent work of art by Bill Reid, a sculptor of Haida and non-aboriginal ancestry, contains thirteen distinct passengers from Haida mythology: raven, grizzly, eagle, wolf, frog, mouse woman, dogfish woman, beaver, a human paddler named "the ancient reluctant conscript," and, standing amid this motley crew of confederates, a chief with speaker's staff in hand who bears the wonderfully enigmatic name of "who is he going to be?"[2]

This complex sculpture is said to express the strange and wonderful "multiplicity" that "wants to be," not only in the nation of Haida Gwaii, the islands of the people, but also on the larger island of Kanata (Canada) or Great Turtle Island. What are the major features of this strange multiplicity that is striving for recognition in Canada as it paddles homeward in the uncertain dawn of the twenty-first century? I believe it is possible to discern four main features of this multiple federation of voyageurs.

First, each figure in the canoe has its own identity, history, and mythology, which it brings to the federation, potlatch-style, as opposed to a uniform federation in which each member is constituted in the same way by the act of federation. Second, in contrast to a symmetrical federation, each seems to relate to the central chief in different yet appropriate ways, and the chief appears to be governed by the consensual movement of the crew as much as he or she governs them. That is, no one would mistake this plural association for an integrated unity, much less a melting pot. Rather, the word that comes to mind is "coordination." Third, although the members are discrete, they overlap, crisscross, and share in a multitude of fascinating ways, unlike a "watertight" confederation or a mere alliance, without losing their identities. The fourth and most strikingly native and Canadian feature is that no member is itself uniform in composition. Each is pluralistic: a federation within itself. The dogfish woman has the hooked nose of both the hawk and the spawning male salmon to remind us of the multiplicity and kinship of identities. The wolf paddles with humanlike hands. Countless passengers and stowaways emerge from within the folds of the main figures. Just so in native and non-native Canada. For example, Haida Gwaii, the Haida nation, while a member of the Assembly of First Nations, is made up of clans, families, members of other First Nations, and non-native Canadians; and British Columbia, while a member of the Canadian federation, is made up of a francophone minority, multicultural groups, individuals, and native people living off-reserve. Each is striving for an appropriate form of political recognition.

The Charter was introduced into Canadian political life in 1982 just when this strange multiplicity that wants to be was striving for constitutional recognition. From the vantage point of 1992 one can see that while the Charter recognized and affirmed many important features of Canadian diversity, it also overlooked and threatened to assimilate others to a uniform or non-federal conception of Canada. One can see this now because 1992 is not only the 10th anniversary of the Charter. It is also the 125th anniversary of the federation of four ancient provinces, the 200th anniversary of representative government in Quebec and of the first federation of Lower and Upper Canada, the 220th anniversary of the Royal Proclamation of 1763 that recognized the First Nations as independent nations, the 280th anniversary of the great treaty federation of the Iroquois, Algonkian, French, and English nations of 1701, the 330th anniversary of the classic Two Row Wampum treaty between the Iroquois and the Dutch, the 350th anniversary of French settlement at Hochelaga/Montreal, the 600th aniversary of the constitution of the Iroquois confederation, and the 5,000th anniversary of the Gitksan and Wet'suwet'en federation, and so on.

Yet, as Quebec, the First Nations, and the provinces have sought to point out since 1982, the Charter fails to recognize and respect these ancient and complex federal relations, along with their time-honoured traditions and conventions, which historically constitute this strange multiplicity and preserve the cultural, legal, and political diversity of its members. The Charter seems to them to be a kind of voice over all the other passengers; as if it sought to lay down its vocabulary as canonical for the whole conversation, rather than seeing itself as one new voice in a federation of many voices with their own forms of expression. For, if it is to be a genuine charter of Canada rather than of a country reconstituted in a uniform manner, then we should find a way to acknowledge in the Charter itself this wonderful multiplicity that has always been called by all its members, through all its centuries of federations and refederations, by its original Micmac-Huron-Iroquois-French-English polysemic name of "Canada."

So, while Bill Reid has given expression to Canada's multiplicity in formline sculpture, Canadians have been struggling over the decade to do the same in their Charter and constitution. The underlying problem has been to find a shared language of Canadian politics that is not drawn from one tradition or region, but rather is itself richly federal enough to enable all the diverse voices to express themselves in their own terms, and so to celebrate all these intersecting anniversaries together. The following sections survey the debate over the Charter and federalism to see if such a language has been found. The first section outlines the federalist criticisms of the Charter, and the second summarizes the traditions on which the criticisms are based. The conclusion asks if the report of the special joint committee on a renewed Canada (28 February 1992), the Beaudoin-Dobbie report, which is based in part on these traditions, does not begin to provide a language of Canadian constitutionalism that does justice to the federal articulation of Canadian multiplicity, and to our rights and freedoms.

THE CHARTER VERSUS FEDERALISM

The Charter sought to establish and foster a pan-Canadian juridical identity across the federation of provinces, territories, and First Nations. The nature of the pan-Canadian Charter-identity has been described in various ways.[3] For our purposes we can start with what are called the three equalities by the report of the commission on the political and constitutional future of Quebec, the Bélanger-Campeau report: (1) the equality of citizen-rights across the provinces, territories, and First Nations; (2) the equality of cultures and cultural origins; and (3) the aggregate equality of the provinces expressed in the amending formula that requires the consent of seven provinces with 50 percent of the population.[4] In the words of Alan Cairns, the "Charter generates a roving normative Canadianism, oblivious to provincial boundaries." It generates "a homogenising Charter-derived-rights-bearing Canadianism."[5]

Consequently, it was not the content of the Charter that initially drew criticism. It was the way in which section1 of the Charter lays it down that Canada is one undifferentiated juridical society rather than a federation of coordinate societies, thereby establishing a non-federal framework for the interpretation of all other sections. Once the sovereignty of this picture of Canada is in place, the federal dimension of Canada appears in section 33, the notwithstanding clause, as subordinate to it. That is, the provincial governments are granted a partial and temporary suspension not from the rule of the Charter itself, to which they remain subject, but rather from federal judicial review of their duty to legislate in accordance with the Charter.[6] According to Cairns, this non-federal Charter framework explains the opposition to it:[7]

> The Charter's message is not ... indifferent to the distinction between provincial communities and the coast-to-coast pan-Canadian community. The Charter's message is a Canadian message. The rights it enshrines are Canadian rights. The community of citizen membership that it fosters is the overall Canadian community. It is the Canadianism of the Charter that explains the continuing lesser sympathy for, and the previous opposition to, the Charter by provincial governments.

The first defence of the Charter was to argue that it does not establish a uniform juridical identity since it contains collective as well as individual rights.[8] The rights of French and English minorities, multicultural groups, women, and aboriginal peoples, and group rights in general, are all present in the Charter along with individual rights. The Charter there-by recognizes an important Canadian tradition of diversity. Moreover, both the proposal of the Government of Canada to amend the constitution (*Shaping Canada's Future Together: Proposals* 1991), and the Beaudoin-Dobbie report have affirmed collective rights as part of Canada's legal and political traditions.

A number of authors then went on to argue that since the Charter enshrines collective rights, there need be no further objections to it by Quebec and the First Nations. Their demands can be understood as demands of cultural minorities and sub-national groups, and so accommodated within the language of the Charter.[9] But, as writers in Quebec and the First Nations replied, this misrepresents and finesses the point they are trying to make.[10] The languages and cultures that Quebec and the First Nations preserve and promote are not of the same status as the languages and cultures that immigrant groups and minorities bring to and develop within already established states and seek to preserve and foster through section 27 multiculturalism. These minorities seek recognition and affirmation of their languages and cultures within the public languages, cultures, and political institutions of an already established country. Quebec and the First Nations are not minority cultures or subnational groups within Canada in any way. They are nations that have been governing themselves for centuries, and their languages and cultures are constitutive of these forms of government and their public discourse; no different in this respect from British Columbia or any other self-governing member of the federation. To think otherwise would be the same as placing the English language or British Columbia in section 27 of the Charter.

In retrospect we can see that the theorists who sought to construe the demands for recognition by Quebec and the First Nations in the language of collective rights of cultural minorities and subordinate nationalities within a framework that envisions Canada as a single society simply failed to appreciate the federalist criticism of the Charter. Indeed, from the perspective of Quebec and the First Nations, the unwillingness of these well-meaning theorists even to question their premise of a single society in which Quebec and the First Nations were seen as cultural minorities belied a residual "colonial" or "Lord Durhamite'" attitude of assimilation.[11] This tendency to misinterpret the criticisms of the Charter was reinforced by two habits of thought: a tendency to ignore the indigenous traditions in which the criticisms were articulated, and a tendency to recast the criticisms in the traditions of recent Anglo-American liberalism and communitarianism, both of which share the non-federal presupposition of an undifferentiated society.[12]

Having removed this misinterpretation, we are in a position to listen to what the critics of the Charter are saying in their own terms. Speakers for Quebec and the provinces voiced two criticisms. First, the Charter was imposed without the consent of the people of Quebec through their provincial government, the National Assembly. The Charter thus violates the oldest principle of federalism, and one of the oldest principles of western law, the principle on which the justice of our political institutions rest. *Quod omnes tangit ab omnibus tractari et approbari debet* – "what touches all must be approved by all."[13] Therefore, the Charter is unjustly applied to Quebec unless and until Quebec consents to it.

Pierre Trudeau replied that if one aggregates the votes of federal MPs from Quebec and the votes for the Charter in the National Assembly one will have a majority. This reply disregards the federal nature of Canada. If Canada is a federation, then the consent of the elected government of the province of Quebec is required. A second reply was that the unanimous consent of the provinces is not required.[14] Again, this flies in the face of the federal principle that what touches all must be approved by all. The Charter manifestly touches the provinces and their governments, and thus requires their consent. As Pierre Trudeau himself has stated, the provinces, the majority of justices in the patriation reference (1981), and well as the authorities cited in the patriation reference affirmed that provincial consent is a convention of the Canadian federation.[15] Moreover, unanimous consent of the provinces is a legal requirement for all fundamental amendments, and it is difficult to think of anything more fundamental than the Charter.

Let us call the principle that "what touches all must be approved by all" the principle of unanimous consent," or simply consent. In classical liberal theories, such as those of Locke and Rousseau, the principle underwrites the requirement that each individual member must consent to the formation of a political organization. In classical Lockean and Canadian federalism it underwrites the requirement that each member province must consent to the formation or amendment of the federation.[16] In Canada the latter requirement is fulfilled by the veto each province has over any amendment to the amending formula. Of course, the principle does not require that unanimous consent is required for every amendment or even for every amendment that touches a province. Rather, it requires only that if a non-unanimous amending formula is employed for certain amendments, or if some provinces pool their vetoes into a regional veto, these arrangements must be based on the consent of all the members. Again, the analogy is to classical liberalism, in which unanimous consent is required to bring in the principle of majority rule.

The principle of consent also underpins the Bélanger-Campeau criticism of the aggregate equality of the provinces embodied in the 7 & 50 formula brought in with the Charter. Any non-unanimity formula like this, introduced without unanimous consent, violates the substantive or coordinate equality of the provinces and bypasses the consent, and so the veto, of provinces that nevertheless may be touched by an amendment. It was a further slap in the face, as Premier Bourassa mentioned to Premier Harcourt, that when the government of Quebec objected in 1982 to aspects of the Charter that affected it directly, it was informed that the Charter could go through legally without the Quebec government's consent; yet, when Quebec brought forward a minimum amendment in 1987-90 that hardly affected the other provinces, Quebec was then informed that the unanimous consent of every province was now required.[17]

The second criticism is that the Charter of rights encroaches on provincial sovereignty over property and civil rights guaranteed in section 92 of the Constitution Act, 1867, and, in the specific case of Quebec, it violates the jurisdictional autonomy of Quebec's civil law and civilian tradition guaranteed in the Quebec Act of 1774.[18] On this view, the Charter conflicts with the constitution and one of the basic imperial statutes on which Quebec's membership in the federation rests. If, therefore, the Charter is to be just with respect to Quebec, then it must be in agreement with the civil law and traditions of rights in Quebec (as, for example, the Quebec Charter of rights of 1975 is) and with section 92 and the Quebec Act.

What is the background principle embodied in the Quebec Act of 1774 and section 92? The principle is, again, one of the oldest and most enlightened principles of Canadian and western jurisprudences: namely, when a pre-existing political body federates with others, or is conquered by another political body, its laws, customs, and forms of self-government continue into the new federation. Let us call this second principle the principle of "legal and political continuity," or simply continuity', as it has always been called in international law.[19] The principle of legal and political continuity stands in opposition to the practice of discontinuity: namely, the view that a federation or a conqueror may destroy the laws and forms of government of the federated or conquered nation. The principle of continuity does not of course freeze a nation to the laws and customs at the time of conquest or federation. Rather, it recognizes the right of the people to continue to govern themselves in accordance with their laws and customs as they develop and change them over time, or to delegate specific powers to the federal government. The principle preserves a people's right of self-government or popular sovereignty.

These two principles of consent and continuity in turn define the compact theory of Canadian federalism: (1) provinces are pre-existing constitutional entities, which the federation recognizes rather than creates; (2) their legal and political institutions of self-government continue through federation; (3) they share coordinate sovereignty with the federal government which is recognized in the unanimous consent formula for any fundamental constitutional change; and hence (4) the federation is based on "consent" or "compact."[20]

Quebec and the provinces turned to Québécois and English Canadian traditions of compact federalism to put their criticisms of the Charter on a philosophical foundation. When the trust between the federal government and the member provinces is broken, the compact theory of federalism works in the same way as Locke's theory of government. If the conventions of the federation are violated, as they were in 1982, then the trust that binds the members to the federation is dissolved, and the powers that were delegated to the federal government in 1867 devolve back to representatives of the sovereign people of the province whose rights have been violated. The province then may renegotiate federation or prepare for secession. The government of Quebec has followed this traditional theory to the letter, from the attempt to renegotiate federalism and amend the Charter in the Meech Lake Accord, and then, when this was refused, through the right to devolve powers back to Quebec in the Report of the Constitutional Committee of the Quebec Liberal Party, A Quebec Free to Choose, and the popular consultation in the Bélanger-Campeau commission, to the preparations for refederation or secession in Bill 150.[21] Before turning to these traditions I will describe the criticisms advanced by the First Nations.

The criticisms of the Charter by the First Nations are similar to those advanced by the defenders of Quebec and the provinces. During the failed first ministers, conferences on the aboriginal right of self-government (1984-6) during the Meech Lake round (1987-90) and (since 1991) by Ovide Mercredi, the grand Chief of the Assembly of First Nations, the objection has been that the Charter was imposed on the First Nations without their consent.[22] This violates the basic principle of aboriginal federalism, the principle of unanimous consent. It is embodied in the Assembly of First Nations itself, in the history of treaty-making, in the exemplary constitution of the Iroquois confederacy, *Kaianereko:wa*, the great law of peace (c. 1390), and in the practice of aboriginal federalism over the centuries.[23]

The second criticism made by the First Nations is that the Charter is unacceptable because it does not emanate from and accord with native traditions of jurisprudence. Native legal scholars such as Aki-kwe (Mary Ellen Turpel) argue that much of the Charter is based on English Canadian traditions of jurisprudence, and, as a result, conflicts with native jurisprudence.[24] If the Charter is to be applied by the First Nations, then it must be based on their consent and reflect their traditions. The reason why the Charter must conform to native legal traditions is exactly the same as why it must conform to the civil law tradition for Quebec: the principle of legal and political continuity. As section 84 of the Iroquois great law of peace states this general principle of aboriginal federalism, "Whenever a foreign nation is either conquered or has by their own will accepted the Great Peace [that is, joined the confederacy] their own system of internal government may continue."[25] The aboriginal traditions of unanimous consent and political continuity inform native understanding of the peace and friendship treaties between natives and newcomers from 1624 to the James Bay and Northern Quebec Agreement of 1975.

The reason why the principles of consent and continuity have been flouted in the case of the First Nations is that the Charter does not recognize them as independent self-governing nations on the same jurisdictional footing as the other members of the federation. Yet this in turn is seen by the aboriginal people as a violation of the Royal Proclamation of 1763, which recognizes their continuous status as self-governing nations and stipulates that all agreements with the Crown must be consensual. Since the Royal Proclamation is constitutionalized in section 25 of the Charter, the imposition of the Charter on the First Nations constitutes a violation of the Charter itself.[26]

In summary, Quebec saw the imposition of the Charter as a violation of two basic principles of the federation and an attempt to assimilate Quebec to a minority status in a unitary state. It was thus seen as the renewal of the policy of assimilation initiated by Lord Durham in 1840, which Quebec had tried to block by confederation based on the compact theory in 1867. The First Nations also saw the Charter as a violation of these two principles and as an attempt to assimilate the aboriginal peoples to cultural minorities within a unitary state. It was thus seen as the continuation of the policy of assimilation initiated by the first Act for the gradual civilization of the Indian tribes (1857), the successive Indian Acts since 1876, and through to the white paper on Indian policy (1969). As Elijah Harper, Ovide Mercredi and Konrad Sioui (the former chief of the Quebec association of First Nations) have stressed, the objections of

Quebec and the First Nations are complementary and rest on complementary traditions.[27] It is to these traditions that I would now like to turn.

TRADITIONS OF FEDERALISM

The First Nations

The First Nations drew on their own traditions of federalism to formulate their objections to the Charter. They have a shared understanding of their inherent rights of self-government grounded in thousands of years of practice before the arrival of Europeans. The status of self-governing nations is founded on the principle of "long use and occupation," constitutionalized in the great law of peace, and recognized across Great Turtle Island. This normal type of government is a federation of nations and they have experimented with countless forms over the centuries, developing elaborate and formal skills of negotiation, diplomacy, and consensus-building. Ever since Europeans arrived, the aboriginal peoples have tried to accommodate the newcomer nations into their traditional practices of multinational federalism by means of treaty-making. All of the more than five hundred treaties have been informed by the background picture of federation represented in a belt of two parallel rows of white wampum beads. This is its meaning:[28]

> These two rows will symbolise two paths or two vessels travelling down the same river together. One, a birch bark canoe, will be for the Indian people, their laws, their customs, and their ways. The other, a ship, will be for the white people and their laws, their customs and their ways. We shall each travel the river together, side by side, but in our own boats. Neither of us will try to steer the others' vessel.

A two-row treaty constitutes the reciprocal recognition of two or more coexisting and self-governing nations, and it embodies the principles of consent and continuity. After consent is reached on this understanding, the parties go on to negotiate various forms of sovereignty association for land use, commerce, military partnership, shared jurisdictions, and the like. In a manner similar to the compact theory of federalism, once mutual recognition is achieved, the nations are free to make agreements on the establishment of a government of the federation, as in the Iroquois Confederacy and the Assembly of First Nations, and on the delegation and sharing of powers.

Two-row and multirow wampum belts are the traditional lingua franca of federal politics in Canada. They were exchanged by First Nations and the French and English as early as 1624 and as recently as 1990 in the signing of the trilingual and trinational protocol agreement between the Iroquois confederacy, Quebec, and the federal government at the Hilton Hotel in Dorval, 12 August 1990, during the defense of Kanesatake (Oka). At the turn of this century the great law of peace was translated from wampum into the written Iroquois and English languages. In 1924 the history and theory of two-row wampum federalism was codified by the Six Nations in *The Redman's Appeal for Justice: The Position of the Six Nations That They Constitute an Independent State.*[29] The First Nations have kept this jurisprudence alive over the centuries – applying it in their relations with native and newcomer nations, explaining it to George III, taking it to the League of Nations in 1924 and the United Nations in 1975, presenting it to parliamentary committees, and explaining it to John Ciaccia and Claude Ryan at Kanesatake in the summer of 1990 and to Chief Justice Allan McEachern in the Gitksan and Wet'suwet'en sovereignty case (Delgamuukw) in British Columbia.[30]

From Chief Pontiac and Joseph Brant in the 1760s to Georges Erasmus and Ellen Gabriel today, the Royal Proclamation of 1763 is seen by native people as the British Crown's formal recognition of the two-row wampum relation of sovereignty association or "treaty federalism" between First Nations and the French and British Crowns.[31] The British Crown also understood the proclamation in this way. From 1696 on, the British Crown held that the Indians were to be treated by the Crown as nations under international law. This was repeated throughout the period and in the background papers leading up to the Royal Proclamation. In addition, Canassatego, the great Senecan diplomat, lectured Sir William Johnson time after time on the fine points of two-row wampum federalism right up to the Royal Proclamation. By recognizing the native peoples as first nations under international law, the Crown legally removed Indian-white relations from the hands of colonial assemblies and land speculators and brought them under its own exclusive foreign policy jurisdiction. The land not purchased by or ceded to the Crown in America was proclaimed to be Indian land under native laws and customs. The only way land could be acquired was through Crown negotiations with chiefs, in public, with their consent and without duress. There is no suggestion in writing or in practice that the Crown would try to govern the Indian nations.[32]

This interpretation of the Royal Proclamation was affirmed by Chief Justice John Marshall in 1831–2 in *Worcester v. the State of Georgia*.[33] He states that the Royal Proclamation was understood by the Crown and the colonists to recognize Indian sovereignty. Marshall explains that the Crown had a two-step theory of establishing sovereignty in America, which accorded with the prevailing conventions of consent and continuity in the law of nations. In the first step a European nation would claim sovereignty over an area of America on which it settled or traded. This first claim of sovereignty was solely with respect to other European nations, asserting a monopoly vis-à-vis other European nations, of settlement and trade with the Indian nations. This step did not touch the Indian nations. In the second step, the European nation would go on to negotiate treaties of trade and settlement with the Indian nations within the designated territory. Here the European nation would recognize the continuing sovereignty of the Indian nations and the Indian nations would recognize the co-sovereignty and coexistence of European nations. Once this reciprocal recognition was established, they would then go on to negotiate settlement, trade, co-use, alliances, and so on, giving rise to relations of treaty federalism between Crown and First Nations. (The status of the First Nations of the United States today, of self-governing "domestic dependent nations" in relations of treaty federalism with the federal government, is derived from the Marshall cases.) Moreover, the early modern recognition of the aboriginal peoples as nations, equal in status to European nations, has been substantiated by scholars of international law who have shown that the First Nations meet the criteria of sovereignty in international law.[34]

Thus, at the formative period of the Canadian federation, native and newcomer traditions of federalism complemented one another. It is important to see that the native and Crown traditions of reciprocal recognition are the philosophical and historical foundations not only of the continuity of the First Nations' self-government but also of French, British, and now Canadian sovereignty in America. Because America was already occupied by self-governing nations and those nations were not conquered, the only legitimate title to sovereignty of the Crown under international law was the consent of the first nations. Consequently, the legitimacy of Canada as a sovereign state, as well as Quebec and the rest of Canada if they separate, rests on the consent of the First Nations, as given in treaties, and the continuity of the First Nations as self-governing nations.

Quebec and the Provinces

The traditions that Quebec and the other provinces turned to in the 1980s go back to the Quebec Act of 1774. Like the Royal Proclamation, the Quebec Act is founded on the principles of continuity and consent. In the conquest of one civilized country by another, the law of nations holds that the customs and laws of the conquered nation continue through the conquest. Ratified by the consent of the people of Quebec, this is one of the most liberal acts in eighteenth-century politics. William Knox, the undersecretary of American affairs, explained it in the following way.[35] When the British arrived in Quebec in 1759 they found a nation that had been governing itself by its own laws and customs for over a century. The French Crown was nothing more than an external sovereign. Moreover, whenever Britain had destroyed the laws and customs of a conquered country in the past, civil strife and enmity had followed; whereas when it had permitted the laws and customs of the people to continue, Britain gained a peaceful ally. Therefore, he concluded, both principle and prudence recommend the recognition of the continuity of Quebec's customs, laws, religion and system of property, and the role of external sovereign only for the British Crown.

As a result of 1763 and 1774, the British empire constituted a "multitude kingdom" of nations with varying degrees of coordinate sovereignty.[36] The leading Whigs supported both Proclamation and Act. Knox himself was one of many Lockean loyalists. Adam Smith praised the Quebec Act and defended the whole pluralistic imperial system in book four of *The Wealth of Nations*. Opposition to the Quebec Act was led by Edmund Burke, the founder of modern conservatism.

The Whigs rallied to the principle of continuity because they understood their liberal freedoms and rights to be founded on the "ancient Constitution." The ancient constitution was the form of government the Angles and the Saxons enjoyed in Briton prior to the Norman conquest and the imposition of the Norman yoke (feudal law). By the principle of continuity, the ancient constitution of Saxon liberties and parliamentary government survived through the conquest. Therefore, the liberal institutions of modern British society were believed by the Whigs to rest on the principle and practice of continuity; to deny it would have been to undercut the ground on which liberalism stood.

The revolutionaries in the colonies to the south condemned both the Proclamation of 1763, which blocked the western expansion of the colonies into Indian lands, and the Quebec Act of 1774, which protected the French language, laws, and religion in Quebec. Both of these were identified in the Declaration of Independence as acts of tyranny and arbitrary government, and were presented as justification for the war of independence. The First Nations, the Canadiens, and the Loyalists realized that the American war of Independence was a contest between two types of federation: the Canadian federation of three orders of government put together in 1763 and 1774 versus the uniform federation of the revolutionaries in the thirteen colonies. The majority of First Nations fought on the Loyalist side, for they argued that the Royal Proclamation was the best way to protect their sovereignty. The Canadiens refused to join the revolution even when the king of France pressed them to take up arms, for they argued that their laws and customs were protected under the Quebec Act.[37] As surprising as it may seem to some today, when the American revolutionaries invaded Canada in 1775, an ad hoc army of Mohawks, Canadiens, and Loyalists, recently displaced from upstate New York, turned them back.

In the 1860s these Loyalist and Canadien traditions shaped the understanding of confederation for many of the proponents. The provinces were understood as autonomous political bodies with their own constitutions. Section 92 of the Constitution Act, 1867, recognized the continuity of the broad powers they had exercised independently. In the classic words of Lord Watson:[38]

The object of the Act [of Confederation] was neither to weld the provinces into one, nor to subordinate provincial governments to a central authority, but to create a federal government in which they should all be represented, entrusted with the exclusive administration of affairs in which they had a common interest, each province retaining its independence and autonomy.

T.J.J. Loranger brought these conventions together in his famous compact theory of confederation, *Letters upon the Interpretation of the Federal Constitution* (1884), which has provided the foundation of Quebec's resistance to domineering federalism and defence of the Constitution Act, 1867, for over a century.[39] A similar compact theory of confederation was held by many Upper Canadians and Maritimers.[40] Lords Haldane and Watson continued the old Privy Council traditions of provincial autonomy and coordinate sovereignty in twentieth-century traditions of judicial review. According to Pierre Trudeau, the compact theory of federalism was held by the majority of provincial premiers from the dominion-provincial conference of 1927 to 1982. The distinctive language of compact federalism can be heard in the exchange between Premiers Harcourt and Bourassa in May 1992.[41]

So the Charter was seen by Quebec, the First Nations, and the provinces as a violation of two founding principles of the Canadian federation that have guided the practice of federalism for over three hundred years. It was seen as a vehicle of centralization and assimilation. In 1960 Prime Minister Diefenbaker was asked why he did not entrench the Canadian Bill of Rights in the constitution and make it binding on the provinces. He replied:[42]

> They say, if you want to make this effective it has to cover the provinces too. Any one advocating that must realize the fact that there is no chance of securing the consent of all the provinces ... [T]he consent of the provinces to any interference with property and civil rights cannot be secured ... . I also want to add that if at any time the provinces are prepared to give their consent to a constitutional amendment embodying a bill of rights ... there will be immediate co-operation from this government.

Prime Minister Diefenbaker had the tradition of compact federalism exactly right and was clearly loyal to it. After the failure of successive governments to reach agreement on constitutional amendment, Prime Minister Trudeau grew impatient with the time-honoured convention of unanimous consent of the provinces and went ahead without it. He covered over this violation with the vision of a uniform pan-Canadian society of the three equalities, grounded in the Constitution Act, 1982, and legitimated by references to the counter-tradition of centralism and assimilation. This new stage-setting made it appear that the Charter was independent of the ancient constitution of the federation, and generated Charter patriots who read the Charter solely in the context of 1982. As a result, they misinterpreted the federalist objections presented by Quebec and the First Nations as demands for minority status and group rights in a pan-Canadian society. They then expanded, but did not question, the conceptual framework that had been set it place in 1982.

In the patriation reference the Supreme Court warned that a breach of the consensual conventions of the federation is redressed politically not legally. True to their respective traditions, the government of Quebec and the First Nations began the process of redress by seeking amendments to the Charter and the Constitution Act, 1982, that would bring them in accord with the principles of Canadian federalism. As Ovide Mercredi explained to Pierre Trudeau, "Consensus is the truest form of democracy ... Maybe if you watch how we operate for a while, you will learn something."[43] Since 1984 the native and non-native people of Canada have come to appreciate the importance of the consensus of the people through their constitutive governments to fundamental constitutional change in our complex federation and to begin to learn, by trial and error, the difficult activity of reaching agreement among the diverse members.

MULTIROW FEDERALISM

During the years following 1982 there was resistance to the idea that the First Nations have an inherent right to govern themselves by their own laws and customs and a presumption that Canada could impose the Charter on them without their consent. During the Meech Lake years there was a parallel resistance to the idea that Quebec has an inherent right to govern itself by its own laws and customs and a presumption that Canada could impose the Charter on it without its consent. These assumptions conflicted with the two principles of Canadian federalism. Since 1990 these assumptions and the underlying picture of a non-federal society have been called into question and debated.[44] Now that these assumptions, which underpinned the sovereignty of the Charter over the federation, have been exposed, the following question remains: Are the Charter and federalism irreconcilable, or is there a place for the Charter in the federation?

I would like to ask if the Beaudoin-Dobbie report, which has majority support in Quebec and the rest of Canada, does not suggest two ways of reconciling the Charter with the two principles of federalism.[45] First, as we have seen, the problem underlying the contest between the Charter and its critics is that they are speaking within two incompatible traditions: Canada as a uniform society and Canada as a plural federation. The Beaudoin-Dobbie report appears to offer a common political language in the terms of which both federal and Charter aspects of the Canadian multiplicity can be discussed without distortion. The Charter rubs elbows with federalism, individual and collective rights stand side by side, the inherent right of self-government of the First Nations is finally recognized in the same terms of compact federalism used by Loranger and Lord Watson to describe the sovereignty of the provinces, Quebec is described as an autonomous political community in terms derived from the Quebec Act of 1774, and the key terms of compact federalism – such as delegation, concurrent powers with provincial paramountcy, opting in and out – also find a place.

The complex federation of political languages in the Beaudoin-Dobbie report is not as elegant as "The Spirit of Haida Gwaii," but does it not express in a complementary way the strange multiplicity that wants to be in Canada at the dawn of the twentieth-first century? For the first time since the great trilingual multirow wampum treaty negotiations of the early modern federation, it is the actual gathering together of this strange multiplicity of voices, in their own terms and as they themselves have spoken about and defined their place in Canada over the last decade in countless committees. In a typically Canadian fashion, everyone disagreed with the specific way in which they were characterized in the report, yet they did not reject the report as a whole.[46] Rather, they all began to argue and articulate their demands in terms laid down by the report, and the language of the report has gradually become the common ground of the negotiations. The participants have thus overcome the earlier impasse of articulating their demands in two incommensurable languages of Canadian politics. If consensus is reached on this new ground, then, even if every detail of the report is changed the terms of the report will have become the language of the renewed federation.[47]

In accordance with the traditions of federalism sketched above, Quebec, the First Nations, and any province could in principle opt out of the Charter in whole or in part and establish its own. Quebec already has a Charter of Rights. Québécois(e) scholars are currently reconceptualizing Quebec as a multicultural and multinational society and working on ways to recognize in the Quebec Charter the autonomy of the eleven First Nations, the anglophone minority, and ethnipluralism.[48] Some aboriginal people have argued that aspects of the Charter conflict with native traditions of responsibilities and government, while others, especially a number of native women's organizations, have argued that certain guarantees in the Charter, such as gender equality in sections 15 and 28, should be applied to aboriginal self-government. To overcome this difficult problem, native people have sought to develop their own Charter and aboriginal rights tribunals that would hear grievances based on native traditions (which often display more gender equality than nonnative traditions or the patriarchal Indian Act), the Canadian Charter, and international law.[49]

It is also possible in principle for both Quebec and the First Nations to consent to the Charter once it is amended to accord with the principle of continuity. This seems to be the more likely possibility in practice at the time of writing. On 11 June 1992 the four organizations representing most of the native peoples of Canada at the multilateral meetings on the constitution agreed to the application of a suitably amended Charter to aboriginal self-government.[50] And 73 percent of Québécois(e) identify "beaucoup" or "assez" with the Charter.[51] One could, for example, dissolve the decade of conflict between the Charter and federalism by amending section 1 to read "a free and democratic federation," rather than "society" as it now stands. This would give recognition to provincial autonomy and the different legal culture of each in the interpretation and application of the Charter.[52] It would also permit recognition at the outset of the treaty federalism of the First Nations with the Government of Canada and the sui generis "trust" relation that the Crown has as a result of the treaties.[53] As the Gitksan and Wet'suwet'en hereditary chiefs explained in Delgamuukw, in almost classic multirow federation terms, once the inherent right of self-government of the First Nations is recognized, then "we see a layering of responsibilities among the Gitksan and Wet'suwet'en, the Federal government, and the Provincial government being resolved in an ongoing series of negotiations." [54]

The second way in which the Beaudoin-Dobbie report seeks to reconcile federalism and the Charter is by characterizing the distinct society clause for Quebec in terms drawn from the Quebec Act of 1774 and to place it in the Charter, thus reaffirming the principle of continuity. The report recommends placing this clause in section 25, hand-in-hand with the Royal Proclamation of 1763, which is already there.[55]

In section 25(1) the continuity principle is also applied to protect the anglophone and francophone minority communities, as Quebec has always done with respect to its anglophone minority in 1774, 1791, and 1867 and in the Meech Lake Accord:

25. The guarantee in this Charter of certain rights and freedoms shall not be construed so as to abrogate or derogate from any aboriginal treaty or other rights or freedoms that pertain to the aboriginal peoples of Canada including (a) any rights or freedoms that have been recognized by the Royal Proclamation of October 1763; and (b) any rights or freedoms that now exist by way of land claims agreements or may be so acquired.

[The Beaudoin-Dobbie Amendment] 25.(1) This Charter shall be interpreted in a manner consistent with (a) the preservation and promotion of Quebec as a distinct society within Canada; and (b) the vitality and development of the language and culture of French-speaking and English-speaking minority communities throughout Canada [the Quebec Act of 1774 subsection].

(2) For the purposes of subsection (1), "distinct society" in relation to Quebec includes (a) a French-speaking majority; (b) a unique culture; and (c) a civil law tradition.

In what way does the reaffirmation of the Quebec of 1774 Act and the Royal Proclamation of 1763 address the concerns of the critics of the Charter and reconcile the antinomies we have considered? First, it serves to recognize Quebec and the First Nations as the oldest self-governing and autonomous nations of the federation. It thus suggests that the continuity of Quebec and the First Nations as self-governing nations is as fundamental as other Charter rights, and provides them with a shield against assimilative and centralizing interpretations of other sections. Furthermore, in advancing this specific amendment, the report appears to be asking Canadians if they have the civic virtue to recognize three orders of government in Canada and thereby live up to the degree of legal and political pluralism that the First Nations, Canadiens, and Loyalists were able to achieve in 1763 and 1774.

In conclusion, there seems to be an even deeper layer of meaning in this amendment. The Royal Proclamation and the Quebec Act literally constituted the federation of First Nations, Quebec and Britain on the principles of consent and continuity. From 1776 to 1814 these confederates went on to defend and cherish this strange federal multiplicity from invasion by the United States, which, in 1776, had declared independence from the principles of the Canadian federation.[56] Thus, it would appear that the report is asking Canadians to reaffirm, in the Charter itself, the principles that define our federation and provide the foundation of our rights and freedoms.

NOTES

1 Sir Isaiah Berlin, "Return of the Volksgeist," (1991) *New Perspectives Quarterly* 4–10.
2 See Robert Bringhurst and Ulli Steltzer, *The Black Canoe: Bill Reid and the Spirit of Haida Gwaii* (Vancouver 1991).
3 See Alan C. Cairns, *Charter versus Federalism: The Dilemmas of Constitutional Reform* (Montreal and Kingston 1992)l; Guy Laforest "L'esprit de 1982," in Louis Balthazar, Guy Laforest & Vincent Lemieux, eds., *Le Quebec et la restructuration du Canada 1980–1992* (Sillery 1991), 147–65; Guy Laforest "La culture politique Canadienne a L'heure de la Charte des Droits et Libertés," Analyse préparée pour les Commissions sur le processus de détermination de l'avenir politique et constitutionnel du Quebec mises sur pied par l'Assemblée nationale du Quebec par l'entremise de la loi 150 (Université Laval, 13 December 1991, unpublished); Peter Russell, "The Political Purposes of the Canadian Charter of Rights and Free-

doms,"(1983) 30 *Canadian Bar Review* 30–54; and Peter Russell's essay elsewhere in this volume.

4 *Report of the Commission on the Political and Constitutional Future of Quebec* (Quebec, March 1991), 33–6.

5 Alan C. Cairn, "Constitutional Change and the Three Equalities," in Ronald Watts and Douglas M. Brown, eds., *Options for a New Canada* (Toronto 1991), 80. Compare Laforest, "La culture politique," 19.

6 See Brian Slattery, "A Theory of the Charter," (1987) 25 *Osgoode Hall Law Journal* 701–47, at 739–41.

7 Alan C. Cairns, "The Charter, Interest Groups, Executive Federalism, and Constitutional Reform," in David E. Smith, Peter MacKinnon and John C. Courtenay, eds., *After Meech Lake: Lessons for the Future* (Saskatoon 1991) 13–31, at 21. Compare Laforest, "La culture politique," 17.

8 See David Elkins, "Facing Our Destiny: Rights and Canadian Distinctiveness," (1989) 22 *Canadian Journal of Political Science* 699–716.

9 See P.G. Barton and R.N. Bronaugh, eds., (1991) 4 *Canadian Journal of Law and Jurisprudence* and Will Kymlicka, *Liberalism, Community and Culture* (Oxford 1989).

10 *Report of the Commission on the Political and Constitutional Future of Québec* 29, 35–6' Laforest, "La Culture Politique"; Christian Dufour, *A Canadian Challenge* (Lantzville 1990); Ovide Mercredi, "Aboriginal Peoples and the Constitution," in David E. Smith, ed., *After Meech Lake* 219–23; Frank Cassidy, ed., *Aboriginal Self–Determination* (Lantzville 1991; Aki-kwe (Mary Ellen Turpel) , "Aboriginal Peoples and the Canadian Charter: Interpretive Monopolies, Cultural Differences," in Richard F. Devlin, ed., *First Nations Issues* (Toronto 1991) 40–73.

11 Ovide Mercredi, "Eighth Annual Guest Lecture," *McGill Law Journal,* Faculty of Law (McGill University 31 March 1992); Guy La forest, "Libéralisme et nationalisme au Canada à l'heure de l'Accord du Lac Meech," (1991) 13 *Carrefour* 68–90. For the background to this "colonial" way of thinking in Canadian legal practice, see Patrick Macklem, "First Nations Self-Government and the Borders of the Canadian Legal Imagination," (1991) 36 *McGill Law Journal* 383–456.

12 Compare Charles Taylor, "Shared and Divergent Values" in Watts and Brown, *Options* 53–72; and Charles Taylor, "The Bleak Future of Canadian Dualism," (McGill University 1992, unpublished).

13 For *Quod omes tangit* see Arthur P. Monahan, *Consent, Coercion and Limit: the Medieval Origins of Parliamentary Democracy* (Montreal and Kingston

1987) 97–120. For the long term effect of proceeding with patriation and amendment without the consent of the government of Quebec in 1982 see *Report of the Commission on the Political and Constitutional Future of Québec* 28, 30, 37, 45, 71; *A Québec Free to Choose*, 3, 11–12; and Gil Rémillard, "Québec's Quest for Survival and Equality via the Meech Lake Accord," in Michael D. Behiels, ed., *The Meech Lake Primer: Conflicting Views of the 1987 Constitutional Accord* (Ottawa 1989) 28–42, at 29: "The 1981 agreement was incomplete, unfinished and fundamentally unacceptable." See Roy Romanow, John Whyte, and Howard Leeson, *Canada ... Notwithstanding: The Making of the Constitution 1976–1982* (Toronto 1984).

14 Pierre Elliott Trudeau, "Fatal Tilt: Speaking Out About Sovereignty," in *Point of View* (Toronto 1991) 7–9, 15. See David Milne, "The Canadian Constitution" (Toronto 1991), 69–123.

15 Trudeau, "Fatal Tilt," *The Attorney General of Manitoba et al. v. Attorney General of Canada et al. (Patriation Reference)* 1981, in Peter H. Russell, Rainer Knopff, and Ted Morton, eds., *Federalism and the Charter* (Ottawa 1990) 706–59, at 746–50.

16 A theory of Lockean or classical liberal federalism was first developed by William Molyneux in *The Case of Ireland's Being Bound by Acts of the Parliament of England* (Dublin 1698). It was employed in the thirteen colonies in the 1770s and by Canadian compact federalists from the early nineteenth century onward. See Patrick Kelly, "Perceptions of Locke in Eighteenth-Century Ireland," (1989) *Proceedings of the Royal Irish Academy* 17–35; Paul Romney, "The Nature and Scope of Provincial Autonomy: Oliver Mowat, the Québec Resolutions and the Construction of British North America Act" (1992) 25 *Canadian Journal of Political Science* 3–28.

17 Stephen Hume, "Bourassa: 'There's no other cheek' to turn" *The Gazette*, 5 May 1992, B3.

18 14 George III, c. 83 (1774). See George Matthews, *Quiet Resolutions: Québec's Challenge to Canada* (Toronto 1990) 70–6; Pierre Fournier, *A Meech Lake Post-Mortem*, (Montreal and Kingston 1991) 11–13; Beaudoin-Dobbie report 25–6; *A Québec Free to Choose*, 7–10, *Report of the Commission on the Political and Constitutional Future of Québec* 11–12, 29–30, 48–9; and see François Rocher, "Québec's Historical Agenda," in Duncan Cameron and Miriam Smith, eds., *Constitutional Politics* (Toronto 1992), 23–36.

19 Brian Slattery, *Ancestral Lands, Alien Laws* (Saskatoon 1983), 10–2.

20 Bruce Ryder, "The Demise and Rise of the Classical Paradigm in Canadian

Federalism: Promoting Autonomy for the Provinces and First Nations,"(1991) 36 *McGill Law Journal* 308–81; Romney, "The Nature and
Scope of Provincial Autonomy."

21 For these events see Alain-G. Gaignon and Daniel Latouche Allaire, *Bé-
langer, Campeau et les autres* (Montréal 1992). As Premier Bourassa later
clarified, the twenty-two powers in the Allaire Report are the powers which
a province has a right to reclaim when the federal trust is breached – not
that he intends in fact to reclaim them. Michel Venne, "Québec accepterait
des pouvoirs partagés," *Le Devoir* 25 January1992, A1.

22 Mercredi, "Eighth Annual Guest Lecture"; Elijah Harper, keynote speech,
"Lessons from Oka – Forging a Better Relationship," Aboriginal Law Association of McGill University (McGill University 13 February 1991), 78–
84; Georges Erasmus, "Introduction," in Boyce Richardson, ed., *Drumbeat: Anger and Renewal in Indian Country* (Toronto 1989), 1–42 at 24–7;
David Hawkes, *Aboriginal Peoples and Constitutional Reform: What Have We
Learned?* (Kingston 1989).

23 A.C. Parker, ed., *The Constitution of the Five Nations or the Iroquois Book of
the Great Law* (Ohsweken 1984). See Menno Boldt and J. Anthony Long,
'Tribal Traditions and European-Western Political Ideologies: The Dilemma of Canada's Native Canadians," in Boldt and Long, eds., *The Quest for
Justice: Aboriginal Peoples and Aboriginal Rights* (Toronto 1985), 333–46; J.
Anthony Long, "Political Revitalization in Canadian Native Indian Societies," (1990) 23 *Canadian Journal of Political Science*, 751–73 at 764–9.

24 Aki-kwe, "Aboriginal Peoples and the Charter,"; Mercredi, "Eighth Annual
Guest Lecture"; Leroy Little Bear, "Dispute Settlement among the Naidan-
ac," in Devlin, *First Nations Issues*, 4–12; Boldt and Long, "Tribal Traditions"; Noel Lyon, "First Nations and the Canadian Charter of Rights and
Freedoms," (1992) 2 *The Network* 4–5.

25 Parker, ed. *The Great Law* 53.

26 Bruce Clark, *Native Liberty, Crown Sovereignty: The Existing Aboriginal
Right of Self-Government in Canada* (Montreal and Kingston 1990).

27 Mercredi, "Eighth Annual Guest Lecture"; Harper, keynote speech; Konrad Sioui, "Roundtable on Native Sovereignty and the Constitution," Department of Political Science, McGill University (26 March 1992).

28 Michael Mitchell, "An Unbroken Assertion of Sovereignty," in Richardson,
ed., *Drumbeat*,107–38, at 110.

29 The Six Nations, *The Redman's Appeal for Justice: The Position of the Six Nations That They Constitute an Independent State* (Brantford 1924).

30 See Francis Jennings, ed., *The History and Culture of Iroquois Diplomacy* (Syracuse 1985); Geoffrey York and Loreen Pindera, *People of the Pines: The Warriors and the Legacy of Oka* (Toronto 1991); Gisday Wa and Delgamuukw, *The Spirit in the Land: The Opening Statement of the Gitksan and Wet'suwet'en Hereditary Chiefs in the Supreme Court of British Columbia* (Gabriola Island 1989).

31 "The Royal Proclamation of 7 October 1763," in W.P.M. Kennedy, ed., *Documents of the Canadian Constitution 1759–1915* (Oxford 1918) 18–21. See Brian Slattery, *The Land Rights of Indigenous Canadian People as Affected by the Crown's Acquisition of Their Territory* (Saskatoon 1979). For the concept of "treaty federalism" see James Youngblood Henderson, "The Doctrine of Aboriginal Rights in Western Legal Tradition" in Boldt and Long, *The Quest for Justice*, 185–220.

32 For this interpretation and the following two paragraphs, see James Tully, "Rediscovering America: The Two Treatises and Aboriginal Rights," in Tully, *An Approach to Political Philosophy: Locke in Contexts* (Cambridge 1993).

33 *Worcester v. the State of Georgia* (1832) 6 Peter 515 (USSC), reprinted in John Marshall, *The Writings of John Marshall* (Boston 1839) 419–48.

34 Maureen Davies, "Aspects of Aboriginal Rights in International Law," in Bradford Morse, ed., *Aboriginal Peoples and the Law* (Ottawa 1991) 16–47; John Howard Clinebell and Jim Thomson, "Sovereignty and Self-Determination: The Rights of Native Americans under International Law," (1978) 27 *Buffalo Law Review* 669–714.

35 William Knox, *The Justice and Policy of the Late Act of Parliament for Making More Effectual ... the Government of Québec...* (London 1774).

36 For the background to the concept of a "multiple kingdom" see Conrad Russell, "The British Problem and the English Civil War," (1987) 72 *History* 395–415; and M. Percival-Maxwell, "Ireland and the Monarchy in the Early Stuart Multiple Kingdom," (1991) 34 *The Historical Journal* 279–95.

37 See James Tully, "Placing the Two Treatises of Government 1689–1832," in Quentin Skinner and Nicholas Philipson, eds., *Political Discourse In Early Modern Britain: Essays In Honour of John Pocock* (Cambridge 1993).

38 Lord Watson, in *Liquidators of the Maritime Bank v. Receiver General of New Brunswick* (1892), cited in the patriation reference (1981) 441–2, in Russell, *Federalism and the Charter* 749.

39 T.J.J. Loranger, *Letters upon the Interpretation of the Federal Constitution Known as The British North America Act 1867* (Québec 1884).

40 Ralph C. Vipond, *Liberty and Community: Canadian Federalism and the*

Failure of the Constitution (Albany 1991); Romney, "The Nature and Scope of Provincial Autonomy."

41 Alan C. Cairns, "The Judicial Committee and Its Critics," (1971) 4 *Canadian Journal of Political Science*, 301–45; Trudeau, "Fatal Tilt"; Vaughn Palmer, "Behind the Scenes as Harcourt Meets Bourassa," *The Gazette*, 13 May 1992, B3.

42 House of Commons Debates, 1960 5648–9, cited in the patriation reference, in Russell, *Federalism and the Charter* 748.

43 André Picard, "Ex-PM Debates with Mercredi," *The Globe and Mail*, 14 December 1991, A4.

44 Taylor, "Shared and Divergent Values"; Taylor, "Bleak future." For the theorists who had construed Quebec and the First Nations as cultural minorities within a non-federal Canadian society, the breakthrough appeared to come in April 1991. See Donald G. Lenihan, ed., "Seminar on Rights," (1991) 19 *Taking Stock: Network on the Constitution* (July 1991) 19.

45 Polls show that 65 percent of Québécois(es) and a majority of Canadians support the report. Hubert Bauch, "Pollsters Say We're Ripe for Constitutional Horse-Trading," *The Gazette*, 25 April 1992; Terence Wills, "Majority Would Back Beaudoin-Dobbie, If It Came to a Vote," *The Gazette*, 3 May 1992, B1.

46 Michel Venne, "Robert Bourassa flaire un 'fédéralisme dominateur,'" *Le Devoir*, 4 March 1992, A1.

47 Compare Graham Fraser, "This is New Age Federalism," *The Globe and Mail*, 2 March 1992, A6.

48 See Simon Langlois, "Le choc de deux Sociétés Globales," in Balthazar, Laforest and Lemieux, *Le Québec et la restructuration* 95–101; Guy Laforest, "A la recherche d'un patriotisme pour le Québec," *Cégep Saint-Laurent* 4 March 1992; José Woehrling, "La protection des droits et libertés, et le sort des minorités," in Alain-G. Gagnon and Francois Rocher, eds., *Répliques aux détracteurs de la Souveraineté du Québec* (Montreal 1992), 131–67; Eric Gourdeau, "Québec and the Aboriginal Peoples," in J. Anthony Long and Menno Boldt, eds., *Governments in Conflict: Provinces and Indian Nations in Canada* (Toronto 1988), 109–27. Like most of the other provinces and the Government of Canada, the Government of Québec recognizes the aboriginal right of self-government "within," not "with," Canada and Quebec. For the full right of self-determination of the First Nations of Cheewitinscee–Eeyowscee (Northern Québec) see Matthew Coon Come, "La secession et les droits des Cris," (1992)2 *Le Réseau* 11–12.

49 Wendy Moss, "Indigenous Self-Government in Canada and Sexual Equality under the Indian Act: Resolving Conflicts Between Collective and Individual Rights," (1990) 15 *Queen's Law Journal* 279–305; Gail Stacey-Moore, "Aboriginal Women, Self-Government, the Canadian Charter of Rights and Freedoms, and the 1991 Canada Package on the Constitution," Native Women's Association of Canada (Ottawa, 3 December 1991).

50 Status Report of the Multilateral Meetings on the Constitution (rolling draft as at 11 June 1992).

51 Jean-François Lisée, "Le Canada dans la peau," *L'Actualité* (July 1992) 27.

52 The courts have already moved in this direction in their application of the Charter. See Judge LaForest in *Edwards Books and Art Ltd v. The Queen* (1986), 35 DLR (4th), at 72 (SCC): "The simple fact is that what may work effectively in one province ... may simply not work in another." Cited in Slattery, "A Theory of the Charter, " 737.

53 See Brian Slattery, "First Nations and the Constitution: A Matter of Trust,"(1992) 71 *Canadian Bar Review* 26–93.

54 Gisdaywa (Alfred Joseph), Delgamuukw (Earl Muldoe), Yaga'lahl (Dora Wilson), and Maas Gaak (Don Ryan), "Closing Statement of the Chiefs 14 May 1990," in Don Monet and Skanu'u (Ardythe Wilson) *Colonialism on Trial: Indigenous Land Rights and the Gitksan and Wet'suwet'en Sovereignty Case* (Gabriola Island 1992), 181–4, at 183.

55 Report of the Special Joint Committee on a Renewed Canada, 26–7. The status report of the multilateral meetings moves the distinct society clause to another section of the Charter and to the Canada clause, and the present section 25 is strengthened, but these alterations do not affect the recognition of Quebec and the First Nations recommended in the Beaudoin-Dobbie report.

56 See Colin Calloway, *Crown and Calumet: British-Indian Relations 1783–1815* (Norman, Oklahoma, 1987).

13   JOHN RUSSELL

Nationalistic Minorities and Liberal Traditions

It is a common criticism of liberal political theory that it cannot accommodate the claims of minority cultures to any sort of special status or rights to self-determination within a liberal constitutional regime. The conventional wisdom holds that liberalism denies the legitimacy of such, or indeed of any, so-called collective rights – or if liberalism is prepared to admit them, individual rights cannot be overridden in their name. Liberalism purportedly rejects these claims because of its *individualism:* as a normative political theory it apparently accords individuals a certain pre-eminent status, settling in their favour any conflict of rights that opposes individual and collectivist claims.

It must be allowed that this is a plausible view of liberal theory, especially recent liberal theory. But if this turns out to be an accurate assessment of the limitations of liberalism, it appears to pose severe practical and philosophical problems for the many countries around the world that are normally regarded as liberal democracies but that have seen fit to entrench certain rights of minority cultures into their constitutional structures. In Canada's case, the matter is all the more pressing, since it is engaged in a process that, though now stalled, seems destined, if the country is to remain together, to entrench yet further and even more powerful rights on behalf of certain minority cultures. A crucial question that is posed by these circumstances is whether countries like Canada have compromised their liberal principles and are embarked on the pathological and ultimately illiberal folly of trying to combine liberal individualist with communitarian collectivist programs in a modern liberal democratic constitutional setting. From a different viewpoint, another way of getting at the same issues is to ask whether these events reflect any deep poverty in liberalism, spelling the need for developments in political theory that will leave behind the old liberal paradigm.

My aim in this paper is to essay a relatively optimistic liberal response to these questions. Yes, there is a version of liberalism that can accommodate recognition of certain minority rights without doing a disservice to animating liberal values. And so liberalism *is* capable of going an important distance in meeting and responding to the exigent pressures of cultural diversity; it is *not* yet ready to be discarded. Undoubtedly, many will not share this optimism or agree that liberalism can go far enough in addressing these claims. However, I am interested in seeing how far liberalism can go in this area, where it has to draw lines, and how it defends those boundaries. That should be of interest even to critics of liberalism, since a sympathetic assessment of the capacity of liberal theory to address these issues must be the point of departure for constructive dialogue and competition with other views. Moreover, it is evident today, both in this country and in many other places, that there is an urgent practical need to see whether this project can be worked out. In a Canadian context, the last ten years of controversy over the capacity of the Charter of Rights and Freedoms to accommodate the claims of aboriginals and French-speaking Quebeckers can be seen either as expressive of the need to withdraw or retreat from the core liberal values, such as respect for liberty and equality (sections 7 and 15) and a basic underlying commitment to individual autonomy, or as an indication of the need to work out these values more fully, attempting to meet the claims of these minorities by rendering their implications more specific and concrete. The latter path will undoubtedly strike many contemporary readers as unusual for a liberal to pursue, though I shall argue that it has an important, though recently overlooked, place in the history of liberal thought.

But if we are seriously interested in seeing how far liberalism can go in accommodating the claims of groups like Canadian aboriginals and French-speaking Quebeckers, we must be prepared to engage liberalism at the level of normative political theory. Here we naturally look first to the work of the contemporary theorists who have provided us with the most recent detailed formulations of liberal theory. That is to say, we look to the work of John Rawls and Ronald Dworkin. Unfortunately, Rawls and Dworkin have themselves provided us with no direct commentary on this subject, but an important attempt to extend their positions to address these issues has recently been offered by the Canadian political philosopher Will Kymlicka.[1] I propose, therefore, to centre much of the substantive part of my discussion on the difficulties contemporary liberalism faces in meeting the claims of certain minority cultures, and then to offer a critical analysis of Kymlicka's attempt to amend that view to accommodate these claims. I conclude that Kymlicka makes a strong case for extending contemporary liberalism to recognize the general legitimacy of claims of certain minority cultures; but I argue that contemporary liberalism à la Rawls and Dworkin fails to provide adequate guidance in identifying and adjudicating the extent and limits of those claims, and that this threatens its liberal program and reveals serious shortcomings within the theory.

However, a review of contemporary liberal thought may not be sufficient by itself to come to an understanding of liberal views on this subject. We should also be sensitive to what earlier liberal theorists and traditions might have to contribute. There is special need of this in the present case, because there is an important but often overlooked liberal position, known as "the new liberalism," that emerged early in this century and that is unique within liberal theory in having devoted a substantial amount of its energies toward addressing the problems created for the modern state by the nationalistic aspirations of certain minority cultures. The tradition that these liberals are part of has its origins with John Stuart Mill and T.H. Green and finds its main expression in the works of the early twentieth-century philosopher L.T. Hobhouse and the economist J.A. Hobson. Mill, in particular, set the philosophical stage for the new liberals' sympathetic consideration of the position of minority cultures by noticing the central role that culture plays in providing the context for the meaningful exercise of freedom and self-development, and by arguing that peoples who constitute nations have prima facie claims to self-government.[2] There were also historical reasons for later interest in this area. As in our own time, Hobhouse and Hobson were also faced with a pressing need to consider and respond to issues of cultural pluralism that were due, in particular, to the fissures that had developed in the structure of late nineteenth century British colonialism.[3] But even more important for our purposes, the new liberals' normative theory is interestingly distinct from more recent liberal views. They advance a broadly Aristotelian liberalism, which regards state action as essentially concerned with ensuring the availability of the common goods essential to promoting the fully adequate healthy functioning of individuals within a well-ordered community. This view represents a distinct, but seldom acknowledged, liberal competitor to the neo-Kantian approaches found in contemporary liberal theory. And indeed, it will be my thesis here that it provides substantially better liberal guidance in addressing the problems posed for the modern state by certain minority cultures.

These conclusions should be of obvious interest and importance to policy-makers, jurists, and students of political theory. For if I am right about the success of an earlier liberal tradition in addressing the issues raised by certain minority cultures, another avenue is opened for liberal policy makers and jurists to gauge their practical deliberations in this area. At the level of political theory, the success of an earlier position in such an important area should help to affirm its credentials as a contender among current liberal theories.[4]

The paper is organized into the following segments: (1) a discussion of the terminology that is used in this debate; (2) an analysis of the difficulties contemporary liberalism faces in recognizing claims to special rights or status for certain minority cultures; (3) a statement of Kymlicka's proposed solution; (4) a brief defence of Kymlicka; (5) criticism of Kymlicka's position; (6) a discussion of new liberal views in this area; and (7) some concluding reflections on the implications of these arguments for Canada's current situation.

TERMINOLOGY

The language that is used in this debate is often of little help in focusing discussion, so it will be useful to begin by briefly suggesting some revisions. First, although it is fairly common to talk about the claims of "minority cultures" or "distinct minority cultures," I prefer to speak of "nationalistic minorities" in this context. The difficulty with using the former terms is that they are enormously elastic and create the impression that we are addressing a much wider range of issues and cases than is normally intended. There are obviously very many distinct minority cultures in every modern society, based primarily on ethnic or religious background. Not every one of them seeks to or can make plausible claims to special treatment or status; and it is reasonable to think that, even if many are entitled to some form of special status or treatment, a wide range of moral considerations, principles, and outcomes will apply in different cases. Moreover, we shall see that the groups whose interests we are particularly concerned to address raise special issues and problems that arise because of the status they can reasonably claim as *nations*. We do better, then, to focus the discussion by talking of "nationalistic minorities." Roughly speaking, nationalistic minorities are minority cultures that are bound together by ties of sentiment and a distinctive history and traditions, and that seek for themselves certain institutional safeguards and prerogatives as means to ensuring the preservation and development of their culture against the encroachment of majoritarian cultural and democratic influences. Such institutional mechanisms usually include claims to special political, mobility, property, and language rights and, by implication, restrictions on those same rights for others. Another related feature of nationalistic minorities is their interest in exercising some form of special jurisdiction or rights to self-determination over a distinct geographical area that is within the common control of a broader polity. Inevitably, given their interest in exercising some form of special control or autonomy over a particular territory, nationalistic minorities tend to view their aspirations as involving a choice between accommodation within or separation from a larger polity; and we see examples of this with Canadian aboriginal peoples and French-speaking Quebeckers.[5]

A second terminological matter that deserves attention is the use of the term "collective rights" to identify the distinctive claims made by nationalistic minorities. Although this term is used in a variety of ways in different theories, for our purposes it is common to think of a collective right as expressing the idea that communities are in some sense independent or original sources of valid moral claims. Since liberalism is usually taken to hold that the individual is the ultimate unit of moral worth, or as Rawls puts it, only individuals can be "self-originating sources of valid claims,"[6] the notion of a collective right thus appears to be an anti-individualistic and anti-liberal idea. But it is controversial whether defenders of collective rights really deny that individuals are the ultimate units of moral worth or whether they just mean to reject a certain individualistic orientation to which liberalism is apparently committed. Moreover, the sorts of claims that are commonly made by nationalistic minorities – claims to special political, mobility, property, and language rights – are not always made merely for the sake of promoting the interests of a community per se. On the contrary, they are, if anything, more commonly than not claimed as expressing certain rights and interests that are essential to the well-being of some individuals.[7] So using a term like "collective rights" in the current context can be both controversial and misleading. Again, we do better to avoid it. We can avoid confusion and the appearance of begging any important questions by simply speaking of the "special rights" of nationalistic minorities.

With these revisions in mind, we can now rephrase the purpose of our inquiry as one of assessing the extent to which liberalism is capable of accommodating the legitimate special rights, if any such exist, of nationalistic minorities. [8]

NATIONALISTIC MINORITIES AND CONTEMPORARY LIBERALISM

The worry that liberalism is not able to address the claims of nationalistic minorities is well reflected in the commitments of recent liberal theory. But we should be careful how we diagnose the difficulty that contemporary liberalism faces. I have already suggested that the common way of thinking about these issues, namely, as a dispute between individualism and collectivism, is overly simple and misleading. More fertile ground for analysing contemporary liberalism and comparing different points of view can undoubtedly be found in attempts to identify the nature of the individualistic position to which contemporary liberalism is apparently committed. But the results of these projects in recent years have also proved to be highly controversial. It is unclear that any substantial progress has been made by opponents of contemporary liberalism in critically portraying the sort of individualism that liberalism stands for; and therefore it is also unclear that progress has been made by these commentators in identifying the boundaries of liberal individualism. In fact, it is fair to say that recent critiques of liberal individualism as resting on "atomistic," "deontological," or "possessive individualist" conceptions of the self have frequently been shown to rest on significant misreadings or on a failure to appreciate the flexibility of the positions under attack.[9] This is not to say that there is nothing that will ultimately be shown to be of importance in these critiques. Rather, it is to say that, at present, if we want to come to an understanding of the capacity of contemporary liberalism to address the issues raised by nationalistic minorities, we put ourselves at a significant disadvantage if we start from premises about that position that are widely contested.[10]

Fortunately, we do not need to look so deeply into the background of contemporary liberal theory to find an uncontroversial characterization that will permit us to make progress on the matters at hand. A satisfying account that explains the difficulties contemporary liberalism faces in meeting the claims of nationalistic minorities is pretty much apparent on the surface of the theory. Contemporary liberalism is now commonly characterized as a *resourcist egalitarian theory*. What this means is that, rather than using the state to establish an institutional framework that attempts to meet needs or to promote welfare or excellence, contemporary liberals limit its authority on matters of justice to devising institutions that will promote, roughly speaking, an egalitarian distribution of resources among members of a particular political community.[11] It is obviously crucial to understanding this position to know what the resources are that liberals plan to distribute. Following Rawls, these are often referred to as "primary goods." They are in a sense universal goods in that they are held to be necessary means to the pursuit of a person's system of ends, whatever those ends happen to be, though as means they are insufficient by themselves to constitute a system of ends or (what is the same thing) a conception of the good. They are therefore goods or resources that it is purportedly rational for all persons to want, and to want more rather than less of, whatever their conception of the good happens to be.[12] Rawls's index of primary goods includes the standard political and civil liberties, opportunities, the powers and prerogatives of office, income and wealth, and the social bases of self-respect.[13]

Now it is fairly easy to see that there are two important aspects of this position that make it difficult for contemporary liberals to address the claims of nationalistic minorities. First, limiting the role of the state to overseeing the proper distribution of resources, that is, to the distribution of universal primary goods or necessary means, prevents it from undertaking any action that would involve taking a stand for, or directly promoting, any permissible conception(s) of the good over other permissible conceptions. This essentially anti-perfectionist view of the limits of state authority, often referred to as "liberal neutrality," apparently rules out the possibility that the state could give special preference or status to nationalistic minorities by according them special rights that would promote or ensure the continued viability of their particular cultures. This last observation suggests a second difficulty. Since contemporary liberalism is committed to an egalitarian distribution of resources, any conferral of differential rights for certain citizens or groups seems to violate that egalitarian commitment. To take the most basic cases, rights to equal liberty and opportunity are apparently violated by granting nationalistic minorities special differential political, mobility, or property rights.

Both the egalitarian commitments of contemporary liberalism and what I shall call the "resourcist anti-perfectionism" implied by its particular resourcist conception of value apparently rule out the according of any special rights to nationalistic minorities. So there appears to be a serious problem with combining contemporary liberalism with special rights for nationalistic minorities. Moreover, it must be admitted that the egalitarian and resourcist anti-perfectionist components of contemporary liberalism give expression to deep and long-standing currents of thought in the liberal tradition, drawn primarily from liberalism's commitment to autonomy and pluralism and to treating persons as equals. If these components express unassailable liberal principles, then it must be admitted that liberalism is incompatible with the aspirations of nationalistic minorities, and that a choice will have to be made between liberalism and another conception of political morality.

KYMLICKA'S DEFENCE OF CONTEMPORARY LIBERALISM

This position has recently been challenged by Will Kymlicka, who has developed a defence of "minority rights" which he argues follows from the general commitments of contemporary liberalism. Kymlicka admits that the contemporary position as stated by Rawls and Dworkin does not seem to leave room to address the claims of minority cultures. But he argues that this is not due to any ineluctable theoretical limitation. Rather, it is due to their failure to see how their own commitments should have led them to recognize special rights for certain minorities. In particular, he argues that Rawls should have incorporated the value of cultural membership as one of the primary goods in his resourcist program. This follows, in large measure, from the central role that is ascribed to self-respect in the theory of primary goods. According to Rawls, self-respect represents the "sense that one's plan of life is worth carrying out."[14] Self-respect thus requires the realization of an effective capacity for autonomy – the capacity to choose, to revise, and generally to make intelligent decisions about what one holds to be valuable in life. It is therefore "perhaps the most important primary good," and to be preserved "at almost any cost."[15] Rawls assumes that self-respect, and thus autonomy, will be properly secured mainly by giving priority to an equal distribution of liberty over the distribution of other primary goods, since he believes that that is apparently sufficient to ensure a viable "context of choice" within which it is possible to autonomously form and revise beliefs about what pursuits or plans of life will have value for us. But Kymlicka notices that this picture is incomplete in an important sense. It assumes only part of what is necessary to establish an adequate context of choice in which deliberation about value and plans of life can effectively take place. Drawing in part on passages from Rawls's own work, Kymlicka argues that being embedded in a vivid and healthy cultural structure is a necessary starting-point or precondition for the meaningful use of liberty in developing a capacity for autonomous deliberation.

> Our language and history are the media through which we come to an awareness of the options available to us, and their significance; and this is a precondition of making intelligent judgements about how to lead our lives. In order to make such judgements, we do not explore a number of different patterns of physical movements, which might in principle be judged in abstraction from any cultural structure. Rather, we make these judgements precisely by examining the cultural structure, by coming to an awareness of the possibilities it has, the different activities it identifies as significant.

What follows from this? Liberals should be concerned with the fate of cultural structures, not because they have some moral status of their own, but because it's only through having a rich and secure cultural structure that people can become aware, in a vivid way, of the options available to them, and intelligently examine their value.[16]

The lack of such a structure leads to "despondency and escapism" and a general inability to exercise liberty in a meaningful manner. On the basis of these considerations, Kymlicka concludes that Rawls omits a crucial component in his own argument for self-respect and liberty, and ultimately for autonomy, by failing to recognize membership in a viable cultural structure as a primary good. Putting the matter in Rawlsian terms, Kymlicka says that the parties in the "original position" (a hypothetical context of choice constructed to select principles of justice) would have powerful reasons to adopt cultural membership as a primary good.[17] In less abstract terms, Kymlicka's argument purports to show that the fact that cultural membership deserves to be treated as a primary good also explains why countries that recognize certain minority rights seem to be acting on an intuition that respect for persons needs to be divided into two components within a theory of justice, namely, that persons are owed respect (1) as citizens, and (2) as members of a cultural community.[18] The former is satisfied, according to Rawls, by giving a certain priority to liberty in the distribution of primary goods; the latter, Kymlicka argues, is satisfied by recognizing cultural membership as a primary good alongside liberty.

If Kymlicka is correct that the index of primary goods should be extended to include cultural membership, this may represent the basis for satisfying one of the aspects of liberalism that I suggested was opposed to granting special rights to nationalistic minorities, namely, its commitment to resourcist anti-perfectionism. That is, according to this argument, cultural membership should be incorporated into the index of primary goods alongside the other generally necessary means to the pursuit of valuable lives. We turn next to consider what Kymlicka has to say to address the apparent conflict in contemporary liberalism between its egalitarianism and special differential rights for nationalistic minorities.

On the face of it, this too is bound to be controversial, since the proposal for giving effect to the importance of cultural membership involves distributing standard liberal rights unequally among minority and non-minority members. According to Kymlicka, the apparent liberal interest in equal distribution of such rights follows from an interpretation of what treating people as equals requires. Kymlicka's aim must be to challenge this interpretation. The argument just canvassed is part of this effort. Within an egalitarian framework, the idea that cultural membership is a primary good purports to demonstrate that part of treating people as equals involves recognizing that they are entitled to equal concern and respect *qua* members of a culture. What Kymlicka must show in order to preserve a general egalitarian framework is that treating people with equal concern and respect as members of a culture may justify unequal distribution of conventional liberal rights across certain cultural boundaries within a multinational state. What stands in the way of this project is the idea that respect for cultural equality can be sufficiently achieved through normal distribution of the standard index of primary goods, including liberty, opportunities, income and wealth, and so on. If so, cultural membership does not require any treatment within a theory of justice, and it could in fact be dropped, for all practical purposes, from the account of primary goods.

Kymlicka's first line of response to this objection is to note that it is contrary to fact. Certain minorities seek protection to preserve a cultural context of choice because they are constantly under threat of being outbid in the economic marketplace or outvoted in the development of public policies in areas that are essential to the survival of that context. Faced with the prospect of a real, though perhaps unwitting, tyranny of the majority, and on the basis of the often tragic history of assimilation of minority cultures, it appears undeniable that in many circumstances egalitarian distribution of the conventional index of primary goods will be insufficient to secure a viable context of choice for certain cultures. But as we noted, the problem then is that granting special political, language, and other rights to minority cultures imposes costs on others, apparently putting them at a disadvantage or in an unequal position with respect to the exercise of those same rights, and so such a policy looks to violate the egalitarian commitments of liberal theory.

According to Kymlicka there is no deep conflict with equality in this picture. Admittedly, the conventional account of liberal equality holds that equal distribution of liberties and other standard primary goods will ensure fairness in the formation and aggregation of all individual choices in a political or economic context, and thus it assumes that any legitimate claims of minority cultures are satisfied by this model. But Kymlicka says that this does not provide us with the full story. The emphasis in this model on fairness in forming and aggregating people's political and economic choices presupposes an important liberal distinction between those things that are *chosen*, and those things that are a matter of people's *circumstances*, not their choices. This distinction between circumstances and choices plays an important role in liberalism, especially in Rawls's and Dworkin's theories, and Kymlicka uses it here to explain how to defend a right to cultural equality. The distinction can be summarized as the view that people do not deserve to suffer from disadvantages that result from circumstances that are unchosen and thus are beyond their control, such as their race, or sex or lack of natural endowments, though they can be legitimately required to suffer the disadvantages that result from their free choices. Now since the majoritarian processes that operate to form and aggregate social choices in political and economic contexts represent circumstances that are beyond the control of the members of a cultural minority, the disadvantages these forces create for them establish the basis for state action to ameliorate those disadvantages, in particular, to ensure that minority cultures have their own viable cultural structures. In the Canadian context, Kymlicka puts the matter this way:

> We can defend aboriginal rights as a response, not to shared choices, but to unequal circumstances. Unlike the dominant French or English cultures, the very existence of aboriginal cultural communities is vulnerable to the decisions of the non-aboriginal majority. They could be outbid or outvoted on resources crucial to the survival of their communities, a possibility that members of the majority cultures simply do not face. As a result, they have to spend their resources on securing the cultural membership which makes sense of their lives, something which non-aboriginal people get for free. And this is true regardless of the costs of the particular choices aboriginal or non-aboriginal individuals make.[19]

Because majorities get for free what certain minorities have to pay for, namely, a secure cultural structure, and because this situation has nothing to do with the choices of the minorities, an egalitarian distribution of the standard list of primary goods creates an unchosen disadvantage for those minorities that a theory of justice should correct. This position is egalitarian in that it is premised on the idea of an equal right to cultural membership. That right can, in turn, be used to justify special differential political, property, mobility, or language rights for minorities in order to secure equal access to membership in a viable cultural structure. Thus it also ensures that differential distributions of political, mobility, and other standard liberal rights flow from a general egalitarian position.

DEFENDING KYMLICKA

Kymlicka's argument is substantially original and, I think, compelling in terms of the case it makes for recognizing the legitimacy of the special rights of certain minority cultures and, in particular, of certain nationalistic minorities. The argument is also general in the sense that it is not necessary to be a contemporary liberal to accept its force. If we accept that a secure cultural structure is a crucial component of a valuable life, and that certain minority cultures are at a distinct and unchosen disadvantage because they have to pay for, whereas others get for free, a secure cultural context, then a general argument exists for recognizing the need to respond to that disadvantage. I propose to accept this argument and incorporate it as part of the position I defend here. The question to be considered in the next section is whether this argument creates special problems for contemporary liberalism that can be handled better by another theory. However, before we get to this, we need to clear away two fairly natural objections that have been raised against Kymlicka's position, since an answer will be necessary to the success of any project for recognizing the special rights of nationalistic minorities that makes use of his general position.

Kymlicka regards it as crucial to defending his position that, ultimately, cultural membership is an unchosen circumstance and not a choice. While he mainly focuses on the political and economic processes for forming and aggregating social outcomes as the unchosen circumstances that disadvantage minority cultures, if it turned out that cultural membership was itself not such a circumstance, then people could presumably be held responsible for the disadvantages that flowed from their cultural membership, including the problems they face competing for goods available through political and economic institutions. But, strictly speaking, this is not a clear case of an unchosen circumstance, since it seems possible for a normally autonomous person to choose to form or revise or even to reject an allegiance to a culture, and Kymlicka goes to some lengths to establish this.

John Danley has recently argued that the possibility of choosing to revise or reject cultural allegiances raises a fatal objection to Kymlicka's view.[21] Although this seems a fairly natural objection, Kymlicka does not try to answer it at any point. Nevertheless, it is fairly easy to suggest a number of responses on his behalf. To begin with, the liberal tradition has a long history of treating such matters as political and religious beliefs pretty much alongside gender, race, natural endowment (etc.) as a type of "circumstance" that requires special measures to prevent individuals from suffering certain disadvantages, even though such beliefs are usually thought to be matters of choice. Another relevant example may be sexual preferences, since these are often revised over the course of a life, creating some controversy over the extent to which they are chosen. And of course liberals have also been concerned to protect persons against disadvantages that result from consensual sexual practices. Thus, even if cultural membership were a matter of choice in some sense, this would not necessarily rule out some forms of special protection. Rather, the problem might be that the circumstances/choice distinction fails to capture adequately all of what liberals have in mind when they try to protect people against certain disadvantages. Another possibility is that the distinction itself requires further specification or interpretation.[22] We might say, for example, that such matters as religious or political beliefs, sexual preference, or cultural affiliation tend, at any particular time, to be so deeply constitutive of our personal identities that treating them as choices subject to review and revision in the normal sense is misleading and impractical, and threatens important social aims, including promotion of conditions for self-respect and for the exercise of a capacity for autonomy on these matters and more generally. Hence, they should be treated for all, or many, intents and purposes as circumstances not choices. I don't think that this represents merely an ad hoc response to Danley, though further argument is required to elaborate and defend this position.[23]

We can follow up this last point by noticing that cultural membership involves aspects that reflect more straightforward examples of differences due to circumstances for which one is not responsible. A cultural membership involves a shared set of traditions and beliefs, like a religion, but it is also a circumstance over which people will very often have limited capacities to exercise control. This is especially true for children, who have no choice whatsoever about the cultural context in which their beliefs about value will initially be formed. Their situation fits squarely within the circumstances/choice distinction, and given the undoubted importance to children of having a rich and viable cultural context in which to make sense of their lives and to be able to exercise meaningful choices about the options available to them, this example provides good grounds for establishing Kymlicka's position by itself. And indeed this is the example that he generally uses to drive his case.[24] Also, it seems correct to say of adults that their cultural membership is a matter of choice in at least a limited sense. That much is admitted by Danley,[25] and while that may also provide some reason for limiting the claims that adults might be able to make, it is not clear how significant this will be, especially if we add in the other considerations mentioned here. I conclude, then, that while Kymlicka may owe us a more careful explanation of the manner and the extent to which cultural membership should be treated as a "circumstance," his position is not fatally undermined by his failure to address this objection.

Another charge that Danley levels is that Kymlicka's conclusions are more ambitious than he apparently intends. As we have seen, Kymlicka is concerned to defend the "minority rights" of "minority cultures." But as I mentioned earlier this covers an enormous range of groups, and Danley suggests that the result of Kymlicka's argument would allow a country like the United States "to become 'Balkanized,' with a crazy quilt of different jurisdictions and different languages, a jumble of different sets of rights."[26] Danley is, in fact, right that Kymlicka does not say directly how to avoid this conclusion. He seems only to contemplate limiting state action to preserve minority cultural structures where these are not "vulnerable" to encroachment and assimilation through majoritarian political and economic practices. But minority cultures are always being assimilated into larger cultures, and as Danley says, this seems to commit Kymlicka to granting special rights to Polish Americans, German Americans,

Italian Americans, Korean Americans, and all other groups that face assimilation. Again, however, Danley is a little too quick and unsympathetic toward Kymlicka's position. The examples that inform Kymlicka's discussion suggest that he is mainly concerned to address the claims of what I have called "nationalistic minorities." I think that with a little imagination it is possible to see how Kymlicka can point to a variety of morally relevant reasons for limiting the claims of certain minority cultures that would steer his position clear of grossly counterintuitive consequences. For as Danley himself notes, there are a variety of morally relevant reasons to distinguish the case of Polish Americans and others from the cases of North American aboriginals. The former often *chose to leave* a certain cultural structure for an opportunity to lead more prosperous economic lives with different and often more diverse options for themselves and their children. These are surely relevant choices that should mitigate or maybe vitiate their claims. Perhaps there is a problem, then, with economic and political refugees who may have little choice but to leave an existing cultural structure. But here the fact that they may be geographically dispersed, or that they may represent a small population, or that their acceptance into the community itself involves certain costs and sacrifices on the part of others, including the community's having no effective choice over whether to accept them, should all count as morally relevant considerations. I have assumed that reasons such as these permit us to concentrate on the issues raised by nationalistic minorities, and it seems to me that, given the emphasis of his discussion, Kymlicka could have made the same point and left these details aside.[27] It is nevertheless an interesting question how Kymlicka's view would affect the treatment of minority cultures generally in a multicultural community like Canada, but I see no reason to think that his position commits him to the consequences Danley envisions.

CRITIQUE OF KYMLICKA

As I said earlier, Kymlicka thinks that contemporary liberalism is committed to respecting persons as citizens, but that it fails by not recognizing that people are also due respect as members of particular cultures. This creates a potential conflict of egalitarian principles, since it is not always possible to distribute both equal rights and resources for citizens and equal rights to cultural membership. Kymlicka resolves this conflict, in effect, by giving a certain priority in some circumstances to respect for persons as cultural actors over respect for persons as citizens. As a result, an unequal distribution of the rights of citizens across certain cultural boundaries is defended to secure equal cultural rights. However, the potential conflict is deeper and more difficult to resolve than Kymlicka has recognized. The signal difficulty is to say to what extent equal respect for persons as cultural actors can justify unequal distribution of rights for persons as citizens *and still retain proper respect for them as citizens.* Kymlicka essentially overlooks this issue. At the one point where he recognizes that aboriginal claims could impose undue burdens or costs on others, for example by requiring control over large tracts of undeveloped land and by imposing unequal political rights, he simply goes on to say that the proper way *to defend* such measures is to see them as correcting for certain advantages non-aboriginal people have before anyone makes choices about how they will lead their lives.[28] But this overlooks what is arguably the most important issue: how much can a nationalistic minority demand to make a secure cultural structure for itself? This is hardly a trivial matter. It raises a clear and fundamental question of distributive justice for any society that faces these conflicts,[29] and failure to address it properly could seriously undermine the prospects for social unity between nationalistic minorities and majorities. Moreover, it is a question that is surely relevant to the claims of Canadian aboriginals and French-speaking Quebeckers.[30]

The following hypothetical example should help to clarify many of the issues at stake. Imagine a situation where securing the cultural structure of a nationalistic minority would require a transfer of resources of land, wealth, and political rights that together would substantially hamper the capacity of a majority community to develop its economic potential, so that it found difficulty maintaining or improving what is, let us say, already little more than a minimally adequate standard of living. Now cultural equality might be the product of this situation. Both the minority and the majority could be able to preserve its cultural heritage in ways that Kymlicka thinks important. That is, each will maintain its own language, a sense of shared history, and shared patterns of life. But the majority society will also be quite strongly prevented by the minority from pursuing its aspiration to improve its material well-being and range of options from a relatively meagre level. [31]

Now this is hardly a fanciful example. It suggests a problem that might arise severely in a country like Brazil or in any number of developing countries in the Third World.[32] It also expresses in fairly clear terms the motivation behind much recent commentary in international law encouraging formal recognition in international human rights covenants and in international law of a *right to development* as a right of *peoples*.[33] Moreover, it poses a conflict that will always have the potential to arise when special rights are granted to minority cultures, namely, that such rights will interfere, perhaps severely in many cases, with the capacity of majorities to maintain or improve living conditions for their members. On the one hand, it is reasonable that in some cases of actual or threatened conflict the minority should not be able to impede the aspirations of the majority in this way. On the other hand, it is not obvious that majorities would always have substantial grounds to defend measures aimed at improving living conditions. If their aspirations included undertaking efforts to provide everyone with enough means to acquire a large suburban house with two cars, a swimming-pool in the backyard, a jacuzzi, a solarium, and foie gras on the table each night, we might legitimately doubt that these could be justified.

One way to resolve this question is to say that nationalistic minorities are entitled to special rights to secure a cultural structure to the extent that those rights do not threaten the *fully adequate healthy functioning*[34] of other communities and of the lives of their members. Where there is such a threat, some compromise will have to be reached that tries to respect as well as possible the interests of each community and its members to secure a fully adequate basis for pursuing valuable lives, including – in addition to membership in a viable cultural structure – access to good food, clothes, shelter, health care, education, recreation and leisure activities, adequate transportation, meaningful career opportunities, social interaction, political participation, and so on. This response, at least at first glance, seems to have the potential to mediate the sort of conflict just described. It would recognize that communities should be entitled to promote the well-being of their members where these efforts are necessary to provide a context that can ensure the fully adequate healthy functioning of its members; but where resources are required that go beyond this, as in the suburban shangri-la just described, claims of others to those resources may take precedence. It is to be preferred over another main alternative, a conventional utilitarian welfarist approach, which sees questions of justice in terms of maximizing satisfaction of aggregated preferences. That approach would tend to place nationalistic minorities at an immediate and severe disadvantage in resolving conflicts with any majority group.[35] As an aside to this discussion about conflicts, notice too that a functional approach may be able to provide a more satisfactory interpretation of the circumstances/choice distinction used by Kymlicka and other liberals, since it would treat as a person's circumstances (to which a theory of justice should respond) all those social and natural impediments that stand in the way of achieving fully adequate healthy functioning. This is a more complex issue than I can deal with here, but as far as I can see there is nothing implausible about treating such impediments as circumstances, since they are in the most important respects matters about which we have no choice and since, arguably, it would be possible to treat certain elements of "choice" as part of one's circumstances where they must be respected in order to permit fully adequate healthy functioning.

We need also to notice that conflicts between nationalistic minorities and the larger polities within which they reside will arise frequently in a modern context. Our present knowledge of what healthy human functioning consists in and our modern circumstances combine to make quite severe demands on such resources. Many of the demands modern societies make on material resources are unquestionably excessive, but there is little doubt that promoting valuable lives on this scheme will also involve substantial demands, and that these will create competition between communities for scarce resources in an increasingly populated world. Having a framework to identify and resolve legitimate conflicts is therefore in many ways an essential precondition to the establishment of just and harmonious social arrangements between these groups. What is provided here that is both needed and lacking in Kymlicka's account is such a framework for mediating claims that nationalistic minorities and majorities may want to make upon each other. Kymlicka has provided us with powerful reasons to accept that nationalistic minorities are entitled to certain claims to special resources; but he hasn't said to what extent these claims may be pressed, nor has he said to what extent a majority can legitimately make claims upon a nationalistic minority when its own interests are importantly at stake.[36]

These are crucial issues for a variety of obvious reasons. One that should not be overlooked arises indirectly from the fact that nationalistic minorities quite naturally and appropriately tend to think of themselves as *nations*. But we need to be wary of the use of their conception of themselves as nations as the basis for invoking the principle of national autonomy in their relations with other communities. That principle by itself purports to establish absolute barriers on the claims that nations can make upon each other. It is in many ways a tragic anachronism in international politics, particularly because of the impediment it creates to efforts to promote international institutions of justice.[37] But the extent to which it is outmoded as an international instrument can only be compounded if it is applied as a principle *within* the modern state to the intimate and necessarily reciprocal relationships that will exist between nationalistic minorities and the wider polity with which they are associated. Without an alternative framework for conceptualizing this relationship and adjudicating the sorts of claims these entities can legitimately make upon each other, we may encourage the perception that a right to cultural equality implies some version of a principle of national autonomy. That could be enormously damaging, and the consequences of such an approach have been, and will probably continue to be, dire in many cases. Again, the functional framework that I am advocating seems to have the potential to begin at least to mediate the conflicts between respect for culture and respect for citizenship that may arise between nationalistic minorities and the wider polities in which they reside.

While this seems like a fairly natural response, it is unlikely that it is a position that contemporary liberals can endorse, given their commitment to what I described as resourcist anti-perfectionism. As we have seen, that position limits the state's role on matters of justice to the distribution of resources and therefore prevents it from taking a position on the value of various permissible ways of life that may be pursued within its jurisdiction. But if the state is to make judgments about what is sufficient for the healthy functioning of its members, it must inevitably make some at least vague judgments about the adequacy or superiority of some ways of life as compared with others. It must be able to tell us when a hydro-electric project on undeveloped aboriginal land is foie gras and when it is needed to further the interests of certain persons in ways that deserve serious consideration. It is difficult to see how a contemporary liberal theory can make such assessments without violating its resourcist anti-perfectionism, since policy on these matters will require making choices about the relative merits of certain lives as compared to others, favouring or rejecting the claims of certain permissible ways of life over others to more resources on the basis of their intrinsic merit. And this it is not permitted to do within a contemporary liberal theory. More important, perhaps, it is difficult to avoid the conclusion that when we face these sorts of conflicts what is most fundamental is a concern for the promotion of healthy human functioning generally; and this favours a teleological or good-based approach to liberal normative theory against the neo-Kantianism of Rawls and other contemporary liberals, or at least it is difficult to see how such an approach can be rejected. A functional theory will recognize that a viable cultural context is a vital component in healthy functioning of an individual, representing an essential part of the basis for self-respect and autonomous deliberation and choice over ends. It will therefore regard any proposal that will interfere with that context as requiring very substantial justification, placing the onus on governments to interfere as little as possible with that context. Where such interference is justified, it will require governments to make all reasonable efforts to make available the resources required to repair damage to a cultural context, providing adequate compensation money, training, ongoing social support, and so on, and even requiring relocation of communities to appropriately congenial circumstances or extension of their boundaries where appropriate.[38]

A different sort of difficulty, but one with a similar solution, arises for Kymlicka through his effort to blend respect for cultural equality with contemporary liberalism's commitment to resourcist anti-perfectionism. The basic problem is that some cultural contexts of choice may be better than others in providing a meaningful and rich set of options through which individuals may pursue satisfying lives, even though the distribution of liberties and other resources generally meets contemporary liberal standards. For example, even if tomorrow all communities distributed resources fairly,[39] it could still be the case that some communities would provide a narrow range of often unhealthy options for children who are raised there. A slightly different example would involve the choices women are encultured into making in many societies to sacrifice their health and their educational and economic prospects, usually to further the interests of male family members. A contemporary liberal who is committed to resourcist anti-perfectionism will have a difficult time defending any official response on the part of an external (or internal) government in these cases, since that would require taking a stand on the limitations of certain permissible ways of life and on the superior value of other ways of life. This is, in effect, a rephrasing of the objection that contemporary liberalism desires pluralism, but can do nothing to promote it.[40] Again, unlike a resourcist anti-perfectionist theory, a functional theory has no difficulty recognizing and responding to such cases in principle, or fitting responses to them into a recognizably liberal program. They represent harms to fully adequate healthy functioning that are significantly the product of others' activities. A response therefore may be justified in terms of an application of the liberal harm principle.[41]

Now I am far from suggesting that these sorts of cases will easily justify coercive intervention on behalf of the afflicted parties. But we commonly accept a role for government in using moral suasion in these matters, and in funding and encouraging projects that would point the way to more enlightened practices. We also recognize the appropriateness of limiting diplomatic or trading relations with other nations as ways of encouraging or coercing countries to adopt more humane and just policies. The problem for contemporary liberalism is that to defend any sort of response to the types of cases just described and others like them, it has to draw, at least tacitly, on some other theory both to identify and to say how to respond to a problem. But this shows that the theory is impoverished by itself and needs supplementing, and once more a functional theory looks like the obvious candidate.[42] Social institutions should be arranged in ways that ensure the fully adequate healthy functioning of each member of a community. Where they do not, some official response is appropriate, though not necessarily a coercive one. In the case of women, it should not seem at all out of place to develop measures designed to encourage them to make better use of the resources available to them, to become more socially independent, and to participate directly in the life of the community and its governing institutions. Moreover, a theory that makes use of a conception of a fully adequate healthy functioning woman would provide the basis for a searching critique of the patriarchal institutions of the community, something that a theory that is committed to resourcist anti-perfectionism has difficulty doing.

NATIONALISTIC MINORITIES AND NEW LIBERALISM

It is important to make a space in liberal theory for the sort of position just advanced. Though there have been recent functional critiques of contemporary liberalism, their liberal credentials are often ambiguously asserted and are sometimes denied.[43] This is largely due to the crudely ahistorical approach to normative theory that dominates today, and to the related acceptance of Rawls's thought as setting the terms for the liberal paradigm. But liberalism is not *monolithic.* There are competing theories within liberalism, just as there are within Marxism, socialism, anarchism, feminism, and so on. Thus, we should make the effort to notice that there is a distinct tradition in political thought, with solid liberal credentials, that would have recognized the limitations of contemporary liberalism that have just been described and endorsed the solution I have posed. That tradition has its early origins in the work of John Stuart Mill and T.H. Green and finds its main expression in the works of the new liberal thinkers, L.T. Hobhouse and J.A. Hobson.[44] Although I cannot properly defend this thesis here, a full investigation would show that the new liberals took from Mill a sharp awareness of both the essential importance and the insidious pitfalls of culture; and they further developed Green's view of government as a regulator of social institutions for the purposes of providing citizens with opportunities to develop their distinctive capacities in ways that permit them "to make most and best of themselves." As a result they saw government in essentially functional terms, as an agency whose role is to promote a social context in which the common needs essential to promoting the physical, moral, emotional, and intellectual aspects of individual well-being were met. Moreover, they recognized that justice might not be satisfied simply by a fair distribution of resources, but that government might have to play an ongoing role in securing conditions for "ample opportunities of recreations ... art, music, travel, education, [and] social intercourse."[45] Moreover, it is interesting that they saw the more critical and constructive role that they prescribed for government as having the potential to break down some important barriers between themselves and their adversaries and to put disagreement on common ground:

On all sides men are agreed that problems of poverty, problems of education, problems of physical, mental and moral efficiency, are matters not merely of individual and private but equally of public and governmental concern. They do not deny the duty or depreciate the responsibility of the individual for himself or of the parent for his family, but they superimpose upon these a duty of the citizen to the state and a responsibility of the state for the individual. [46]

Within this context, the new liberals recognized the legitimacy of claims to "cultural equality" based on the crucial role cultural membership plays in facilitating the healthy functioning of individuals. Such claims might of course conflict with the standard rights of citizens; and they saw, as we do now, the resolution of this conflict as one of the most immediately challenging tasks facing the modern state.

[Finding the right place] for national rights within the unity of the state, to give scope to national differences without destroying the organization of a life which has somehow to be lived in common, is therefore the problem that the modern state has to solve if it is to maintain itself. It has not only to generalize the common rights of citizenship as applied to individuals, but to make room for diversity and give some scope for collective sentiments which in a measure conflict with one another.[47]

The new liberals recognized that such conflicts might be deep and difficult to resolve, but they held that a functional approach provided the right sort of guidance for identifying these tensions and mediating their resolution. That approach also led them to recognize the need to pursue matters of justice into a variety of spheres that are in many cases only now being put back onto the liberal agenda, including justice in the family, in international relations, between cultures, and for women. [48]

It is also important to see that this view gives significant expression to the egalitarian and anti-perfectionist currents in liberal thought. It is egalitarian in that it is based on an ideal of equality that can be characterized in terms of an equal right of all persons to fully adequate healthy functioning. It is anti-perfectionist in the sense that the state is essentially concerned with establishing social conditions that will tend to produce individuals with the skills and wherewithal, and therefore the capacity, to make meaningful choices to function in a fully adequate and healthy human manner. But the state does not require that individuals use their skills or resources to achieve healthy human functioning; nor does it determine what ends they must pursue. Rather, it aims to achieve the capability of persons to exercise certain types of choices that reflect fully adequate healthy functioning, but it leaves the choosing up to them.[49] This may not be anti-perfectionist enough for some, since the state must regulate social arrangements in ways that tend to produce persons who are capable of exercising meaningful choices to behave in certain ways. And that may require the diversion of resources to and regulation of institutions with some vague (and revisable) conception of healthy human functioning in mind. But it is anti-perfectionist in the sense that contemporary liberalism finds most objectionable, and that Kymlicka was most concerned to show a commitment to providing viable cultural contexts of choice did not entail, namely, that particular ways of life are not imposed on recalcitrant individuals. Moreover, it reflects the practices of all modern liberal societies which have accepted, with little or no objection from liberals, an important state role in promoting healthy recreational opportunities and lifestyles, the arts and sciences, participation in public affairs, meaningful career opportunities, continuing adult education, and so on. So to the extent that this theory incorporates what might be called "soft" perfectionist elements,[50] the argument that it is illiberal for these reasons looks pretty thin. On the contrary, there is no reason to reject it as a liberal theory or to fail to rank it as a competitor among contemporary liberal theories.

An important departure of this view from contemporary liberalism is its rejection of a narrow, often formalistic focus on autonomy as a central and distinctive animating value in liberal theory. Like all liberal theories, new liberal thought tends to favour autonomy, but unlike many other liberal theories, it is unambiguous about not separating realization of a capacity for autonomy from living well generally. Thus the theory is drawn away from a narrow focus on a capacity for autonomy toward integrating the realization of that capacity as an element among, and product of, securing the essential capabilities for functioning well over a whole life, for "physical, mental, and moral efficiency," as Hobhouse puts it. By contrast, the contemporary liberal theory of Rawls regards the conditions for the realization of a capacity for autonomy as met mainly through legal endowment of certain rights and liberties; and he regards the realization of this capacity, along with a capacity for a sense of justice, as the prime end of a liberal theory of justice.[51] As we have seen, Kymlicka important-ly extends that position by arguing that realization of a capacity for au-tonomy requires, in addition, a viable cultural context of choice from which one can deliberate effectively about life plans and personal pur-suits. But if the argument of the last section is correct, even this may not be sufficient at times, and it suggests that a capacity for autonomy may not be separable, at least not over a whole life, from leading lives that ex-press capacities essential to function with physical, mental, and moral ef-ficiency. If so, a highly exclusive focus on autonomy per se may represent too thin and misleading a basis for a defensible political theory. And in-deed, independent evidence for this latter thesis is given in the preceding section. We saw there that the plausibility of a functional framework for mediating potential conflicts between nationalistic minorities and major-ity communities points, in effect, to the need for state action to be con-cerned with other ends besides autonomy where matters of justice are involved, namely, with securing what is essential to the fully adequate healthy functioning of individuals across certain institutionalized cultur-al boundaries.

I am of course not suggesting that this earlier liberal tradition had all the answers in these areas. Much more work needs to be done to elabo-rate and defend the position that they began and that I have sketched here. What I am suggesting is that the liberal framework that this earlier tradition began to develop should be taken seriously today because of its potential to address and mediate some of the most vexing problems faced by the modern state.[44]

CONCLUSION: IMPLICATIONS FOR CANADA

On the basis of the foregoing analysis, we can see that the main prob-lem from the point of view of justice concerns the recognition of the spe-cial rights of Canadian aboriginal peoples. French-speaking Quebeckers already have a viable and secure cultural context of choice and standards of living that are roughly comparable to other parts of Canada. The claims of Quebeckers to preserve their cultural structure are broadly satisfied by these circumstances, though further constitutional instruments may be required to give more formal recognition to their distinctness and their rights to protect their culture in certain circumstances. Canadian aboriginals often lack both viable cultural structures and adequate standards of living; and the recovery and development of their cultures may impose substantial costs and burdens on Canadians. In both cases, however, there is a potential for conflict between respect for the minorities' cultures and respect for other citizens' rights and interests in leading valuable lives. What is needed and has been proposed is a way of conceptualizing the handling and adjudication of such disputes. As well, it is an advantage of this framework that its application is general and fits with a solution to broader but related conflicts that raise matters of justice. In particular, it can be part of a more general approach that recognizes that we live in a small and increasingly crowded and demanding world, and that these circumstances require the claims of nationhood to be weighed against other claims of justice in ways that will, and should, change the way we think of the prerogatives of nations. For Canada and the nationalistic minorities that reside here, there is also an opportunity to help to lead the way in approaching these issues by adopting mechanisms and applying them in ways that are consonant with this broader purpose.

Finally, it should be apparent that the work of theorists like Kymlicka and the new liberals shows that there need be no deep antagonism between animating liberal principles and the aspirations of nationalistic minorities. On the contrary, current provisions in the Charter that recognize special language rights, aboriginal rights, and respect for multiculturalism can be seen as expressions of, not derogations from, liberal values of equality, liberty, and respect for autonomy. At this writing, proposals for rendering these and other special rights more specific and concrete have just been rejected. That rejection was based significantly on the belief that such rights were inconsistent with respect for fundamental liberal values. I have argued that this is a mistake. Given proper interpretation, these special rights can fit within a liberal framework, and can provide important guidance for politicians, judges, and community leaders without overlooking or threatening cultural diversity.[53] This will not satisfy some who think that liberal principles do not go far enough in making space for the special rights and distinctness of certain cultural groups. But I believe that the position advanced here makes substantial room for the realization of their legitimate interests in preserving and developing their cultures while recognizing the legitimacy of many of the competing demands that must be accounted for and resolved given the conditions of modern life and our current knowledge of human affairs. That suggests the fundamental soundness of applying liberal principles to the multinational, multicultural circumstances of a country like this one. At the very least, it outlines the ground for possible agreement between disputants, and should help to provide the basis for an informed and productive examination of competing positions.

NOTES

A shorter version of this paper was presented at the conference "The Charter Ten Years After" in Vancouver on May 16, 1992 in Vancouver. I would like to thank the participants for their helpful comments. Following the conference, I circulated a longer draft and received many useful comments and suggestions from Philip Bryden, David Copp, David Lyons, and Allen Wood. Will Kymlicka generously made available to me some of his forthcoming work which had a bearing on issues addressed in this paper, and he made a number of other useful suggestions. Throughout my work on this paper Colin Macleod and Avigail Eisenberg provided resourceful and constructive criticism and ready access to stimulating discussion about these issues. I express my appreciation to all these individuals for their help. Work on this paper was supported by a doctoral fellowship from the Social Sciences and Humanities Research Council of Canada.

1 Will Kymlicka, *Liberalism, Community, and Culture* (Oxford University Press, 1989) hereinafter referred to as *LCC.* Since publication of this work, Kymlicka has published a number of articles that have clarified and extended his views. See "Individual and Group Rights," in Judith Baker, ed., *Group Rights* (University of Toronto Press, forthcoming); "Liberalism and the Politicization of Ethnicity,"(1991) 4 *The Canadian Journal of Law and Jurisprudence* 239–56; "The Rights of Minority Cultures: Reply to Kulkathas," (1992) 20 *Political Theory* 140–6; and "Two Models of Pluralism and Tolerance," (1992) 13 *Analyse & Kritik* 33–56.

2 John Stuart Mill, *On Bentham and Coleridge* (1838 and 1840; New York: Harper Torchbooks 1962) 73, 82; *The Logic of the Moral Sciences,* chapter 6 of *A System of Logic* (1834; La Salle: Open Court 1988) 27–8, 46ff, 93–

4; *On Liberty,* in *Utilitarianism* (1861), *On Liberty* (1859), and *Representative Government* (1861) (London: J.M. Dent and Sons 1968) 118, 129–31; *Representative Government,* chapters 16–17.

3 J.A. Hobson, *Imperialism* (1902; London: George Allen and Unwin, revised edition 1938). L.T. Hobhouse, *Democracy and Reaction* (London: T. Fisher Unwin 1904).

4 There is another liberal tradition that deserves mention in this context. That is a Lockean approach grounded in the idea of a social compact based on consent and respect for continuity of government. James Tully has recently applied this position to the relations between certain minority cultures and the majority communities with which they are associated. (See his essay elsewhere in this volume.) I will not consider the specific merits of this view in this paper except indirectly. Like the position I defend, it has the virtue of providing a framework for resolving conflicts between certain minority cultures and other groups, albeit an austere one that recognizes, among other things, the legitimate exercise of the principle of national autonomy by these minorities. If I am right that contemporary liberalism lacks a framework for dispute resolution in many instances, then the alternative I propose and Tully's Lockean position may be the main liberal contenders for the attention of policy-makers, jurists, and students of political theory. Resolution of this competition will depend on which view we think better expresses the ideals of liberalism and provides a more satisfying basis for helping to resolve the problems posed by cultural pluralism.

5 A precise formulation of the notion of a nationalistic minority is not possible, and undoubtedly this rough definition will require amendment either to extend or restrict its application in certain cases (cf. Mill, *Representative Government* 259–60). By focusing on these groups I am not denying that arguments for granting them special rights will have purchase in defending the special claims of other cultural minorities. Nor am I asserting that such groups that fall within the broad definition of a nationalistic minority can always make legitimate claims for special types of protection or recognition, though I shall write as though I am addressing such groups with legitimate claims.

6 John Rawls, *A Theory of Justice* (Cambridge, Mass.: Harvard University Press 1971) 8–9.

7 Cf. Kymlicka, *LCC* 139–40 and "Group Rights."

8 In this section, I have criticized some of the terminology employed by Kymlicka in his main work on this subject (*LCC* 138–40). However, after

preparing this paper, I discovered that he had quite recently adopted a terminology similar to mine but for slightly different purposes. He now uses the term "special rights" to describe what he thinks certain minority cultures are most interested in asserting in a Canadian context. As I read him, however, he gives this term a narrower meaning referring, roughly, to "rights accorded to individuals as members of certain communities," though such rights may at times have to be accorded to communities in order to be effective (for example, special Indian fishing rights are accorded to a community on behalf of the special rights of its members). Such rights are to be contrasted with another form of collective or community rights, namely, "group rights," which refers to rights communities have that are independent of, and may conflict with, the rights of the individuals who comprise the community. Kymlicka seems to think that liberalism can recognize such special rights but not group rights. I tend to agree, and my discussion here will be consistent with that position, though I do not want to foreclose the more general debate. See his very informative review of these matters in "Group Rights."

Kymlicka has also proposed recently that for the purposes of discussions like this one, we can regard the terms "national minorities" and "minority cultures" as roughly interchangeable ("Liberalism and the Polticization of Ethnicity" 239–41). I think that the latter term is too vague for reasons given in the text. I also have some reservations about his definition of the term "national minorities" and some minor qualms about the term itself. Kymlicka uses it to refer to groups that represent "a historical community, more or less institutionally complete, occupying a given territory or homeland, sharing a distinct language and history" within a particular multinational state. This seems to express quite naturally what is implied by the notion of a *national* minority, but this definition has the odd consequence of recognizing national minorities only *after* they have achieved some sort of formal nation-like status, either by being voluntarily incorporated within a multi-nation federation by having a history of being institutionally complete within a particular territory. What I am mainly worried about is that this conception of a national minority is too narrow to capture the range of cases that we should be concerned to address. The problem is that the notion needs to be broad enough to entertain the possibility that cultural groups who are not yet institutionally complete or have historical territorial claims may in some circumstances, say, through immigration or forced migration, have legitimate aspirations to status as national minorities in these respects. Palestinian refugees in the countries bordering Israel might be good candidates in some scenarios. Also, we should perhaps not discount the possibility that sometime in the distant future areas of some of the southern United States may become so dominated by Latino culture that some special provisions recognizing their distinct national character should be adopted.

These may be reasons to prefer the term "nationalistic minorities." It more clearly expresses the idea of national aspiration as an important element in identifying these minorities, and this is less obviously implied by the alternative and, indeed, is formally missing from Kymlicka's discussion. Perhaps more clearly than the term "national minorities," it also suggests that although the formal conditions establishing the national status of groups can be unsettled or developing in some respects, the groups can still be recognized as nations. It also conveys something of the vagueness of the idea of nationhood as applied to these groups. In some important sense they are nations, but the closeness of their ties to other groups or nations tends also to blur the boundaries of their nationhood, at least as that notion is conventionally understood. As we shall see, I take this to be an important fact that needs to be recognized (though not only in this context), and that may tend to be discounted by too narrow a focus on the notion of nationhood.

9 For the liberal critics' side see Adina Schwartz, "Moral Neutrality and Primary Goods," *(1973) 83 Ethics* 294–307; Michael Sandel, *Liberalism and the Limits of Justice* (Cambridge University Press 1982); Alasdair MacIntyre, *After Virtue: A Study in Moral Theory* (University of Notre Dame Press 1984); Charles Taylor, "Atomism," in *Philosophy and the Human Sciences: Philosophical Papers,* Vol. 2 (Cambridge University Press 1985). For some recent and incisive liberal responses see Joel Feinberg, *Harmless Wrongdoing* (Oxford University Press 1988) chapter 29A; Kymlicka, *LCC,* chapters 4–5 and passim; Thomas Pogge, *Realizing Rawls* (Ithaca: Cornell University Press 1989) ch.2.

10 It is perhaps worth specifically noting one way of portraying the commitments of contemporary liberalism that is too controversial for our purposes, even though it is commonly invoked by critics and proponents alike. According to this characterization, contemporary liberalism represents an individualistic *rights-based* approach to questions of fundamental justice. But while liberalism is undoubtedly concerned with individual rights to an important extent, it is not represented as a rights-based theory by the theorists

who have provided us with its most careful contemporary formulations. Rawls has expressly refused to endorse this idea; and though Dworkin at one time described his and Rawls's views as rights-based, he has since withdrawn this characterization. See Rawls, "Justice as Fairness: Political Not Metaphysical," *(1985) 14 Philosophy and Public Affairs* 236n, and Dworkin, "In Defense of Equality,"(1983) 1 *Social Philosophy and Policy* 34–5. Rawls and Dworkin are, I think, right to avoid this way of describing their positions, but this is not to rule out the possibility that a rights-based formulation could be given. It would, however, be prima facie a mischaracterization of contemporary liberalism, and a great deal of subtle argument would be required to show otherwise – argument that would take us well beyond the bounds of this paper.

11 Cf. Kymlicka, *LCC* 36–7.

12 Rawls, *A Theory of Justice* 92ff.

13 See also Rawls, "Social Unity and the Primary Goods," in Amartya Sen and Bernard Williams, eds., *Utilitarianism and Beyond* (Cambridge University Press, 1982) 162; "The Priority of the Right and Ideas of the Good," (1988) 17 *Philosophy and Public Affairs* 255–60; Dworkin, "Liberalism," in Stuart hampshire, ed., *Public and Private Morality* (Cambridge University Press 1978); and "What Is Equality? Part 2: Equality of Resources," (1981) 10 *Philosophy and Public Affairs* 283–345. There are, of course, interesting differences between Rawls's and Dworkin's resourcism, but they do not affect the substance of my discussion. There is also some controversy in the literature over whether Rawls's "difference principle" is egalitarian. I shall leave this aside and take at face value the egalitarian credentials of his view.

14 Rawls, *A Theory of Justice* 178.

15 Ibid., 440.

16 Kymlicka, *LCC* 165. Cf Rawls, *A Theory of Justice* 563–4.

17 Kymlicka, *LCC* 166.

18 Ibid., 150ff.

19 Ibid., 187.

20 Ibid., 51.

21 John Danley, "Liberalism, Aboriginal Rights, and Cultural Minorities," (1991) 20 *Philosophy and Public Affairs* 168–85.

22 Kymlicka, *LCC* 38.

23 In the next section, I develop further these very sketchy remarks, and suggest a rationale for treating such apparent choices as circumstances; but I do not claim to make a definitive case for this position, nor am I convinced

that the position I defend must ultimately rely on such a distinction.

24 Kymlicka, *LCC* 165–6, 186, 189, 240.

25 Danley, "Liberalism, Aboriginal Rights, and Cultural Minorities" 177.

26 Ibid., 176.

27 This issue is discussed by Kymlicka, who arrives at a similar conclusion. See "Liberalism and the Politicization of Ethnicity" 249–53.

28 Kymlicka, *LCC* 186–9, 199–200.

29 Which is to say, in effect, that the parties to the original position deliberating behind the veil of ignorance would have compelling reasons to determine the weight or priority of these competing principles, as they did for Rawls's original principles.

30 To take just one example from this country's current deliberations, Canada's Inuit people have recently voted to accept a land claims settlement that would pay them $1.15 billion and give them outright ownership of 335,000 square kilometres of land (an area roughly half the size of Alberta). Paul Woods of Canadian Press reported these concerns about the proposal: "Some people have questioned whether Canada can afford Nunavut [the territory to be created by the settlement]. Aside from the $1.15 billion Ottawa is to pay the Inuit, establishing a new territorial government could cost another $632 million. Operating costs could eat up another $200 million a year, a government study said. That's a lot of money considering the region has only 22,000 people – about the size of Brockton, Ontario." Quoted in the Vancouver *Sun*, 4 May 1992, A5.

31 Notice that this situation can also be presented as a disadvantage that is due to circumstances not choices. Both Kymlicka and Rawls assume that a viable cultural structure will be one in which a rich diversity of options will be present (Kymlicka *LCC* 165; Rawls, "Social Unity and the Primary Goods" 166, 182). If this is not so for the majority, they face disadvantages that may not result from their own choices. This could be one way of framing the conflict here as a question of justice.

32 I chose Brazil as an example, since it has a comparatively small aboriginal population and a non-aboriginal population for whom even a radical egalitarian redistribution of liberties, opportunities, and income and wealth would not provide a very prosperous standard of living, though it would probably provide a minimally adequate standard of living for most.

33 This issue is canvassed in many of the articles in a recent collection of essays edited by James Crawford entitled *The Rights of Peoples* (Oxford University Press 1988). See in particular Roland Rich, "The Right to Development: A

Right of Peoples?" and Lyndel Prott, "Cultural Rights as People's Rights," especially 102–3.

34 It is more common to speak of "healthy functioning" but I add the modifier "fully adequate" to emphasize what is usually left implicit in the former term, namely, that a functional approach aims to respect and encourage diversity and to establish the basic conditions for human flourishing. See Russell, "A Defense of Ideal Liberalism," Ph.D. dissertation, Cornell University, 1994, for a more complete development of this position.

35 More egalitarian welfarist approaches – for example, a much discussed recent proposal for equality of opportunity for welfare – would, I suspect, result in generally unstable arrangements between cultures assuming (what seems plausible) that some cultures instil in their members a greater (or lesser) capacity for realizing welfare based on the consumption of comparatively fewer (or greater) resources. Cf. G.A. Cohen, "On the Currency of Egalitarian Justice," (1989) 99 *Ethics* 925. See David Brink, *Moral Realism and the Foundations of Ethics* (Cambridge University Press 1989), chapter 6, for a non-conventional utilitarianism based on an objective conception of value that could perhaps be extended to incorporate the position I defend.

36 Perhaps one thing that Kymlicka would say is that a contemporary liberal framework would try to resolve these issues as a matter of "expensive tastes." But it is important to see that, for practical purposes, there may often be no agreement between cultures on what constitutes an expensive taste. For example, demand by non-aboriginals for pulp lumber on aboriginal land may be regarded as an expensive taste by aboriginals, just as the aboriginals' desire to preserve a natural environment might be regarded as an expensive taste by non-aboriginals. So we still need some framework to resolve disputes, and a functional framework looks like the most plausible candidate. Also, it is important to see that the functional approach shares with contemporary liberalism a concern about expensive tastes. It would take at least another paper to explain the differences with contemporary liberalism in this respect and to argue for the relative superiority of a functional theory on these matters, and so I can't do justice to this issue here. One of the reasons for preferring a functional theory in this respect is that it seems to do a better job of identifying and meeting special needs where on a contemporary liberal view such needs are narrowly defined and many such legitimate needs arguably end up being described as expensive tastes (see Martha Nussbaum, "Aristotelian Social Democracy," in R. Bruce Douglas, Gerald

M. Mara, and Henry S. Richardson, eds., *Liberalism and the Good* [New York: Routledge 1990] 211–13). If so, it provides a better framework for identifying and resolving these issues as well. However, the different issues of identifying the limits of such needs and explaining how motivation for accepting distribution of resources would work on such a scheme need careful treatment, although I doubt that they are more troubling for this view than for its main competitor.

37 See Charles Beitz, *Political Theory and International Relations* (Princeton University Press 1979) 71ff.

38 There is no reason to think that minorities will not be able to withstand the pressures of majorities or that majorities will always have an easy time making their argument for access to such resources. The serious difficulty that the current James Bay hydro-electric project is encountering in Quebec has resulted in significant part from New York State's decision not to purchase the project's electricity on the grounds that it would not be used to meet the sort of needs that could justify interference with aboriginal culture in the James Bay region.

39 In this respect, it is worth noting that Kymlicka generally defends a conventional contemporary liberal egalitarian distribution of resources *within* different communities (*LCC* 196–7).

40 These issues remain mainly unaddressed even in Rawls's recent work. He envisions requiring children's education to further understanding and support for a *political* conception of justice, but the issue of using state authority for wider educational purposes or to promote pluralism is rejected ("Priority of the Right and Ideas of the Good" 267–8). Dworkin is slightly more sensitive to the potential for problems to arise, and he has suggested that the state may play a role in the promotion of culture ("high" culture in particular) where the market fails ("Can a Liberal State Support Art?" *A Matter of Principle* [Cambridge, Mass.: Harvard University Press 1985]). But it is difficult to see how this fits with his overall scheme, and his critics have argued quite persuasively that such proposals represent ad hoc amendments to his theory. See Samuel Black, "Revisionist Liberalism and the Decline of Culture," (1992) 102 *Ethics* 244–76.

41 Kymlicka has recently stated that respect for autonomy may justify certain types of responses to illiberal minorities (see "The Rights of Minority Cultures" and "Two Models of Pluralism"). His discussion and proposals are vague enough that he may be in close agreement with the position I advance here. If so, it is difficult to see how he can take the position he does

without adopting a functional approach or violating liberal neutrality or, as I have characterized it, resourcist anti-perfectionism.

42 One other thing contemporary liberals have to say about these types of cases is that they mean to defend an ideal theory, or a theory where full compliance with the requirements of justice is assumed. They hold that a clearer view of how to handle cases under non-ideal circumstances is gained by this approach (Rawls, *A Theory of Justice* 8–9). We can see that this is false for the cases just described. Other theoretical commitments need to be adopted to assess the extent of the problem, even to identify the existence of a problem, and to say how to respond.

43 The most prominent of these critiques have perhaps come from Martha Nussbaum and Amartya Sen. See in particular Nussbaum, "Aristotelian Social Democracy"; Sen, "Equality of What?" in Sterling M. McMurrin, ed., *The Tanner Lectures on Human Values* (Salt Lake City: University of Utah Press 1980); *The Standard of Living* (Cambridge University Press 1987); and "Well-being, Agency, and Freedom: The Dewey Lectures," (1985) 83 *The Journal of Philosophy* 169–221. Nussbaum emphasizes the parallels between her view and liberalism, though she does not claim to present a liberal position. Sen rarely addresses this issue.

44 Kymlicka acutely draws attention to the contributions of this earlier tradition to the question of nationalistic minorities, but he does not consider the relative merits of their normative view as against the position he defends (*LCC* 207–10).

45 J.A. Hobson, *The Social Problem* (London: J. Nisbit and Co., 1901) 79.

46 L.T. Hobhouse, *Social Evolution and Political Theory* (New York: Columbia University Press 1911) 184.

47 Ibid., 146–7. See also Hobhouse, *The Elements of Social Justice* (London: George Allen and Unwin 1922) 45–6, 193–4 and *Social Development: Its Nature and Conditions* (London: George Allen and Unwin 1924) 297.

48 It is particularly surprising to me that Hobhouse's contributions to feminism have not been noted in any of the important surveys of women in western philosophy. Particularly surprising is the fact that Hobhouse argues that social justice requires "equality in marriage and parenthood," anticipating Susan Moller Okin's position in *Justice, Gender, and the Family* (New York: Basic Books 1989). Cf. Hobhouse, *Social Development: Its Nature and Conditions* 120–1, 279; *Democracy and Reaction* 89–90; *Morals in Evolution* (London: Chapman and Hall 1906) part I, chapters 4–5; *Liberalism* (1911; New York: Oxford University Press 1964) 60ff, 93–4; *Social Evolution and*

Political Theory 65–6, 168–9; and *The Elements of Social Justice* 146–7. See also my "Okin's Rawlsian Feminism? Justice in the Family and Another Liberalism" (unpublished).

49 See Hobhouse, *Social Evolution and Political Theory* 199–201. The most perspicuous contemporary account of a similar position comes from Nussbaum, who draws up a compelling list of "basic functional capabilities" that share with primary goods an aim for universality of application in the lives of all persons, though they depend on a "thick vague" conception of value ("Aristotelian Social Democracy" 214, 224–5). In a recent paper, David Copp explains how meeting basic functional needs can be extended to apply to special needs ("The Right to an Adequate Standard of Living: Justice, Autonomy and the Basic Needs," (1992) 9 *Social Philosophy and Policy* 252–5.

50 I use this term to refer to a normative framework that seeks to establish social conditions that permit realization of capabilities to achieve fully adequate healthy functioning. In contrast to "hard" perfectionist theories, "soft" perfectionism does not seek to force people to function in certain ways or to maximize human excellence.

51 Rawls, "The Priority of the Right and Ideas of the Good" 260.

52 The best account of new liberal thought is Michael Freeden, *The New Liberalism: An Ideology of Social Reform* (Oxford University Press 1978) and *Liberalism Divided: A Study in British Political Thought* (Oxford University Press 1986). The issues surrounding nationalistic minorities, however, are not addressed in these works. Freeden has also developed a theory of rights that follows significantly from new liberal views. See *Rights* (Minneapolis: University of Minnesota Press 1991) and "Human Rights and Welfare: A Communitarian View,"(1990) 100 *Ethics* 489–502. I develop the normative theory sketched here in Russell, "A Defense of Idea Liberalism."

53 I don't mean to deny, however, that some aspects of the recently rejected Charlottetown accord were inconsistent with liberal principles. In particular, I doubt that the accord provided proper protection for the rights of native women, native offenders, and dissidents or non-traditional native minorities living on reserves. This was the apparent implication of exempting native communities from the constraints of the Charter in order to protect native languages, traditions, or cultures. It should be clear by now that I reject such an approach as unwise, unnecessary, *and* illiberal.